SEXU

In this wide-ranging survey Joseph Bristow introduces readers to the most influential contemporary theories of sexual desire. Revealing how nineteenth-century scientists invented 'sexuality', he investigates why this term has been the source of such controversy in modern culture.

Demonstrating the lasting influence of late-Victorian sexology, *Sexuality* turns a critical eye on many conflicting accounts of eroticism. Bristow shows why Freud and Lacan have been widely discussed within the fields of cultural studies, literary history and feminist theory. He explains the importance of Bataille, Baudrillard, Cixous, Deleuze, Irigaray and Kristeva, among many others. Analysing the work of Michel Foucault, Bristow considers how *The History of Sexuality* paved the way for queer theory in the 1990s. The conclusion looks at the decisive postmodern emphasis on erotic diversity.

Presented in a clear and concise style, *Sexuality* makes complex theoretical ideas accessible to readers who wish to discover more about this exciting and rapidly developing field.

Joseph Bristow is Professor of English at the University of California, Los Angeles. He previously taught at the University of York, England. He is the author of several books, including *Effeminate England: Homoerotic Writing after 1885*, and is joint editor of *Nineteenth Century Women Poets: An Oxford Anthology*.

THE NEW CRITICAL IDIOM

SERIES EDITOR: JOHN DRAKAKIS, UNIVERSITY OF STIRLING

The *New Critical Idiom* is an invaluable series of introductory guides to today's critical terminology. Each book:

- provides a handy, explanatory guide to the use (and abuse) of the term;

- offers an original and distinctive overview by a leading literary and cultural critic;

- relates the term to the larger field of cultural representation.

With a strong emphasis on clarity, lively debate and the widest possible breadth of examples, *The New Critical Idiom* is an indispensable approach to key topics in literary studies.

- See below for new books in this series.

Gothic by Fred Botting
Historicism by Paul Hamilton
Ideology by David Hawkes
Metre, Rhythm and Verse Form by Philip Hobsbaum
Romanticism by Aidan Day
Stylistics by Richard Bradford

SEXUALITY

Joseph Bristow

PROPERTY OF
BAKER COLLEGE
Owosso Campus

ROUTLEDGE

LONDON AND NEW YORK

First published 1997
by Routledge
11 New Fetter Lane, London EC4P 4EE

Simultaneously published in the USA and Canada
by Routledge
29 West 35th Street, New York, NY 10001

Reprinted 2002

Routledge is an imprint of the Taylor & Francis Group

© 1997 Joseph Bristow

Typeset in Garamond and Scala Sans by Routledge

Printed and bound in Great Britain by
TJ International Ltd, Padstow, Cornwall

All rights reserved. No part of this book may be reprinted
or reproduced or utilized in any form or by any electronic,
mechanical, or other means, now known or hereafter
invented, including photocopying and recording, or in any
information storage or retrieval system, without permission in
writing from the publishers.

British Library Cataloguing in Publication Data
A catalogue record for this book is available from the British Library

Library of Congress Cataloging in Publication Data

Bristow, Joseph.
Sexuality / Joseph Bristow.
p. cm. – (The new critical idiom)
Includes bibliographical references and index.
1. Sex. 2. Sex and history. 3. Sexology. I. Title. II. Series.
HQ12.B68 1997   96–32461
306.7–dc20   CIP

ISBN 0–415–12268–6(hbk)
ISBN 0–415–08494–6(pbk)

CONTENTS

Series Editor's Preface

The New Critical Idiom is a series of introductory books which seeks to extend the lexicon of literary terms, in order to address the radical changes which have taken place in the study of literature during the last decades of the twentieth century. The aim is to provide clear, well-illustrated accounts of the full range of terminology currently in use, and to evolve histories of its changing usage.

The current state of the discipline of literary studies is one in which there is considerable debate concerning basic questions of terminology. This involves, among other things, the boundaries which distinguish the literary from the non-literary; the position of literature within the larger sphere of culture; the relationship between literatures of different cultures; and questions concerning the relation of literary to other cultural forms within the context of interdisciplinary studies.

It is clear that the field of literary criticism and theory is a dynamic and heterogeneous one. The present need is for individual volumes on terms which combine clarity of exposition with an adventurousness of perspective and a breadth of application. Each volume will contain as part of its apparatus some indication of the direction in which the definition of particular terms is likely to move, as well as expanding the disciplinary boundaries within which some of these terms have been traditionally contained. This will involve some re-situation of terms within the larger field of cultural presentation, and will introduce examples from the area of film and the modern media in addition to examples from a variety of literary texts.

PREFACE AND ACKNOWLEDGEMENTS

Sexuality aims to provide a clear and concise introduction to the meanings and myths attached to a key critical term. In covering a wide range of theoretical writings, I have tried to give a fair and balanced representation of contending intellectual positions. Given the strict limits on space, the discussion has been obliged to condense a great many complex points in the most direct manner possible. So that readers may gain further insights into this diverse field, parenthetical references indicate noteworthy secondary sources. Wherever possible, I have explained cultural allusions that might be unfamiliar to some readers. Dates of birth and death have been provided for the large number of historical figures mentioned in the discussion.

This book was completed while I held a Senior External Research Fellowship at the Stanford Humanities Center during 1995–96. The Director of the Center, Keith Baker, together with the administrative staff – Sue Dambrau, Gwen Lorraine, and Susan Sebbard – made me feel particularly welcome during my stay. Research for this study was assisted by the help I received from the staffs of both the Cecil H. Green Library and the J. Henry Meyer Memorial Library at Stanford. Two fellows at the Center – Eric Oberle and James I. Porter – kindly pointed me in the direction of sources I would not otherwise have found. Richard W. Schoch, a Whiting Fellow at the Center, offered warm and sustaining friendship during the writing process. The Associate Director of the Center, Susan Dunn, showed great generosity in loaning me personal copies of books that were proving hard to obtain while I was drawing this project to a close. Last but by no means least, Talia Rodgers has been an extremely patient and encouraging editor, as has the series editor, John Drakakis. My thanks to all of them.

Stanford University, May 1996

INTRODUCTION

What is sexuality? To this blunt question, the answer would seem clear enough. Sexuality is surely connected with sex. But if we find ourselves pressed to define what is meant by sex, then the situation becomes somewhat more complicated. In the English language, the word sex is certainly ambiguous. A sign with various connotations, sex refers not only to sexual activity (*to have sex*), it also marks the distinction between male and female anatomy (*to have a sex*). So it would perhaps be wise to think twice about the ways in which sexuality might be implicated in these distinct frameworks of understanding. Is sexuality supposed to designate sexual desire? Or does it refer instead to one's sexed being? If we find ourselves answering yes to both enquiries, then sexuality would appear to embrace ideas about pleasure *and* physiology, fantasy *and* anatomy. On reflection, then, sexuality emerges as a term that points to both internal and external phenomena, to both the realm of the psyche and the material world. Given the equivocal meaning of sex, one might suggest that sexuality occupies a place where sexed bodies (in all their shapes and sizes) and sexual desires (in all their multifariousness) intersect only to separate. Looked at from this dual perspective, there are many different kinds of sexed body and sexual desire inhabiting sexuality. Small wonder this immensely significant term has for decades generated a huge amount of discussion from conflicting critical viewpoints.

Given the diverse theoretical approaches to sexuality, this introductory guide outlines the major twentieth-century debates about eroticism, all the way from late-Victorian sexology to queer theory. Each chapter in turn shows why there is still little agreement among leading theorists on the most appropriate method for interpreting sexual desire. While some would argue that sexuality articulates a fundamental human need, others would recommend that we examine closely how such an assumption arose in the first place. Contending arguments have been made that sexuality needs to be understood in relation to widely varying phenomena, from physiological drives to structures of language. The fact that it remains hard to obtain consensus on what sexuality is – or, for that matter, should be – prompts a great many urgent questions. Why is it that the twentieth century has witnessed an unending fascination with distinctive types of erotic behaviour? What are critics seeking to discover when devising elaborate theoretical models to understand sex? And why have modern thinkers reached such contradictory conclusions about the meaning of sexuality in our everyday lives?

To get to grips with these fundamental issues, we could do well to begin by considering how, why, and when sexuality originally gained legitimacy as a critical category. Sexuality is a comparatively new term. The word became common currency in late-nineteenth-century Europe and America when anthropological, scientific, and sociological studies of sex were flourishing as never before. In its earliest scientific usage, sexuality defined the meanings of human eroticism, and when marked by a prefix – such as 'bi', 'hetero' or 'homo' – the word came to describe types of person who embodied particular desires. In previous decades, however, the label sexuality was used somewhat differently, and it is worth pondering briefly the rather unexpected contexts in which sexuality appears at these earlier times.

Dip into the *Oxford English Dictionary* and you will see that the first recorded use of sexuality appears in 1836. The word turns up in an edition of the collected works of eighteenth-century English poet, William Cowper (1731–1800). Cowper's editor notes that this eminent writer 'built his poem' titled 'The Lives of Plants' upon 'their sexuality'. The *OED* suggests that in this editorial commentary sexuality means 'the quality of being sexual or having sex'. Yet 'having sex' in this particular instance refers primarily to botany. This example alone plainly shows that sexuality has not always belonged to an exclusively human domain.

A slightly later usage of sexuality may also strike us as a little surprising. The *OED* lists its third definition of the word in a quite familiar manner, as 'recognition of or preoccupation with what is sexual'. Yet here, too, the example employed to support this definition presents 'what is sexual' in an uncommon way. The example in question comes from the authorial Preface to *Yeast: A Problem* (1851), a polemical Condition-of-England novel by English writer, Charles Kingsley (1819–1875): 'Paradise and hell . . . as grossly material as Mahomet's, without the honest thorough-going sexuality, which you thought made his notion logical and consistent'. This sentence may well encourage us to ask why Kingsley should associate sexuality with argumentative rationality. Rarely, if ever, in the twentieth century has sex been thought to underpin the cognitive powers of the mind. To the contrary, some theorists are convinced that sexuality opposes reason because it exerts a hydraulic force which threatens to rise up and subvert the logical intellect.

If these two examples from the *OED* have any value, then it is to confirm that the contemporary perspectives from which we view sexuality have for the most part arisen in the past century – although there are one or two exceptions to the rule. The *Supplement* to the *OED*, for example, notes that the English poet and essayist Samuel Taylor Coleridge (1772–1834) employed the term bisexuality as early as 1804, in *Aids to Reflection*, where he commented on 'the very old tradition of the *homo androgynous*, that is, that original man . . . was bi-sexual'. To Coleridge, 'bi-sexual' evidently means containing both sexes in one body. Although this usage is not completely outmoded today, it is definitely not the same as the modern view that bisexuality means attraction to both men and women. Only by the 1890s had sexuality and its variant prefixed forms become associated with types of sexual person and kinds of erotic attraction. The *Supplement* to the *OED* records that both the words heterosexuality and homosexuality first entered the English language in an 1892 translation of the well-known study, *Psychopathia Sexualis*, by the Austrian sex researcher, Richard von Krafft-Ebing (1840–1902). Thereafter, it took some time before the words circulated widely among the population, and it is clear that when they were generally acknowledged they were perceived as the only sexual options. (It is important to note that bisexuality tended to disappear from public view, being consigned to specialist medical textbooks and psychoanalytic writings.) This fact becomes plain in a frequently cited episode in *My Father and Myself* (1992 [1968]) by English novelist J.R. Ackerley (1896–1967). In this distinguished memoir, Ackerley recalls his bafflement at being asked by a friend shortly after the First World War (1914–18): 'Are you a homo or a hetero?' 'I had', writes Ackerley, 'never heard either term before' (Ackerley 1992: 117). But, as Ackerley points out, 'there seemed only one answer' to this question. Even if he 'did not care for the word "homosexual" or any label', Ackerley claims that the term now enabled him to discern exactly where he stood on 'the sexual map'. As a result, he remained 'proud' of 'his place on it' (Ackerley 1992: 118). Ackerley's remarks certainly point to a curious tension between sexual naming and sexual being, revealing the power of the term homosexual to grant a coherent place within the cultural order, while at the same time expressing some discontent at having one's erotic preference attached to a specific classification. This tension suggests that there is always likely to be a gap between the experience of eroticism and the category used to contain that experience.

This issue has been explored by several influential historians of sexuality. Having devoted much of his research to examining the recent emergence of the word sexuality in its current sense, Jeffrey Weeks remarks that it is vital not to forget that 'what we define as "sexuality" is an historical construction' (Weeks 1986: 15). Warning against the belief that sexuality refers to an essentially human quality known through all time, Weeks claims that sexuality is a '"fictional unity", that once did not exist, and at some time in the future may not exist again'. In other words, the term sexuality is historically contingent, coming to prominence at a time when detailed attention was increasingly turned to classifying, determining, and even producing assorted sexual desires. Consequently, he questions whether sexuality is an entirely suitable expression for discussing the erotic lives of cultures that preceded the late-Victorian moment when sexuality earned its current name.

In a similar spirit, the American classical scholar David M. Halperin sounds a warning note against employing the term homosexuality to describe erotic activity between men in Ancient Greece. Observing that homosexuality is a distinctly modern construction, Halperin declares: 'It may well be that homosexuality has no history of its own outside the West or much before the beginning of our century' (Halperin 1990: 18). Like many cultural historians, Halperin is highly sensitive to the critical hazards involved in using such a loaded modern idiom. Since homosexuality has often been seen as the dissident antithesis to normative heterosexual desire, the term may not be altogether germane to understanding how past societies conceptualized erotic relations between persons of the same sex. Like Weeks, Halperin advances the view that sexuality needs to be understood first and foremost in its own specific historical context because the word itself might only have limited analytical reach if applied to sexual arrangements before the present century.

To illustrate the rise of sexuality as a peculiarly modern phenomenon, Chapter 1 examines the development of sexology, in particular from the 1860s through to the early twentieth century. Sexology was the science that sought to know the name and nature of diverse desires and sexual types, and the comprehensive vocabulary it created retains its influence to this day. Not only did sexology bring the figures of the bisexual, homosexual, and heterosexual to public attention, it also investigated perverse behaviours, including sadism and masochism. Sexological writings often went to inordinate lengths to classify sexual perversions, compiling case histories that featured men and women making frank and startling disclosures about their erotic desires. Countless volumes of this kind provided an imposing, if at times inflexible, system of terms for describing a broad range of sexual types and practices. But such works did not always celebrate the phenomena they investigated. Since early sexology often leant heavily on medical science, it had a marked tendency to codify certain sexual behaviours as categories of disease. It would take many decades before sexology decisively shifted its emphasis away from pathologizing styles of sexual conduct. By comparison, modern scientific inquiries in the sexological tradition often try to refrain from presenting dissident desires as illnesses. Yet despite their liberal-minded gestures, books of this kind still tend to follow a pattern of research established by their Victorian ancestors. Time and again, they seek to typologize an astounding range of erotic phenomena, often taking pains to identify norms against which sexual performance can be measured. The same is largely true of popular works that offer sexual advice. Authors of contemporary guides on sex often focus on developing tried and tested techniques that will lead to orgasm: an event that sexologists almost always concur is the ultimate aim of sexuality. Chapter 1 explains that, no matter how non-judgemental current sexological research might have become, the span of works that fall within its scope seldom does more than quantify forms of sexual stimulation and classify sorts of sexual desire. Despite its taxonomic zeal to expand our knowledge of eroticism, sexology unfortunately has limited explanatory power when investigating all the different sexual identities and behaviours it seeks to evaluate.

If, since the turn of the twentieth century, one field of knowledge has more than any other taken our understanding of sexuality well beyond sexology, then it is surely psychoanalysis. That is why Chapter 2 first considers the researches of Sigmund Freud (1859–1939) into the unconscious, revealing how hard he strived (and sometimes failed) to divorce his analytic methods from those of nineteenth-century hereditarian science, the field of inquiry that fascinated the earlier generation of sexologists. Having explained the powerful influence of Freud's Oedipus and castration complexes, the discussion turns to the intricate range of critical terms devised by his successor, Jacques Lacan (1901–1981). By locating desire within the field of signification, Lacan's work at last disengaged psychoanalysis from its scientific heritage. In many respects, Lacan's work completes one of the main tasks begun by Freud: to dissociate eroticism from biological mechanisms. Psychoanalysis was the first body of theory to produce a detailed account of why sexuality must be understood separately from reproduction. In one the clearest guides to psychoanalytic thought, Jean Laplanche and Jean-Bertrand Pontalis examine why sexual desire does not conform to a biological instinct that drives human beings towards perpetuating the species:

> If one sets out with the commonly held view that defines sexuality as instinct, in the sense of a pre-determined behaviour typifying the species and having a relatively fixed *object* (partner of the opposite sex) and *aim* (union of the genital organs in coitus), it soon becomes apparent that this approach can

> only provide a very inadequate account of the facts that
> emerge as much from direct observation as from analysis.
>
> (Laplanche and Pontalis 1973: 419)

By forcing attention on why sexuality is not necessarily geared to reproductive ends, psychoanalysis develops models that trace the origins of erotic pleasure back to infancy. In theorizing how human beings establish specific sexual identifications, Freud and, subsequently, Lacan reveal that the organization of the sexual drives starts the moment we enter the world. According to psychoanalysis, the early development of the erogenous zones bears a psychic imprint that persists throughout adulthood. Such is the initial impression made by sexuality that psychoanalysis believes it can sometimes prove hard for adults to manage their earliest and thus most insistent unconscious desires. To uphold these leading ideas, Freud identified the two interdependent structures he called the Oedipus and castration complexes. Similarly, Lacan argued that sexuality was structured around the primary symbol of cultural authority he named the phallus. Both writers have gained notoriety for developing what undeniably are paradigms that take the centrality of the anatomical penis, the psychology of penis-envy, and the symbolic power of the phallus entirely for granted. Psychoanalytic phallocentrism would become the subject of intense debate among feminists, both in the late 1920s and early 1930s and again from the late 1960s onwards. The closing section of Chapter 2 considers a range of differing feminist standpoints on the penis and the phallus that absorb Freudian and Lacanian theory respectively. Whereas some feminists claim that this complex body of research is largely a symptom of patriarchal dominance, others argue that psychoanalysis provides significant clues about both the cultural and psychic mechanisms that assist in perpetuating sexual inequality in the West.

One of the main lessons of psychoanalysis is that sexuality comprises turbulent, if not destructive, drives whose early formation can at times prove impossible to eradicate in adult life. Freud's belief that the conflicted libido was caught in a life-and-death struggle would shape much subsequent discussion about the volatile condition of eroticism. Beginning with Freud's powerful theory of the death drive, Chapter 3 draws together two notable debates that focus on sexuality as a seemingly boundless source of impulsive energy caught within a dynamic of creation and destruction. The first part of the discussion looks at the work of several avant-garde theorists – including Georges Bataille (1897–1962), Gilles Deleuze (1930–1995), and Félix Guattari (1930–1992) – who have tried to unravel why sexuality violently oscillates between life and death. The second part of Chapter 3 reveals how this fraught discussion about the life-giving and death-dealing aspects of desire appear most vividly in modern feminist debates about pornography. Undoubtedly, pornography continues to divide feminist opinion about the injurious or emancipatory effects of erotic desire. On the one hand, many radical feminist campaigners against pornography claim that it leads time and again to violent sexual crimes, and should therefore be legally called to account for the serious damage it causes. On the other, libertarian feminists eager to combat punitive state censorship argue that there are affirmative aspects to pornography. They believe that some types of graphic sexual representation can allow women to explore and emancipate desires otherwise suppressed in a patriarchal society.

Yet this widespread emphasis on how sexuality either represses or frees sexual desire strikes French social theorist Michel Foucault (1926–1984) as nothing more than a means through which power has been organized in Western society. In *The History of Sexuality* (1976–84), Foucault prompts us to contemplate the historical circumstances that shape some of the leading claims made by psychoanalysts and philosophers about the explosive condition of eroticism. Chapter 4 examines the distinctive methods Foucault employs to demystify sexuality as a critical category. By concentrating on how power-laden discourses construct desire, he scrutinizes the conceptual regimes that have led many thinkers, from Freud to contemporary feminists, to much the same conclusion: that tempestuous sexual desires are inevitably trapped within a system of suppression and liberation. Repeatedly, Foucault explores the cultural dynamics that have persuaded the modern epoch to believe that sex 'has become more important than our soul, more important almost than our life' (Foucault 1978: 156). So powerful is this idea, he states, that one is led to think that we should 'exchange life in its entirety for sex'. What was it, Foucault asks, that brought many twentieth-century intellectuals to agree that '[s]ex is worth dying for'?

Acutely conscious of how powerful concepts such as sexuality come to dominate our lives, Foucault examines the political fabrication of influential beliefs which profess that erotic behaviours, identities, and styles are fundamental to human existence. In the process, Foucault constantly looks at how sexuality emerged as an intelligible category whose widespread acceptance has played a crucial role in regulating the social order. Although on occasions strongly criticized for treating eroticism as if it were separate from gender, Foucault has none the less inspired a later generation of feminist and queer theorists to confront the cultural interests served by the meanings ascribed to sexual desire. In this regard, critics such as Judith Butler, Gayle Rubin, and Eve Kosofsky Sedgwick have paid close attention to the troublesome ways in which modern society has been remarkably willing to accept essentialist definitions of what it means to be male or female, masculine or feminine, heterosexual or homosexual. Their work stands at the forefront of a vibrant series of critical explorations that reveal why we need to denaturalize the essentialist presumptions about desire that have governed modern approaches to erotic identities and practices.

As we head towards the next century, few would doubt that the established categories through which the West has long understood sexuality are now under considerable strain. In a late capitalist world influenced by fragmentary postmodern styles of thought, sexual identities are undergoing such rapid transformation that the sexological and psychoanalytic classifications that were once readily accepted are starting to look redundant. To show how sexual identities are currently diversifying, the Conclusion briefly sketches the flourishing debates about bisexuality, transgender issues, and sexual communities of colour — all of which contest the antiquated vocabulary that persists in misrepresenting their desires. These increasingly visible erotic minorities have significant implications for the present study. *Sexuality* proceeds on the assumption that there is much to be gained by examining the sometimes coercive theoretical uses to which the category of sexuality has been put. If we can understand what has been done to this concept, then it should be possible to make a constructive response to unforeseen sexual pleasures and unrealized erotic potentialities.

1

SEXOLOGICAL TYPES

SEXUAL CLASSIFICATIONS

Enter any major bookstore in the industrialized world and you are likely to find several shelves (if not more) devoted to studies of sexual behaviour. Such books might be found in the psychology section but the chances are they will be grouped together under a more specialized heading: sexology. Here you will discover a range of works, including updated editions of Alex Comfort's *The Joy of Sex* (1972), that give popular advice on sexual techniques for same-sex and other-sex partnerships. Especially in the 1960s, the number of 'how-to' manuals offering guidance on sexual practices and the improvement of sexual pleasure proliferated as never before. Such writings have been popular since at least the time of *Married Love: A New Contribution to the Solution of Sex Difficulties* (1918) by Marie Stopes (1880–1958). This bestselling book was among the first to broaden common knowledge of human sexual potential, and it remains an open question whether such works are ultimately liberating or oppressive in their repeated insistence that sexual satisfaction is a fundamental human need. Similar kinds of guidance on sexual matters circulate perpetually in the mass media, from advice columns in magazines aimed at young people to live 'adult' radio talk-shows. Given the ample opportunities that now exist to obtain information about many aspects of eroticism, it is perhaps hard to appreciate how dangerous this kind of knowledge was often thought to be when sexology – the science of sexuality – first made its appearance in the late nineteenth century.

According to Janice Irvine, sexology currently serves as 'an umbrella term denoting the activity of a multidisciplinary group of researchers, clinicians, and educators concerned with sexuality' (Irvine 1990: 2). These days, conferences devoted to sexology bring together a vast range of people with very different skills, from promoters of safer sex to medical doctors working in genito-urological clinics. But this was not always the case. Sexology was first associated with the controversial work of scientists examining aspects of sexual disease. Known in German as *Sexualwissenschaft*, the word sexology is attributed to the German physician, historian, and sex researcher Iwan Bloch (1872–1922), among whose works is a rather zany but none the less fascinating study of the sexual habits of the English (published 1901–3). Sexology initially designated a science that developed an elaborate descriptive system to classify a striking range of sexual types of person (bisexual, heterosexual, homosexual, and their variants) and forms of sexual desire (fetishism, masochism, sadism, among them). Bloch's *The Sexual Life of Our Time* (1907) is one of several prominent works that sought to provide a distinctly scientific explanation of various sexual phenomena. Yet, like many such studies that drew on scientific authority to uphold its claims, his work met with considerable hostility in many quarters of society. So great was the mismatch between the scientific intent and the moralistic reception of many sexological texts from the 1880s through to the 1920s, it would be fair to claim these weighty tomes drove at the centre of a major anxiety in Western culture. For there was a constant struggle among those who saw themselves as respectable people to hide what sexology, in all its scientific authority, was determined to uncover.

It was certainly for this reason that copies of one of the most detailed sexological studies, *Sexual Inversion* (1897), written by Havelock Ellis (1859–1939) in cooperation with critic and poet John Addington Symonds (1840–1893), led to the arrest of a London bookseller who sold a copy to an undercover policeman in 1898. This was hardly an auspicious time to bring before the world an array of case studies that revealed complex patterns of same-sex desire. It was, after all, only three years after the Irish author Oscar Wilde (1854–1900) had been notoriously vilified in the press, and subsequently sent to serve a prison sentence of two years for committing 'gross indecency' with other men. Such 'gross' homosexual acts were outlawed – both in public *and* in private – by the 1885 Criminal Law Amendment Act. Never since the day of its seizure has Ellis's liberal-minded exploration of homosexuality ever been published again in Britain – a sign, I think, of the severe prohibition on serious public debate about same-sex desire in a country that only partly decriminalized male homosexuality, first in 1967 and again in 1994.

Sexological writings have been renowned for making discoveries about sexual behaviour that many of the more conservative sections of modern society would prefer not to hear. In the mid-century, for example, the first Kinsey Report, *Sexual Behaviour in the Human Male* (1948), brought together an imposing mass of statistical detail to show that 37 per cent of the adult male population in the United States had achieved orgasm through homosexual contact. Such data flew in the face of what had by that time become a virulently homophobic American culture. Several decades later, the appearance of *The Hite Report: A Nationwide Study of Female Sexuality* (1976) caused a sensation when it divulged that most American women did not reach orgasm through heterosexual intercourse – a point many earlier sexological works that did not become bestsellers also took pains to note. Newspapers, women's magazines, as well as specialized academic periodicals were quick to respond to Shere Hite's findings.

Sexological works of this kind are a curiosity because they have increasingly attracted popular attention, even though they rally huge quantities of information that most people not trained in statistical analysis could not possibly compute. (Social scientists, in fact, pointed out that Hite's research methods were highly questionable.) Presented as monumental 'Reports', these works seek to give an official stamp of approval to the disclosure of unpalatable sexual truths that society often is at first reluctant to accept. In many ways, the bulk and weight of such surveys gives the definite impression that, if researchers keep amassing ever-increasing quantities of data, then the more they will be able to know about it.

Since its inception, sexology has left modern society with a contradictory legacy. On the one hand, it has played a major role in enabling sex to be debated more widely and seriously at all levels of society, at times providing useful technical advice on how to solve sexual problems at both the emotional and physical level. On the other, sexology often remains worryingly insensitive to the historical contingency of the scientific methods it employs to estimate sexual adequacy or inadequacy, deviancy or normativity. Time and again, one finds sexological writings – all the way from the 1890s to the 1990s – seeking to produce some everlasting truth about the sexual capacity of human beings. Such works are habitually filled with deceptive ideas about what is supposed to constitute average performance, in terms of frequency and intensity of erotic sensation, implying there is a common standard against which our sexualities might be measured. Sexological writings are frequently so preoccupied with the quantification of data regarding sexual behaviours and functions that they rarely pause to consider how or why sexuality might resist the structures of categorization that sexual science multiplies at an exponential rate. One only has to look at a mightily compendious work such as *The Social Organization of Sexuality*, published in 1994, to see the confidence with which social scientists present their statistical evidence as 'accurate information'. Although the writers insist that theirs is not an ethical task to make 'judgements about what people "should" do sexually', they assume that sexuality is a perfectly recognizable category that subsumes all forms of 'sexual conduct' (Laumann *et al.* 1994: xxx–xxxi, 31). Assuming that sexuality means sexual activity, they group facts under headings such as frequency of sexual partners, sexually transmitted infections, sex and fertility, and normative orientations towards sexuality. Hardly ever do they question the biases that have for more than a century been inscribed in their methods for organizing this material. So it remains difficult for their readers to gain insights into the cultural conditions and ideological pressures that gave rise to the idea of sexuality in the first place.

The critic who has produced the most incisive accounts of the sexological tradition is Leonore Tiefer, who has extensive professional experience in genito-urological medical practice. Closely acquainted with the research of Alfred C. Kinsey (1894–1956) and his heirs, Tiefer complains that studies of this kind repeatedly fail to identify exactly what might plausibly fall within the field of analysis:

> The most basic, and also most difficult, aspect of studying sexuality is defining the subject-matter. What is to be included? How much of the body is relevant? How much of the life span? Is sexuality an individual dimension or a dimension of a relationship? Which behaviours, thoughts, or feelings qualify as sexual – an unreturned glance? any hug? daydreams about celebrities? fearful memories of abuse? When can we use similar language for animals and people, if at all?
>
> (Tiefer 1995: 20)

Tiefer's call is for modern sexology to deliberate carefully about the assumptions, biases, and downright prejudices it has inherited from a highly developed tradition of research that seldom interrogates the limits to what might or might not be construed as sexual. Her point is that the models often employed by sexologists may well be inappropriate to the phenomena they are attempting to explain. She notes how sociologists John Gagnon and William Simon, in *Sexual Conduct: The Social Sources of Human Sexuality* (1973), adopted 'the metaphor of dramatic scripts to draw our attention to learned, planned, external sources'. The trouble is that such metaphors, like the common usages of 'drive' and 'instinct' to describe sexuality, 'direct the attention of researchers, scholars, and readers to distinct possibilities' (Tiefer 1995: 20–1). Viewed as 'innate', the sexual 'drive' would seem to follow a path to a specific goal, depending on external stimuli. In using such loaded terms, Gagnon and Simon's *Sexual Conduct* does not take pains to scrutinize the assumptions that underwrite them. Tiefer argues that countless studies of this kind remain unaware of the incommensuration between the theoretical model in place and the sexual phenomenon under discussion. In her view, this type of disparity was most astounding when one recalls the battles that took place in the American Psychiatric Association during 1973. During that year, concerted efforts were made to declassify homosexuality as a mental disorder. As Tiefer says, the normality or abnormality of a particular sexual behaviour, identity, or style depends largely on the interpretative lens through which it is observed.

To amplify some of these general remarks, I shall first of all set out to explore some of the more striking problems that beset a handful of notable early works of sexology. Although the first sexologists may well feel to us like relics from the distant past, their conceptual and narrative structures in many ways endure to this day. In these founding texts of sexology, one sees an exhaustive effort being made to derive natural truths from cultural phenomena. Rather than advance the idea that Western society developed customs and practices that emerged from specific historical conditions, these writers often believed that their culture provided a wholly intelligible map for interpreting human nature. To this end, they employed devices that were thought to provide transparent access to the indisputably natural state of sexuality. Above all, they scrutinized bodily behaviours to derive the essential core of desire that erupted from within each human subject.

Particularly important in sexological research is the genre known as the case history. Here the subject of research plots the biographical facts of her or (more usually) his psycho-sexual development. This notable discursive form frequently resembles a confession in which women and men testify to the often shameful inner truth of their sexual being. It is uncommon indeed to find sexologists pondering how the case history is itself a structure of representation that shapes and manipulates information according to generic and narrative conventions. Sexologists rarely hesitate to question whether the subject under investigation might be swayed towards certain conclusions. After all, the conventions used by sexologists to some degree determine what can and cannot be said within the linear and developmental form that characterizes the history containing each case.

The case history, however, is not the only heuristic device that sexologists employ to extract supposedly natural facts from cultural phenomena. Early sexological writings also substantiate their claims by drawing widely – one might say, promiscuously – on a dazzling assortment of data taken from comparative anthropology, an academic discipline that established itself in the 1860s. Here, too, one can see a marked tendency in such writings to align the cultural manifestation of sexual behaviours with what are presumed to be natural conditions. In one study after another, sexologists strive to show the primitive nature of sexual instinct: a word that explains sexuality in terms of social Darwinism. Developed by the English writer Herbert Spencer (1820–1903), social Darwinism emphasized the 'survival of the fittest', a doctrine that proved hugely influential from the 1870s through to the 1930s. Even when not pursuing arguments about the primitive core of civilized society, sexologists often draw amply on biological data to make observations about copulation, mating, and reproductive aims. In this respect, it is perhaps no accident that Kinsey – one of the most distinguished sexologists to emerge in the twentieth century – began his academic career as a zoologist; his early research was into the gall wasp.

So with these issues in mind, let me begin by examining several noteworthy aspects of four different works that fall within the general field of sexual science. Starting with the courageous research of the German sexual liberationist, Karl Heinrich Ulrichs (1825–1895), I move on to contrast the assumptions upon which the psychiatrist Richard von Krafft-Ebing built *Psychopathia Sexualis* (first published in 1886, and revised and expanded in many successive editions). Two further German works open up the complexity of sexological thinking within this period: first, Iwan Bloch's *The Sexual Life of Our Time* (1907), and second, *Sex and Character* (1975 [1903]) by Otto Weininger (1880–1903). Since much of this writing displays considerable confusion about female sexuality, my discussion proceeds to two notable women writers: Olive Schreiner (1855–1920), who drew on aspects of contemporary scientific thought in the name of a progressive politics of social change; and Radclyffe Hall (1883–1943), whose banned novel *The Well of Loneliness* (1928) drew partly on sexological thought to represent the dignity and integrity of lesbianism. Schreiner's vision, if sharing with the sexologists a number of similar assumptions about sex and race, provides an alternative perspective on women's desires in an era when sexuality was for the first time the subject of extensive research and speculation. Likewise, Hall's controversial fiction reveals how and why a woman's desires might not conform to dominant heterosexual conventions. Given the emergence of fiction, plays, and poetry by feminist New Women (such as Sarah Grand [1854–1953]) and Aesthetes and Decadents (such as the aunt and niece who collaborated as Michael Field [1846–1914 and 1862–1913], and Oscar Wilde) with a strong interest in same-sex desire, the period in which sexology emerged has been aptly characterized by Elaine Showalter as one of 'sexual anarchy' (see Showalter 1990).

Among the sexologists, perhaps the most detailed typology of sexual variation was devised by Ulrichs in the 1860s and 1870s. If the intricate terms he created strike us today as rather bizarre, then his work remains undoubtedly significant precisely because of its determination to refine a vocabulary that sought to specify sexual diversity of many kinds. Ulrichs, a Hanoverian legal official, pursued a lifelong campaign in Germany to justify the naturalness of sexual relations between men. He spelled out his views in a series of twelve short books published between 1864 and 1879, most of which were aimed at transforming state legislation. Pioneering in their field, Ulrichs's writings would become a major point of reference for many later researchers, notably Krafft-Ebing. In fact, Ulrichs was the first of a line of zealous researchers whose radicalism would be gradually eclipsed by thinkers who wished to pathologize the types of 'man–manly love' which he did his utmost to defend as healthy and normal. Ulrichs's work circulated widely, especially among homosexual men seeking information that both explained and legitimized their sexual condition. In one pamphlet after another, Ulrichs brought to light significant details about male homosexuality, details revealed to him in countless letters sent by eager correspondents from all over Europe. In the English tradition, his influence can be felt most palpably in the confessional memoirs of the Victorian critic and poet, John Addington Symonds. (For reasons of propriety, Symonds's memoirs had a fifty-year ban placed on their publication when his manuscript passed into the hands of the London Library in 1926. On Symonds, see Bristow 1995: 127–46.)

Homosexuality, however, is not the word that Ulrichs employs in his analysis of sexual desire between men, since his researches predated that term by several years. Deriving his nomenclature from Plato's *Symposium*, Ulrichs draws a clear distinction between what he calls Uranian and Dionian love. In Ulrichs's model, Uranian desire is expressed by Urnings: these are persons who love their own sex, in the manner of the god Uranus. By comparison, those who experience opposite-sex attraction were named Dionings, after the goddess Dione. 'Urnings', declares Ulrichs, 'have existed in all areas, in antiquity, among uncivilized nomads, indeed, actually among animals' (Ulrichs 1994: 34). Found among primitive peoples, in all periods of history, and in nature itself, Uranian love is said to be more prevalent in Germany than commonly perceived, and it may well be increasing. 'No father', remarks Ulrichs, 'is sure if the germ of this orientation is latent in one of his sons and if it will break through at puberty' (Ulrichs 1994: 35). In each of his short studies, Ulrichs seeks to clarify the precise nature of the Uranian disposition, showing how the 'germ' of same-sex desire is implanted *ab ovo* in the very physiology of the man-loving man.

Ulrichs begins his vindication of man–manly love by insisting on the congenital nature of the Urning's desires. 'There is', he writes, 'a class of born Urnings, a class of individuals who are born with the sexual drive of women and who have male bodies'. On this basis, he claims that the Urning 'is not a man, but rather a kind of feminine being when it concerns not only his entire organism, but also his sexual feelings of love, his entire natural temperament, and his talents' (Ulrichs 1994: 36). Since the sexed body and the gendered mind of this erotic type are by definition turned inside out, Ulrichs declares that Urnings constitute a *'third sex'*: 'not fully men or women'. In making this claim, Ulrichs lays the ground on which he establishes his belief that Urnings are beings who contain the soul of the opposite sex in their own bodies. Contrary to its aims, this idea would have a lasting and damaging influence on twentieth-century prejudices against homosexuals. For it set the trend for imagining that lesbians and gay men were 'inverts'. One of the myths that has circulated most widely about lesbians and gay men is that both sexual identities involve the inversion of assumed gender norms – so that the butch lesbian and the effeminate gay man have often been the recognizable stereotypes that serve to caricature and thus condemn styles of homosexual dissidence.

Committed to the belief that Urnings were a separate sexual species whose desires inverted Dionian ones, Ulrichs focuses on effeminacy as the cardinal sign of the Uranian temperament. 'When Urnings get together', he notes, 'they mostly give themselves feminine nicknames. I suppose this is because they feel like women, even if only subconsciously' (Ulrichs 1994: 60). The more Ulrichs developed this model, the more easily he could argue that there might be a corresponding 'fourth sex': 'a sex of persons built like females having woman–womanly sexual desire, i.e. having the sexual direction of men' (Ulrichs 1994: 81). But as his speculations gathered pace, it became difficult for Ulrichs to account for varieties of sexual behaviour purely in terms of male and female Urnings and Dionings. For one thing, he found himself obliged to consider what would become known later as bisexuality. And true to form, he devised a word for bisexuals: Uranodionings.

By the time he wrote his seventh treatise on man–manly love, Ulrichs had constructed an elaborate system that would include many – but by no means all – possible permutations of Uranian and Dionian desire, and it is instructive to see how he pieced together the following tabulation of variant sexual types:

I   Men
II   Women
III Urnings
    1   Mannlings
    2   Intermediaries
    3   Weiblings

IV Urningins
V   Uranodionings
   1   Conjunctive
   2   Disjunctive
VI Uranodioningins
VII Hermaphrodites

(Ulrichs 1994: 314)

If this list of seven specimens, together with their qualifying sub-categories, looks cranky in the extreme, then readers would be well-advised to open the pages of any late-twentieth-century encyclopedia of human sexuality, just to get a sense of the exceptional lengths to which social and medical scientists will go in their effort to identify and comprehend the seemingly endless list of sexual types and behaviours. Ulrichs's meticulous expansion of his list of sexual types indicates the hazards involved in trying to find a language that can adequately describe the phenomena under analysis. Although the clear-cut opposition between Uranian and Dionian desires has already been described, the polarity they represent becomes altogether less stable when we look carefully at the additional terms he uses here to designate different forms of desire.

Among Urnings, for example, there are two internally opposed types: Mannlings (virile homosexuals) and Weiblings (effeminate homosexuals). Between these two stand the Intermediaries who belong to a revealingly liminal category that, in Ulrichs's scheme, allows his readers to understand how a virile Urning might take a passive role in sex, while an effeminate Urning might adopt an active position. Further down the list come the Urningings, later named in the early twentieth century as lesbians, but it is clear from the whole of Ulrichs's writings that he knew next to nothing about lesbianism, or what he sometimes called 'woman–womanly' desire. Thereafter, we find the bisexuals, who also fall into two categories: conjunctive (who experience 'sensual love in a double direction'), and disjunctive (who 'feel only a romantic gentle love for young men'). Regarding the latter, Ulrichs declares: 'Shakespeare perhaps belongs in this category' (Ulrichs 1994: 313–14). No doubt the nineteenth-century critical controversies surrounding Shakespeare's sonnets were on Ulrichs's mind when pondering sexual love between older and younger men. The final two categories identify female bisexuals and intersexual persons who bear the physical characteristics of both sexes.

In Ulrichs's idiosyncratic system for naming all these sexual variants, one point becomes patently clear. It is impossible for Ulrichs to construct his model of erotic identities without taking for granted that all sexualities are grounded on a principle of sexual difference. Ulrichs always assumes that the desire of any one person is predicated on an attraction to an opposite pole. In his first analysis, he renders Uranian or man–manly love intelligible because it reveals how a feminine soul seeks a masculine object. Likewise, when pressed to account for active and passive homosexual behaviours, Ulrichs interprets the positions taken up by each partner as either feminine or masculine. Everywhere we look in his scheme of sexual relations, the same principle obtains. Feminine desires require their masculine complement, and vice versa, whether in Uranian or Dionian forms. In Ulrichs's view, sex was always split into two antithetical but none the less complementary forms. His belief that the Urning embodied an inverted sexual identity is generally thought to mark a decisively new stage in Western conceptions of sex. We might perhaps label this the psychiatric model of sexuality, since there is an assumed discordance between the sexual mind and the sexual body in Ulrichs's theory of Uranian desire. Previous writers on sexual physiology seldom questioned the congruence between the sexed body and the sexed being of a man or a woman. The sexological discourse on homosexuality did much to shatter such an assumption.

What cultural conditions made this particular style of thinking possible in the 1860s? One answer would be that in the nineteenth century the idea that the sexes were polar opposites magnetically attracted to each other had such a tight ideological grip on the culture that it was believed to be an indisputable fact of nature. Ulrichs was hardly alone among sexual radicals in basing his thinking about eroticism on highly conventional notions about femininity and masculinity. It is useful to compare his writings with those of the English socialist essayist, poet, and socialist politician Edward Carpenter (1844–1929), who championed Ulrichs's belief in the 'third sex'. Like Ulrichs, Carpenter would readily acknowledge that the polar opposition between men and women was the fault of existing social relations: 'As a rule they [boy and girl] know little of each other; society has kept the two sexes apart . . . They hardly understand each other'. But such comments would not prevent him, in a radical pamphlet titled 'Woman, and Her Place in a Free Society' (1894), from asserting: 'Man has developed the more active, and Woman the more passive virtues'. In fact, Carpenter would draw on recent scientific inquiries to back up the following view: 'In woman . . . the more fundamental and primitive nervous centre, and the great vaso-motor system of nerves generally, are developed to a greater extent than in men'. On this basis, he could argue: 'Woman is the more primitive, the more intuitive, the more emotional; the great unconscious and cosmic processes of Nature lie somehow nearer to her' (Carpenter 1894a: 6; 1894b, 22; 1894c, 8–9). Although Carpenter followed Ulrichs in championing the dignity of what he called 'the intermediate sex' and 'homogenic love', his work contains classic examples that demonstrate how his well-intentioned liberatory sexual politics construes distinctions between the sexes in strikingly orthodox terms. It would take many decades indeed before a consensus was reached that emotionality, passivity, and primitivity were hardly qualities that could be naturally attributed to women.

The problems involved in Ulrichs's schematic conception of inversion were compounded by the far from radical inquiry into sexuality produced by Krafft-Ebing. A professor of psychiatry at the University of Vienna, Krafft-Ebing was one of Sigmund Freud's most distinguished colleagues. The title of his major work, *Psychopathia Sexualis* (1894), makes it clear that this examination of desire adopts a medical perspective on the psychological and pathological condition of erotic life. As Bloch writes, 'Krafft-Ebing is, and remains, the true founder of modern sexual pathology' (Bloch 1908: 455). The scope of Krafft-Ebing's often intriguing investigation is much broader than Ulrichs's series of short studies. Divided into five sections, the book not only pays attention to the psychology and physiology of sexual love, it also devotes a great amount of space to the itemization of 'pathological manifestations': from 'sexual neuroses' to 'satyriasis and nymphomania' (that is, male and female forms of heterosexual erotomania). The concluding part of the study considers the legal regulation of sexual acts, especially ones of a perverse nature. 'Criminal statistics', writes Krafft-Ebing, 'prove the sad fact that sexual crimes are progressively increasing in our modern civilization' (Krafft-Ebing 1894: 378). This is his clarion call to the power of the state to control as much as possible any 'abnormalities' that are likely to result in 'immorality'. 'From what experience teaches', he insists, 'it may be said that, among the sexual acts that occur, rape, mutilation, pederasty, *amor lesbicus*, and bestiality may have a psycho-pathological basis' (Krafft-Ebing 1894: 382). To modern readers, it surely takes a considerable leap of the imagination to understand how lesbianism might have a similar pathological status to bestiality and rape.

Rather than summarize each and every aspect of Krafft-Ebing's fascination with the diseased features of human sexuality, I want to draw attention to the main assumptions underpinning his belief that eroticism was always proximate to mental and physical disorders. Throughout *Psychopathia Sexualis*, he unwaveringly maintains that sexual desire is a potentially explosive power that it has been the purpose of civilization to tame. 'Sexuality', he declares on the very first page, 'is the most powerful factor in individual and social existence'. He adds: 'Love as an unbridled passion is like a fire that burns and consumes everything; like an abyss that swallows all, – honour, fortune, well-being' (Krafft-Ebing 1894: 1–2). These remarks place such emphasis on the fundamental power of sexual feeling in the male of the species that he never stops to think if this idea is unique to the period in which he is writing. Instead, Krafft-Ebing sets out to show how the highest forms of cultural organization in the West have gone to considerable lengths to assuage, if not completely master, apparently dangerous sexual energies. To support his argument, he is obliged to draw comparisons between pre-eminent Northern European societies and those that have apparently failed to attain such dignified levels of breeding and gentility.

'On primitive ground the satisfaction of the sexual appetite of man seems like that of an animal', Krafft-Ebing asserts. Only with the advent of morality were human beings able to dissociate themselves from this degrading condition. First, the genitals were covered because of a morally uplifting sense of shame. Second, women were treated with increasing respect, no longer abused as 'thing[s] to satisfy lust and to work'. Finally, the civilizing process was complete when monogamy had full rein, a point that comes into focus when Krafft-Ebing attempts to contrast Christian and Muslim attitudes to marriage:

> The fact that in higher civilization human love must be monogamous and rest on a lasting contract was thus recognized. If nature does not more than provide for procreation, a commonwealth (family or state) cannot exist without a guarantee that the offspring shall flourish physically, morally, and intellectually. Christendom gained both mental and material superiority over the polygamous races, especially Islam, through the

equalization of woman and man, and by establishing monogamous marriage and securing it by legal, religious, and moral
ties.

If Mohammed was actuated by a desire to raise woman
from her place as a slave and means of sensual gratification to
a higher social and matrimonial plane, nevertheless, in the
Mohammedan world woman remained far below man, to
whom alone divorce was allowed and also made very easy.

(Krafft-Ebing 1894: 5)

On this view, Christianity makes for a preferably higher set of
sexual arrangements than Islam because monogamy controls the
animal-like passion that constantly threatens to degrade the man.
In making this claim, Krafft-Ebing upholds the commonplace
Victorian wisdom that men are innately aggressive in their sexual
drives, while women embody modesty and passivity. 'Probably',
speculates Krafft-Ebing, 'feminine modesty is an hereditarily
evolved product of the development of civilization' (Krafft-Ebing
1894: 15). He argues that, unlike the restive sexuality of the
male, the woman has her 'native element' in 'love' – a desire for
protection by a husband, which is met in return by the care and
attention she devotes to the man's every need. So it may appear
rather strange that he should stake such a strong claim on the
'superiority' of Christianity in securing the 'equalization' of
woman and man'.

But Krafft-Ebing reveals that even such 'equalization' between
the sexes holds no uncertain dangers. Given his propensity for
linking desire with disease, Krafft-Ebing amplifies his understanding of how civilized men and women create honourable, lov-
ing marriages by appealing to a concept that verges on the brink
of being pathological. The concept in question is the fetish, a
phenomenon that Freud would later theorize in a well-known
paper published in 1927. In *Psychopathia Sexualis*, sexual love
reaches its highest point through the highly individualized, dis-

tinctive, and thus fetishistic pleasures that a man derives from the object of his affections. In other words, sexual love in marriage is based on the unique fetishism enjoyed by the man. This theory helps to explain precisely how men select their partners in a discriminating rather than lustful way:

> It is well-known from experience that accident determines this mental association, that the objects of the fetish may be individually very diverse, and that thus the most peculiar sympathies (and antipathies) arise.
>
> These physiological facts of fetishism explain the individual sympathies between husband and wife; the preference of a certain person to all others of the same sex. Since the fetish represents a symbol that is purely individual, it is clear that its effect must be individual. Since it is coloured by the most intense pleasurable feeling, it follows that possible faults in the beloved object are overlooked ('Love is blind'), and an exaltation of it is induced that to others is incomprehensible, and even silly under some circumstances.
>
> (Krafft-Ebing 1894: 19)

It does not take much to see how this theoretical model has been devised to manage the basic fear that runs throughout Krafft-Ebing's work: that all sexual love, even in its most distinguished and praiseworthy married form, is to some degree tainted with illness. That is why he is at pains to argue that the 'fetish may constantly retain its significance' for the man 'without being pathological'. But this shall only be the case if 'the particular concept' – such as the love of perfume, the shape of a foot, or the colour and texture of hair – 'is developed into a general concept'. If male heterosexual desire in all its refined particularity was ultimately unable to distance itself from its pathological love of the fetish, then such eroticism would remain reprehensibly perverse.

Given the overwhelming quantities of evidence that Krafft-Ebing subsequently produces on the topic of sexual perversion,

Psychopathia Sexualis makes the distinct impression that the highest form of heterosexual love is menaced on all sides by an epidemic of perverse sexual behaviours. The numerous case histories included in his chapters on sadism, masochism, fetishism, and homosexuality attest to what he considers are widespread sexual disorders among men. Take, for example, one of the longer cases studied in the chapter on masochism, the perversion that Krafft-Ebing himself named after Leopold Sacher-Masoch (1836–95), remembered for his fiction of perverse desire, *Venus in Furs* (1870). 'Case 50' features a man of thirty-five who declares that from an early age he has been perpetually excited by fantasies involving whipping. Here is how he tells part of his story:

> Even in my early childhood I loved to revel in ideas about the absolute mastery of one man over others. The thought of slavery had something in it for me, and alike whether from the standpoint of master and servant. That one man could possess, sell, or whip another, caused me intense excitement; and in reading *Uncle Tom's Cabin* [a novel about American slavery, by Harriet Beecher Stowe (1811–96)] . . . I had erections. . . . Though these ideas caused erections, yet I have never masturbated in my life; and from my nineteenth year I had coitus without the help of these ideas and without any relation to them. I always had a great preference for elderly, voluptuous, large women, though I did not scorn younger ones.
>
> (Krafft-Ebing 1894: 105)

As his narrative unravels, 'Case 50' reveals how he has only been able to enact his fantasies by hiring the services of prostitutes. Such experiences have quelled his desires for no more than periods of two weeks, after which he usually suffers his 'next attack' that consequently forces his return to the brothel for another series of punishments from his 'mistress'. Even though he enjoyed a satisfactory sexual relationship in the early months of his marriage, his masochistic desires proved the stronger. Yet rather than admit his masochism is a problem, 'Case 50' almost seems to take pride in his condition: 'in spite of its marked pathological character, masochism is not only incapable of destroying pleasure in my life, but it does not in the least affect my outward life' (Krafft-Ebing 1894: 108). In fact, the more one looks at this case history, the more obvious it seems that the masochistic rituals in which this man engages form a dynamic and vibrant part of his existence – although there is immense cultural pressure on him to believe otherwise.

Faced with such materials that enlarged his contemporaries' knowledge of the irrepressible force of sexual perversion, one might reasonably expect Krafft-Ebing to provide a detailed analysis of the cultural, psychic, or physiological sources of such diseased eroticism. So what exactly does Krafft-Ebing have to say about the causes of perverse desire? Surprisingly little. His chapters on sadistic and masochistic practices form a stream of almost uninterrupted case histories, testimonials, and other documentation drawn from researchers who had already amassed plenty of data on the topic. One has to wade through endless pages of this material before one reaches an explanation. And when the moment comes to pass judgement on precisely what causes such perverse behaviours, Krafft-Ebing follows the majority of his intellectual peers by taking recourse to heredity: 'masochism, as a congenital sexual perversion, constitutes a functional sign of degeneration in (almost exclusively) hereditary taint; and this clinical deduction is confirmed in my cases of masochism and sadism' (Krafft-Ebing 1894: 147).

Significantly, Krafft-Ebing supplies a rather different diagnosis when confronting homosexuality. To be sure, he generally asserts that same-sex desire is, like all other peversities, a congenital condition. On occasions, however, his evidence points to moments when same-sex desire has been expediently 'acquired', rather than inborn. He believes that aberrant episodes of homosexual intercourse occur when cultural factors prevail against the seemingly normal path of desire towards the opposite sex:

> Sometimes the development of higher sexual feelings toward the opposite sex suffers, on account of hypochondriacal fear of infection in sexual intercourse; or on account of an actual infection; or they suffer as a result of faulty education which points out such dangers and exaggerates them. Again (especially in females), fear of the result of coitus (pregnancy), or abhorrence of men, by reason of mental or moral weakness, may direct into perverse channels an instinct that makes itself felt with abnormal intensity. But too early and perverse sexual satisfaction injures not merely the mind, but also the body; inasmuch as it induces neuroses of the sexual apparatus (irritable weakness of the centres governing erection and ejaculation; defective pleasurable feeling in coitus), while, at the same time, it maintains the imagination and libido in continuous excitement.
>
> (Krafft-Ebing 1894: 189)

This extract is highly representative of how Krafft-Ebing anxiously handles the precarious divide between pathological homosexual desire and healthy heterosexual love. Once he concedes that congenital conditions cannot account for each and every sexual perversion, he finds himself remarking that there may indeed be environmental circumstances which discourage women from creating sexual partnerships with men. Throughout this paragraph, one sees how difficult it is for him to align conventional prejudices against the moral weakness of women with the natural state of female heterosexuality. Somehow, a woman is liable to fall short of the desires that are naturally her own. In this respect, Krafft-Ebing is voicing troubled and contradictory thoughts about female sexuality that are very much of his epoch. In spite of itself, his commentary discloses that lesbian desire was perhaps a much greater possibility in late-nineteenth-century culture than a highly moralistic society was willing to admit, not least because there were plausible social reasons why women may well prefer intimate relations with their own sex rather than with men.

Yet even if *Psychopathia Sexualis* did everything it could to uphold normal, healthy, heterosexual desire in marriage, it should be borne in mind that Krafft-Ebing's work was none the less widely censured. By the time the tenth edition of this influential tome appeared in 1902, the *British Medical Journal* said it was 'the most repulsive of a group of books of which it is type'. Lesley Hall and Roy Porter note that, in the course of the decade in which it made its appearance in Britain, Krafft-Ebing's study was finally viewed 'as little more than a scientific work of pornography' (Porter and Hall 1995: 163). Strict social codes of respectability, ones that deemed sex to be a wholly unspeakable topic, often militated against the broad circulation of sexological writings. A similar fate would befall related works in the field. By the time the English translation of Iwan Bloch's *Sexual Life of Our Time* was published in 1907, all copies were deemed fit for burning by the Magistrates' Court in London's Bow Street.

But if such works were condemned by the law courts for the same heinous crime of discussing eroticism, it should not be forgotten that there were many differences of opinion between the sexologists themselves. Although Bloch pays a gracious tribute to the pioneering research of Krafft-Ebing, he remains dissatisfied with the exclusively medical focus of *Psychopathia Sexualis*. Especially misguided, he feels, is Krafft-Ebing's insistence on labelling many sexual behaviours degenerate. To show why perverse sexual behaviours are not necesarily diseases, Bloch turns to the flourishing field of anthropological inquiry, since it is there he finds indisputable truths about the biological basis of human eroticism. '[L]et us', declares Bloch, 'compare the sexuality of the civilized human being with that of the savage; then we shall recognize the vast extension of our visual field for the comprehension of psychopathia sexualis' (Bloch 1908: 456). *The Sexual Life of Our Times* devotes much of its attention to the interaction between the evolution of the species and the civilizing conditions that have served to regulate and ennoble sexual instinct. In trying to reveal how eroticism has been shaped by the cultural environment, Bloch sees sexuality formed from two contrary but innate impulses. Drawing on a rich array of contemporary scientific writings, he argues that both lust and shame are inborn qualities. He claims the practice of wearing clothing stems from an inherent sense of shame that provokes desire. In other words, the cultural practice of covering the genitals derives from two natural sources: an inbuilt erotic drive and a biologically determined sense of modesty. In so-called primitive cultures, he maintains, tattooing and body adornment could be viewed as having the same dual function (see Bloch 1908: 149–57).

In revealing how sexuality was born of spontaneous lust and self-regulating shame, Bloch rallies a huge amount of evidence to maintain his belief that the uneasy feelings associated with eroticism have completely harmless sources. Above all, it is on the topic of masturbation that Bloch breaks with the burden of prejudice that caused some Victorian doctors to perform clitoridectomies to arrest the hazardous excitements presumed to arise from female autoeroticism. Such excitements were thought to lead to insanity, a view Bloch cautiously, and somewhat apologetically, sets out to refute:

> Auto-erotism (including its grosser form, masturbation) is . . . to a certain extent, a physiological manifestation; it becomes morbid only in certain conditions – that is to say, individuals who are previously morbid. This is, indeed, an old medical doctrine, that there exists a physiological masturbation *faute de mieux*, and a morbid masturbation in cases of neurasthenia, mental disorder, and other troubles. . . . The ultimate cause of such auto-erotic manifestations as belong neither to the category of 'vice' nor to that of 'crime' is to be

found . . . in a disharmony in the nature of many in respect of the premature development of sexual sensibility. For this reason we meet with these manifestations among the lowest races of mankind as we do among civilized peoples; even among animals auto-erotism is a widely diffused phenomenon. This can be observed, not only among the monkeys (perhaps already a little civilized) of our Zoological Gardens, which masturbate freely *coram publico*, but it may be seen also in horses.

(Bloch 1908: 411)

'Even elephants masturbate', Bloch goes on to assure us, thus emphasizing the wholly natural basis to what most of his comtemporaries considered a 'gross' practice.

Here and elsewhere Bloch assuredly runs against the grain of Krafft-Ebing's *Psychopathia Sexualis*. But no matter how much Bloch strives to undermine the established sexological tendency to pathologize desire, passages such as this one cry out for an analysis that would reach beyond the extremely limiting explanations achieved by appealing to the natural world. So it is significant that, within a matter of pages, Bloch briefly alludes to Sigmund Freud's innovative *Three Essays on the Theory of Sexuality*, which appeared in Vienna in 1905. In the light of Freud's work, Bloch observes that autoeroticism belongs to a pattern of psycho-sexual development: 'auto-erotism is almost always a precursor of completely developed sexuality, and manifests itself a long time before puberty'. 'Freud', adds Bloch, 'enumerates among the regions of the body by the stimulation of which sexual pleasure is most readily obtained, the lips of the infant, which, in sucking the mother's breast or its substitute, receive an instinctive perception of pleasure, in which the stimulation produced by the warm flow of milk also plays a part' (Bloch 1908: 413). Such comments indicate precisely the grounds on which psychoanalysis would begin to supersede sexology when theorizing the origins of autoerotic pleasure, as theories based in biology proved unable to account for how far culture could and did depart from nature.

But if Bloch reveals an emergent awareness of how biological science could not wholly account for certain sexual activities, then elsewhere he absorbs many of the more reactionary styles of thought that set a definite limit on *Psychopathia Sexualis* and even Ulrichs's defences of inversion. Following its predecessors in the sexological tradition, Bloch's book devotes much space to discussing acquired and congenital forms of homosexuality. Like his contemporary, the sex radical Magnus Hirschfeld (1868–1935), Bloch sees in the congenital man-loving man specific physical manifestations of inversion. The homosexual body becomes the focus of a supposedly scrupulous medical gaze:

> More especially after removing any beard or moustache that be present, we sometimes see much more clearly the feminine expression of face in a male homosexual, whilst before the hair was removed they appeared quite man-like. Still more important for the determination of a feminine habitus are direct physical characteristics. Among these there must be mentioned a *considerable deposit of fat,* by which the resemblance to the feminine type is produced, the contours of the body being more rounded than in the case of the normal male. In correspondence with this the *muscular system* is less powerfully developed than it is in heterosexual men, the skin is delicate and soft, and the complexion is much clearer than is usual in men.
>
> (Bloch 1908: 498–9)

Ridiculous to modern eyes, this professedly medical appraisal of the feminine distribution of fat in male Urnings betrays its voyeuristic fascination when Bloch recollects seeing a group of male homosexuals *en masse*: 'Last winter I attended an urnings' ball, and I was much impressed, when looking at the *décolleté* men, with the remarkable whiteness of their skin on the shoulders, neck, and back – also in those who had not applied powder – and by the fact that the little acne spots almost always present in normal men were absent in these'. Pale and delicate, these Urnings also bore another feature that made them into a separate species: 'The peculiar rounding of the shoulders', writes Bloch, 'was also remarkable, from its resemblance to what one sees in women' (Bloch 1908: 499).

In making these observations, there is no doubt that Bloch wishes to contest Krafft-Ebing's earlier beliefs in the degenerate nature of homosexuality. 'For me', insists Bloch, 'there is no longer any doubt that homosexuality is compatible with complete mental and physical health' (Bloch 1908: 490). But his depiction of the male cross-dressers' ball points to an area of confusion that persists in sexological thought to this day. It is only too clear that his stance as a scientific observer becomes entranced by the delightful forms of sexual display that have lured him into their circle. Surveying a group of men enjoying transgender roles, Bloch is seduced by the spectacular exoticism of this event. His writing discloses little about the sexual condition of the men donning *décolleté* dresses. Instead, he reveals his own wild fantasies about the male homosexual body: a body on to which a great many fears and fascinations have been projected for the past hundred years, and which intensified alarmingly during the first decade of the AIDS epidemic. Even if propounding the belief that homosexuality is a sign of 'complete mental and physical health', *The Sexual Life of Our Time* expresses a prurient interest in establishing the indisputable psychical and bodily difference of male homosexuals from their heterosexual opposites. Bloch is obviously straining hard for minute evidence of distinctive signs whose sexual otherness shall support his claims.

Scientists, however, were not the only researchers who regularly made what now appear outlandish assertions about the sexual phenomena they sought to analyse. The philosopher Otto Weininger's *Sex and Character* (1903), a book notorious for its misogyny and anti-Semitism, produced a revealingly different theoretical model to account for sexual difference. From cover to cover, this largely philosophical work pushes what was a limited vocabulary for comprehending sexual desire to an excruciating limit. An immensely popular study running into many editions, *Sex and Character* was written by a young, self-hating Jewish homosexual who, shortly after his conversion to Protestantism, shot himself at the age of twenty-three. Based on the doctoral dissertation he submitted to the University of Vienna, Weininger's disreputable volume emerged in the intellectual climate that fostered Krafft-Ebing's and Freud's diverging strands of thought about sexuality. In some idiosyncratic respects, *Sex and Character* is possibly more radical than its deservedly bad reputation might lead us to believe. Despite its numerous offensive passages, the twisted logic of Weininger's inquiry intriguingly challenges the stark contrast earlier sexologists such as Krafft-Ebing and Bloch made between men and women, heterosexuality and homosexuality.

Although not strictly a work of sexological research, *Sex and Character* draws liberally on contemporary debates stemming from hereditarian science to support its central belief that sex is always a matter of a degree, rather than a fixed opposition. Here is how Weininger puts his case about the relative position of men and women with regard to sex: 'The fact is that males and females are like two substances combined in different proportions, but with either element never wholly missing. We find, so to speak, never either a man or a woman, but only the male condition and the female condition' (Weininger 1975: 8). In advancing this view, Weininger is expanding in modern form the conviction held by anatomists since the time of the classical philosopher, Galen of Pergamum (*c.* 130–200AD), that masculinity and femininity derived from one sex, not two. (Galen's view, by the way, did not assume that the one sex from which men and women derived ensured equality between the sexes. See Laqueur 1990:

25–8.) 'Sexual differentiation', writes Weininger, 'is never complete. All the peculiarities of the male sex may be present in the female in some form, however weakly developed; and so also the sexual characteristics of the woman persist in the man, although perhaps they are not so completely rudimentary. The characters of the other sex occur in the one sex in a vestigial form' (Weininger 1975: 5). Hence, on this model, a man's nipples are made of tissue that develops into breasts in the female of the species. Likewise, the light growth of facial hair to be found even in highly feminine women is the vestige of the full beard common to the male sex.

Consequently, Weininger asserts that all human beings abide in 'a permanent bisexual condition', a bisexuality that he insists should not be confused with hermaphroditism. If, argues Weininger, we accept the fundamental 'bisexual' state of humanity, then we can appreciate 'all sorts of intermediate conditions between male and female – sexual transitional forms'. Even though we may like to believe that 'ideal types of man' and an 'ideal woman' exist, such types are merely imaginary. But here Weininger's theory takes one of its most infamous turns. Rather than maintain that the 'intermediate' or 'bisexual' nature of all sexual variations is to be celebrated in its diversity, he proposes that 'ideal' types of men and women 'not only can be constructed, but must be constructed'. 'As in art', he writes, 'so in science, the real purpose is to reach the type, the Platonic Idea' (Weininger 1975: 7). Such a view marks the beginnings of a particularly worrying version of social engineering: for society, he believes, must be guided towards producing an 'ideal' sexual antithesis out of a potentially chaotic 'bisexual' order.

Weininger was read and discussed by many modernist writers, such as D.H. Lawrence (1885–1930) and Gertrude Stein (1874–1946), both of whom had a strong interest in same-sex desire. Part of the appeal of *Sex and Character* was its decisive emphasis on how human beings are not as sexually differentiated as many of his contemporaries would like to think. He views homosexuality as a wholly comprehensible part of the broad span of sexual identities stretching out between absolute forms of masculinity and femininity. But that does not mean he approves of homosexual eroticism:

> Homo-sexuality is merely the sexual condition of these intermediate sexual forms that stretch from one ideally sexual condition to the other sexual condition. In my view all actual organisms have both homo-sexuality and hetero-sexuality.
>
> That the rudiment of homo-sexuality, in however weak a form, exists in every human being, corresponding to the greater or smaller development of the characters of the opposite sex, is proved conclusively from the fact that in the adolescent stage, while there is still a considerable amount of undifferentiated sexuality, and before the internal secretions have exerted their stimulating force, passionate attachments with a sensual side rule amongst boys as well as amongst girls.
>
> A person who retains from that age onwards a marked tendency to 'friendship' with a person of his own sex must have a strong taint of the other sex in him.
>
> (Weininger 1975: 49)

Lest it appear that Weininger is referring solely to homosexual desire when he mentions 'friendship' between men, he goes on to claim that there 'is no friendship between men that has not an element of sexuality in it' (Weininger 1975: 49). In other words, closeness between men of any kind carries an element of attraction, thereby making it difficult indeed to distinguish between sex and friendship. From his perspective, each and every same-sex relation is always already eroticized. There seems to be no escape from the all-consuming perversions of sex.

To ensure that the pervasive threat of homoeroticism does not gain full expression in human society, Weininger insists that the sexual distinctions between men and women must be pushed further and further apart. Male and female, he argues, have to be constructed as the ideal antithetical absolutes that shall overcome the disorder created by the 'bisexual' state against which human beings must constantly battle. To this end, Weininger wants to uphold a rigid divide between the male's powers of mind and the female's powers of sensuality:

> The incongruity between the man and woman depends, in a special measure, on the fact that the contents of the thoughts of the man are not merely those of the woman in a higher state of differentiation, but that the two have totally distinct sequences of thought applied to the same object, conceptual thought in the one and indistinct sensing in the other.
>
> (Weininger 1975: 191)

To Weininger, there are certain phenomena that show precisely how and why the male intellect can and must achieve a successful separation from the retarding sensuality of women. He declares the highest form of masculinity is genius, a condition to which women simply cannot aspire. Genius, he claims, marks the triumph of the male to remove itself furthest from what he calls the 'henid' or sexually intermediate stage of humanity. 'In this way', he writes, 'genius declares itself to be a kind of higher masculinity, and thus the female cannot be possessed of genius' (Weininger 1975: 111). Instead, the woman 'is always living in a condition of fusion with all the human beings she knows, even when she is alone'. 'Women', adds Weininger, 'have no definite individual limits', for they lack both an ego and the faculty of reason. Pursuing this point, Weininger concludes: 'she is sexuality itself'. This claim, however, leads Weininger into increasingly contorted argumentation, since he finds himself having to distinguish between (1) the admirable sexuality ascribed to respectable women, whose ideal destiny is motherhood, and (2) the degrading sexuality manifest in the prostitute. The conflict between these competing types of sexualized femininity reaches breaking-point in his argument when he suddenly proclaims: 'Probably most women have both possibilities in them, the mother and the prostitute' (Weininger 1975: 217).

This extreme statement is undoubtedly the result of a long-established tradition of sexist thought that became deeply entrenched during the Victorian period. During the nineteenth century, European and American cultures insisted on dividing femininity into angelic and demonic, virtuous and vicious types – implying, at all times, that these apparently opposite poles of good and bad women were in some respect interdependent. So with this inflexible logic in mind, Weininger hurtles towards the drastic conclusion that men are constantly in danger from the devouring passions of all women, since not even respectable females can suppress their inexhaustible eroticism. Not only is a woman thought to be wholly dependent on a man to satisfy her voracious desires, she is also said to weaken the man by manipulating his vulnerable sexual instincts. Consequently, Weininger advises men to aspire to the high moral ideal of chastity so that they are not lured into the devitalizing excesses of coitus. He assumes it is women's maddening enthralment to sexuality that threatens to make men slaves to it as well:

> If he is going to treat her as the moral idea demands, he must try to see in her the concept of mankind and endeavour to respect her. Even although woman is only a function of man, a function he can degrade or raise at will, and women do not wish to be anything else than what man makes them, it is no more a moral arrangement than the suttee of Indian widows, which, even though it be voluntary and insisted upon by them, is none the less terrible barbarity.
>
> (Weininger 1975: 338)

This extract certainly counts among the most conflicted moments in Weininger's study. For just as he seeks to prove that men can and should have mastery over women, he recognizes at once that such a 'moral arrangement' closely resembles the 'terrible barbarity' of the Indian practice of *sati* – widow-burning – that British colonialists perceived as a horrific expression of primitive brutality. In other words, Weininger is having to balance his high moral ideals against what he considers an inhuman punishment. Perhaps, after all, there really is no difference between civilized and savage attitudes towards women. That, at least, is one consequence of an argument that perpetually imperils its leading claims.

Not accidentally, Weininger is led to consider the links between three areas of contemporary culture that marked some of the greatest inequalities within the West. Jews, African slaves, and women all come under the same contradictory rubric: to be treated in a moral spirit that ensures their rightful subjection:

> Although the humanity of Jews, negroes, and still more of women, is weighed down by many immoral impulses; although in these cases there is so much more to fight against than in the case of Aryan men, still we must try to respect mankind, and to venerate the idea of humanity . . .
>
> The problem of woman and the problem of the Jews are absolutely identical with the problem of slavery, and they must be solved in the same way. No one should be oppressed, even if the oppression is of such a kind as to be unfelt as such. The animals about a house are not 'slaves', because they have no freedom in the proper sense of the word which could be taken away.
>
> (Weininger 1975: 338)

No one could doubt that here we can see the foundations laid for a distinctly fascist style of thought. On the one hand, Weininger speaks a high-minded language of 'respect', while on the other, he remarks that all subordinated groups are analogous to household pets. In conclusion, the 'respect' shown towards those peoples sub-jugated by the males of the Aryan master-race amounts to a con-descending appreciation of the inborn subservience of each inferior group. It should come as no surprise, then, that Nazi pro-paganda was citing Weininger's work as late as January 1945 (see Hyams 1995: 155–68).

In his imposing study of the Nazi *Freikorps* of the 1920s and 1930s, Karl Theweleit shows precisely how this manner of sexual thinking fed into fascist military ideology. Members of this elite were encouraged to create chaste bonds of brotherliness to protect themselves from the ravenous and vitiating sexuality they felt were characteristic of women:

> Women who don't confirm to any of the 'good woman' images are automatically seen [by the *Freikorps*] as prostitutes, as the vehicle of 'urges'. They are evil and out to castrate, and they are treated accordingly. The men are soldiers. Fighting is their life, and they aren't about to wait until that monstrous thing happens *to them*. They take the offensive before these women can put their horrible plans into practice.
>
> (Theweleit 1987: 171)

Like the countless images of *femmes fatales* hung in many a *fin-de-siècle* art gallery, the 'bad' women who haunted the military minds of the *Freikorps* represented the vengeful force of female sexuality. Just as Weininger's *Sex and Character* declares that men must resist sexual enslavement by women, the elite Nazi soldiers feared being engulfed by destructive female desires.

Depressingly, residual forms of Weininger's system of thought still retain a certain currency in some areas of popular cultural criticism. Although hardly fascist in intention, Camille Paglia's *Sexual Personae: Art and Decadence from Nefertiti to Emily Dickinson* (1990) resonates with ideas about the different sexual and artistic capabilities of men and women that echo *Sex and Character*. On Paglia's model, men attain genius precisely because of their sexual anatomy, a feature that enables them to guard against female forces that are a constant danger to civilization:

> What had nature given man to defend himself against women? Here we come to the source of man's cultural achievements, which follow so directly from his singular anatomy. . . . Man is sexually compartmentalized. Genitally, he is condemned to a perpetual pattern of linearity, focus, aim, directedness. He must learn to aim. Without aim, urination and ejaculation end in infantile soiling of self or surroundings.
>
> (Paglia 1990: 12)

In contrast to these penile perpendiculars, women's sexuality is said to be 'diffused throughout her body'. 'Her desire for foreplay', adds Paglia, 'remains a notorious area of miscommunication between the sexes'. While men want sex straight up and down, women require an endless plateau of pleasure – or so Paglia wants us to believe.

According to Paglia, Western culture has been built on an eternal war waged between timeless, inherent, and universal masculine and feminine forces that can be found in two sources: (1) the animus and anima that characterize the psychological archetypes influentially explored by C.G. Jung (1875–1961), and (2) the violent dialectic between male Apollonian aspiration towards art and female Dionysian dwelling in primeval nature discussed by Nietzsche. Espoused to these everlasting principles, Paglia asserts: 'Woman is the primeval fabricator, the real First Mover'. Associated with a formless state of natural being, woman – in Paglia's lurid prose – 'turns a gob of refuse into a spreading web of sentient being, floating on the snaky umbilical by which she leashes every man'. Hence, on this view, it remains man's task to release himself from the serpentine noose that coils around him. 'Reason and logic', insists Paglia, 'are the anxiety-inspired domain of Apollo, premiere god of sky-cult'. The 'Dionysian', by contrast, 'is liquid nature, a miasmic swamp whose prototype is the still pond of the womb' (Paglia 1990: 12). Much as we might be dazzled by her poeticisms, Paglia ironically produces a theory that is as static as the ever-spreading formless femininity that to her mind reveals women's natural propensity not to produce great art. Nowhere does Paglia provide sociological insights that might account for the persistent sexual inequality that remains highly visible in the West. Instead, *Sexual Personae* belongs to an outmoded tradition of thought that consigns masculinity and femininity to antithetical energies deeply embedded in human nature.

FEMINIST CONTENTIONS

For all the influence that they still enjoy in modern culture, the claims made by sexological writings have hardly gone uncontested, not least by feminist thinkers. Indeed, feminists have for decades been involved more than any other group in a vigorous dialogue with this body of research. In this section, therefore, I want to reflect for a moment on a handful of contrasting interventions that feminists have made when engaging with sexology. This part of the discussion shows that feminist theorists have written both within and against the sexological tradition. Like the early male sexologists, some late-Victorian feminists were fascinated by the influential theory of 'sexual selection' laid out in Charles Darwin's *The Descent of Man, and Selection in Relation to Sex* (1871). Similarly, they absorbed aspects of social Darwinism (notably in Herbert Spencer's *First Principles* [1862]) and the science of eugenics or 'race-health' (whose founder was Darwin's cousin, Francis Galton [1855–1920]). It has been argued that sexology came to exert considerable influence over feminist thought in Britain by the time women had gained the suffrage in 1918. Sheila Jeffreys believes that the sexism of sexological discourse in large part neutralized further feminist campaigns for liberation (Jeffreys 1985). Even if Jeffreys's opinion has been questioned by other historians (see Bland 1995: 308), it is fair to claim that feminist thinking in the 1920s was often taken up with promoting the heterosexual woman's power in reproducing the race. Consequently, motherhood became the truest sign of women's cultural authority. This perspective meant that single women and lesbians were at times viewed as contemptible inferior beings who had failed to bear the proper fruits of womanhood. Yet in the same period, it is plain to see that lesbians themselves might choose to adapt rather different aspects of sexological research in the name of their own political empowerment. Let us look in turn at these two conflicting ways in which notable women writers intervened in sexological debate.

The South African political campaigner and author Olive Schreiner was one of several prominent radical thinkers who, in a critical spirit, drew on features of evolutionary thinking to support women's liberation. Renowned for her fine experimental novel, *The Story of An African Farm* (1883), and her distinguished sequence of visionary allegories, *Dreams* (1890), Schreiner was a political activist who divided her time between Britain and South Africa, and on several occasions her life was endangered because of the anti-colonial struggles in which she was involved. After the completion of her first novel, she worked for many years on an ambitious study of sex and evolution. But her first version of the manuscript was destroyed in a raid on her home by British soldiers. Rewriting the work from scratch, Schreiner published *Women and Labour* in 1911. Strictly speaking, this book does not follow the generic pattern of those investigations conducted by the male sexologists when tracing the evolution of sexual behaviours and types. Instead, Schreiner's study draws on a similar body of social Darwinism to indicate how and why the future could be transformed to improve middle-class women's lives. The goal of her carefully considered argument is to show that modern society has accrued certain benefits through material progress while creating conditions that fail to ameliorate the longstanding inequality between men and women. The sexes have been torn apart because of the role played by labour among the professional classes in the West. Over time, she argues, men have gained increasing opportunities to work, while women have been separated further and further from useful toil. Focusing solely on middle-class experience, this is how Schreiner puts her case:

> Never before in the history of the earth has the man's field of remunerative toil been so wide, so interesting, so complex, and in its results so all-important to society; never before has the male sex, taken as a whole, been so fully and strenuously employed.
>
> So much is this the case, that, exactly as in the earlier conditions of society an excessive and almost crushing amount of the most important physical labour devolved upon the female, so under modern civilized conditions among the wealthier and fully civilized classes, an unduly excessive share of labour tends to devolve upon the male. That almost entirely modern, morbid condition, affecting the nervous system, and shortening the lives of thousands in modern civilized societies, which is vulgarly known as 'overwork' or 'nervous breakdown', is but one evidence of the even excessive share of mental toil devolving upon the modern male of the cultured classes, who, in addition to maintaining himself, has frequently dependent upon him a larger or smaller number of entirely parasitic females. But, whatever the result of the changes of modern civilization may be with regard to the male, he certainly cannot complain that they have as a whole robbed him of his fields of labour, diminished his share in the conduct of life, or reduced him to a condition of morbid inactivity.
>
> (Schreiner 1911: 48–9)

Even though Schreiner's critical writings are committed to feminist aims, this passage reveals how her thoughts on what she calls 'sex-parasitism' in some ways echo Weininger's conservative reflections on the draining force of female sexuality. It is intriguing that both examine the same phenomenon – the apparent weakening effect of women upon men. But the conclusion Schreiner draws to change this situation could not make a starker contrast with the final judgement reached by Weininger in *Sex and Character*. For she believes there are areas in human life where sex is not even an incidental factor in determining fitness for specific kinds of work: 'The male and female brains acquire languages, solve mathematical problems, and master scientific detail in a manner wholly indistinguishable: as illustrated by the fact that in modern universities the papers sent in by male and female candidates are as a rule absolutely identical in type' (Schreiner 1911: 183).

Yet in staking this claim, Schreiner promptly adds that middle-class women do indeed perform sexually specific forms of labour. Above all, it is the literal labour of childbearing that places such women at the centre of society, and thus plainly shows women's irrefutable significance in perpetuating the race. Schreiner, however, is keen to emphasize that childbearing and motherhood, if necessarily female work, cannot serve as the only form of toil in which bourgeois women should participate. If, at the same time, women are denied access to types of mental labour, then they will weaken humanity. It is on this issue that Schreiner's evolutionary precepts come into their own:

> No man ever yet entered life farther than the length of one navel-cord from the body of the woman who bore him. It is the woman who is the final standard of the race, from which there can be no departure for any distance for any length of time, in any direction: as her brain weakens, weakens the man's she bears; as her muscle softens, softens his; as she decays, decays the people.
>
> Other causes may, and do, lead to the enervation and degeneration of a class or race; the parasitism of its child-bearing women *must*.
>
> (Schreiner 1911: 109)

Here she states that the stronger a woman grows in intellectual and professional competence, the fitter she will be to produce hardy members of the future race. So female powers of mind shall fortify heredity, enabling both men and women to partake of a healthier and more equal society.

Women and Labour is one of the foremost feminist tracts of its time. Lucy Bland's comprehensive history of feminist campaigning around sexuality in Britain between the 1880s and the First World War certainly shows that Schreiner was hardly alone among radical women in turning to aspects of eugenic and hereditarian thought (Bland 1995). But, unlike Schreiner, some feminists from this era were preoccupied with the supposed hazards of sexual intercourse with men. In *The Great Scourge and How to End It* (1913), for example, the suffragist Christabel Pankhurst (1880–1958) controversially insisted that women had to be saved from the dangers of marriage because, according to her statistics, a very high percentage of men was infected with venereal disease. Likewise, in *Marriage as a Trade* (1909), Cicely Hamilton (1872–1952) observed that sex and motherhood jeopardized women. From her perspective, celibacy was an admirable alternative to heterosexuality. Even if these views hardly became dominant, they signal how feminist attitudes towards sexual behaviour were diversifying at this time. In this ferment of debate, the figure of the lesbian became more prominent than ever before, suggesting new possibilities for women's sexuality.

The distinguished research of Terry Castle and Lilian Faderman has revealed the rich and varied canon of literary writings that focus on woman-to-woman desire in the nineteenth and twentieth centuries (Faderman 1981; Castle 1993). If these writers share a common perspective, it lies in how they recognize the hazards in applying modern conceptions of female homosexuality to literary works produced before the twentieth century. Just as sexology created the term sexuality, so too did the word lesbian emerge at a specific historical moment. The naming of the lesbian was not entirely widespread until the 1920s, by which time several European and American cities had established communities and networks for women-loving women. Even during that decade, the novel that brought female same-sex desire to public attention did not refer to lesbianism as such. Instead, in *The Well of Loneliness*, Radclyffe Hall represents its female protagonist, Stephen Gordon, as an invert: the figure representing a third or intermediate sex. Stephen's first name indicates she has a male soul trapped in a woman's body. But the fact that she was given a male name by her father – who desperately hoped for a son – shows that to some degree external factors have also impinged on the remarkable character of Hall's invention. Indeed, the novel charts Stephen's development in a family where she bonds closely with a father who encourages her in athletic pursuits, while remaining distant from a kind but timid mother who presents an extreme form of femininity with which Stephen cannot identify. Throughout the novel, Stephen confronts the severe social pressures against her desire to form intimate relations with other women. Bearing the name of the first Christian martyr, she ultimately sacrifices her deep love for a feminine younger woman, knowing that her girlfriend would be happier and safer in a sexual relationship with a man.

Since the day it was published, *The Well of Loneliness* has remained the most widely read and debated novel of lesbian desire, and Hall's decision to feature a female invert has been an enduring source of controversy. Some readers, for example, believe Stephen's masculine bearing perpetuates a negative stereotype of butch lesbianism, while others claim that Hall's unapologetic protagonist is an empowering figure who defies the dominant sexual order. Likewise, Hall's conservative politics have made some readers cast doubt on her representation of the woman-loving woman. Yet, at the same time, Hall's work has remained politically important, especially for feminists concerned with the terms on which women might resist heterosexual norms.

In a notable essay first published in 1984, Esther Newton takes the latter view: 'Hall, like the sexologists, uses cross-dressing and gender reversal to symbolize lesbian sexuality. Unlike the sexologists, however, Hall makes Stephen the subject and takes her point of view against a hostile world' (Newton 1989: 290). Even though Stephen, for all her upper-class privilege, experiences considerable emotional cruelty, Hall's novel shows that the invert's desires have both pride and dignity. Reflecting on the 'narrow-hipped, wide-shouldered' body she has inhabited from birth (Hall 1981: 13), Stephen refuses to internalize the animosity aimed against her female masculinity:

> All her life she must drag this body of hers like a monstrous fetter imposed on her spirit. This strangely ardent yet sterile body that must worship yet never be worshipped in return by the creature of its adoration. She longed to maim it, for it made her feel cruel; it was so white, so strong and so self-sufficient; yet withal so poor and unhappy a thing that her eyes filled with tears and her hate turned to pity. She began to grieve over it, touching her breasts with pitiful fingers, stroking her shoulders, letting her hands slip along her straight thighs – Oh, poor and most desolate body!
>
> (Hall 1981: 187)

This stirring passage captures a marked psychological conflict. Even though Stephen sees herself as physiologically 'sterile', she none the less insists she is emotionally 'ardent', filled with the capacity to love. If no one else shall adore her, then she herself will find the resources to respect her seemingly wounded body. In fact, Stephen finally experiences physical love in an episode that the novel treats with the greatest discretion. Just at the moment she has drawn her lover close to her, the narrator quietly adds: 'and that night they were not divided' (Hall 1981: 313). In a novel extending to well over 400 pages, these are the only words that hint at sexual intimacy between women.

But the very suggestion of lesbian sexuality was enough to unleash remarkable animosity from the British press, notably in the reactionary *Sunday Express*. Such was the controversy sparked off by the virulent moralistic attack on Hall's writing that the Director of Public Prosecutions brought the charge of 'obscene libel' against *The Well of Loneliness*. The trial at the Magistrates' Court in Bow Street gathered together many writers whose own work was seeking to represent proscribed sexual identifications. E.M. Forster (1879–1971) and Virginia Woolf (1884–1941) jointly wrote a letter to the press in Hall's defence. Both Woolf's experimental narrative *Orlando* (1928) and Forster's novel *A Passage to India* (1924) have a conspicuous interest in patterns of same-sex desire. Neither work, however, featured explicitly homosexual characters. Indeed, Forster suppressed his short stories featuring violent homoerotic fantasies (on these, see Lane 1995: 145–75). Such works were reserved for posthumous publication only. It is fair to claim that no other writer experienced such public vilification as Hall for her dissident sexuality. The ferocious public response assuredly bore out the moral message of her novel – that lesbians would be martyred in British society. Undoubtedly, the lesbian embodied a signal threat to a culture that was more and more unsettled by women's demands for autonomy both inside and outside the patriarchal family.

After this period, feminist responses to sexology changed as debates about sexuality shifted in themselves. In this context, one of the most vexed areas of discussion from the mid-century has been the relationship between women's sexual freedom and heterosexual desire. These debates intensified since the 1940s with sexological research placing increasing emphasis on the need to maximize erotic potential, culminating in the libertarian sexual revolution of the 1960s. On the one hand, feminist arguments have been put forward in favour of rejecting men, not least because the demand for women to sexualize themselves deepens the already exploitative framework of heterosexuality. Inspired by works such as Jill Johnston's *Lesbian Nation* (1973), the separatist movement known as political lesbianism produced a forceful critique of how heterosexuality involved 'sleeping with the enemy' – on the grounds that this hegemonic institution continued women's sexual subordination. On the other hand, the 1990s witnessed a renewed discussion which maintained that feminism and heterosexuality were not exactly incompatible, since women were in a stronger position to take control of their intimate lives with men.

Lynne Segal is among the leading critics to consider how feminism has contended with the contradictory legacy of sexological thought. Charting the influence of sex advice manuals from the time of Stopes's *Married Love*, Segal considers how researchers such as Kinsey in the 1940s, as well as William H. Masters and Virginia E. Johnson in the 1960s, left women with two opposing ideas about female sexuality. Kinsey, for example, stressed the significance of sexual pleasure for women, arguing that clitoral stimulation rather than vaginal penetration was central to achieving orgasm. Yet the biological imperatives driving his research deflected him from social problems in opposite-sex relations, notably how heterosexual intercourse could well involve women's coercion by men, leading to oppressive relationships, unwanted pregnancies, and disease (see Segal 1994: 92). But despite their shortcomings, as Segal notes, Kinsey's reports (1948, 1953) and Masters and Johnson's *Human Sexual Response* (1966) enabled a later generation of feminist sexologists to produce material that stressed the significance of women's rights to enjoy sexual pleasure – and, what is more, pleasure on women's own terms. None the less, some feminist sex research of the 1970s was still hampered by the restrictive behaviourist framework that claimed orgasm was the ultimate goal of sexuality. Segal shows how, for instance, in *For Yourself: The Fulfilment of Female Sexuality* (1975), Lonnie Barbach confidently asserts that women can always 'recondition themselves to respond positively to erotic stimuli'. Here is how Segal sums up her reservations about this type of feminist engagement with the sexological demand to 'recondition' the sexually responsive body:

> What is disowned with such casual cheeriness is all interest in a woman's complex emotional life, here reduced instead to her cognitive awareness of what is seen as her biological potential for orgasms, and her right to have them. There is no hint or whisper of the often troubling, irrational or 'perverse' nature of sexual desire and fantasy, which may bear little relation to our conscious ideals and commitments as autonomous agents in the world. . . . What arouses desire, as almost any women's fiction can illustrate, rarely obeys the dictate of conscious feminist pursuit, but as often includes inappropriately submissive, aggressive, hostile, or in other ways 'deviant' impulses. Yet in sexology, feminist or otherwise, all experience is seen as manipulable, from the outside in, and the possibility of desire arising from and expressing contradictory, conflicting or quite literally impossible impulses cannot even be expressed, let alone explained, within this framework.
>
> (Segal 1994: 104)

Time and again, argues Segal, twentieth-century sexology misleadingly assumes that sexuality is purely a physical matter that involves external stimuli that must lead to orgasmic results. On this view, sexology regards the human body like a desiring machine, with its erogenous zones aroused for the one climactic performance that exclusively defines sexual success. Since its beginnings, then, sexology has been far too focused on classifying sexual types and measuring sexual behaviours, setting norms and targets for each. Even if sexology has over time shifted away from pathologizing certain sexual desires by placing more and more emphasis on the primacy of individual erotic satisfaction, it cannot comprehend how sexuality may exceed, defy, and confound bodily function. That is why Segal closes her study by demanding a new 'gender order' in which we can 'fashion new concepts and practices of gender based upon the mutual recognition of similarities and differences between women and men, rather than upon notions of their opposition' (Segal 1994: 317). No doubt this as yet unrealized 'gender order' will come into view once our culture no longer believes that popular sexology holds out the promise of a better and more satisfying erotic life.

CONSUMING PASSIONS

Given the persistence of sexology during the past hundred years, readers are probably left wondering exactly what gave rise to this type of research in the first place, and why it has enjoyed such lasting influence. Why should it be in this period that sexuality found a name? And why were theorists impelled to go to such strenuous lengths to make sense of sexual difference and erotic desire? Answers to these urgent questions have been the subject of far less debate than one might expect. In fact, it remains the case that even the more distinguished of the many historical accounts of sexual science repeatedly fail to tell us why this body of knowledge developed as it did. For example, in their impressively well-documented work, *The Facts of Life*, Porter and Hall conclude they have only been able to draw 'a rather coarse diagram to indicate some of the kinds of ideas floating around at particular historical moments in a particular national context upon which individuals have drawn to make their own "sexual knowledge", their sense of the "facts of life"' (Porter and Hall 1995: 283). Such a 'coarse diagram' at times makes it difficult to see how and why an explicit discourse of sexuality came into its own. Admittedly, they acknowledge that 'sexuality could not exist in the culture without words, images, metaphors and symbols to represent it' (Porter and Hall 1995: 8). Yet, even though they pay careful attention to this general point, it is still the case that Porter and Hall's highly detailed research leaves one puzzled about why in the late Victorian era the emergent term sexuality became such a significant topic of scientific investigation.

Rather than assume that there must have been one originating cause that spurred these sexological inquiries into action, it would be advisable to think about the upsurge of interest in sexuality being overdetermined: that is, emanating from multiple sources that constellated together in textbooks of the kind I have been discussing. No one could deny that evolutionary and eugenic thought, the intensification of women's campaigns for the suffrage, and the development of sexually dissident subcultures all had a part to play in establishing this area of inquiry. But these interrelated developments might make more sense if one could find a model that identified some of their common features.

One of the few studies that attempts to do exactly this is Lawrence Birken's *Consuming Desire: Sexual Science and the Emergence of a Culture of Abundance, 1871–1914* (1988). Birken's concise book locates scientific studies of sexuality within a history of philosophical ideas. His argument focuses on how the emergence of the Enlightenment category of the individual in bourgeois society altered how people thought about their economic relations with the world. Given the advancement of property ownership, the individual had increasing opportunities to enter into free economic relations with other individuals. Thus, economies of consumption became fundamental to relations of production, as Western culture placed more stress on choice, pleasure, and taste. On this model, 'sexology conceived of a wider society in which idiosyncratic consumers freely entered into erotic relations with each other' (Birken 1988: 49). Therefore, masochism, even if condemned as pathological, could at some level be perceived as a kind of sexual taste. But, as Birken notes, the freedoms afforded by emergent market principles made for individual subjects whose psychological idiosyncrasies could threaten the social order as a whole. An increasing emphasis on autonomy met with a corresponding response for more regulatory laws to control the potential anarchy unleashed by the proliferation of individual desires. The following sentences pursue this point:

> As economic man realized his freedom only by submitting to the law of the market, so psychological man and woman realize their freedom only by submitting to the law of the sexual market.
>
> In other words, sexology simultaneously discovered and attempted to regulate the idiosyncratic consumer. On the one hand, sexual science emphasized the multiplicity of individual preferences and thus the uniqueness of each person's 'consumption bundle' or 'case'. So the American physician Frank Lydston argued, around 1890, that 'as we may have variations of physical form and of mental attributes, so we have variations and perversions . . . of sexual affinity'. On the other hand, the sexologists attempted to subjugate these varied desires to an immanent law of sex.
>
> (Birken 1988: 49)

If one considers patterns of cultural consumption in the economic realm more broadly, then it becomes clear that nineteenth-century society enlarged the concept that a human subject could be what it desired. The notion that the subject expresses desire through the power to consume can be understood in general developments visible in nineteenth- and twentieth-century culture – from purchasing goods in department stores to obtaining an ever-broadening range of sexual commodities, such as pornography. At the same time, late-Victorian feminist campaigns for the right of middle-class women to obtain professional work of all kinds points to a related aspect of a society that made increasingly close associations between sexual desire and economic power. 'Give us labour!' demands Schreiner, on behalf of her sex (Schreiner 1911: 33). In stating that women have a fundamental reproductive labour to perform, Schreiner is also insisting that women should have a fair share of the market: the world in which female professional workers can thrive for the good of everyone.

Compared to Birken, John D'Emilio provides a similar, if more obviously Marxist, analysis of market forces and desire. In his classic essay, 'Capitalism and Gay Identity' (1983), D'Emilio does not explicitly address the rise of sexology but the framework he develops certainly hold some clues to why sexual minorities became more visible in the nineteenth century, and thus made themselves subjects of scientific inquiry. Keen to quash any notion of the 'eternal homosexual', he combats such essentialist suppositions by considering why gay subcultures developed in the context of the 'free-labour system' that emerged under nineteenth-century American capitalism (D'Emilio 1992: 5). He examines how the white family slowly changed its status from an independent unit of production that formed the cornerstone of society to a grouping that cultivated the affections of its members. No longer was the family 'an institution that provided goods' but one that offered 'emotional satisfaction and happiness' (D'Emilio 1992: 7). As a consequence, marriage shifted its emphasis from procreation to being an institution that nurtured children. Given that capitalism changed the structure of the family, creating divisions between the public world of work and private domestic life, the possibility arose for men and women to create intimate relations that might depart from familial arrangements. D'Emilio argues that growing opportunities to sell one's labour in contexts outside the self-supporting family meant that alternative sexual styles of living became available to many more people than before, especially in urban centres.

Yet given the pronounced hostility to homosexuality under this phase of late capitalism, D'Emilio has to address the structural contradiction between the mode of economic production and the reigning morals of the day. Here is how he approaches this problem.

[T]he relationship between capitalism and the family is fundamentally contradictory. On the one hand, capitalism continually weakens the material foundation of family life, making it
possible for individuals to live outside the family, and for a lesbian and gay male identity to develop. On the other, it needs to
push men and women into families, at least long enough to
reproduce the next generation of workers. The elevation of the
family to ideological pre-eminence guarantees that a capitalist
society will reproduce not just children, but heterosexism and
homophobia.

(D'Emilio 1992: 13)

Put another way, just as changing economic circumstances permit
dissident sexualities to emerge, so too do they consolidate the
pressure on the family to reproduce itself. But there are noticeable limitations to this Marxist approach. How does one balance
the development of homosexual subcultures against the increase
of homophobia? Is it the case that the prevailing morals might be
lagging behind the changing relations of production? Or is it
that the rather unpredictable condition of the free labour market
inspired a strict morality that gave society a sense of control over
its destiny? In D'Emilio's thought-provoking essay, such questions remain unanswered. Ultimately, it remains hard to see precisely why lesbians and gay men, producing their own networks
under the changing free labour economy, have simultaneously
become 'the political victims of the social instability that capitalism generates' (D'Emilio 1992: 13).

In some respects, it could be argued that Birken's and
D'Emilio's respective essays suffer from differing degrees of economic determinism: that is, the belief that economic changes
necessarily dictate all other social and cultural relations. This
mode of thinking can become inflexibly functionalist in its
approach to sexual phenomena. In assuming that a specific set of
economic causes has identifiable cultural effects, such analyses

suggest that the contradictory dynamic between homosexuality and homophobia is a wholly external matter. Even though economic history can throw light on how sexual dissidents forged their communities in specific capitalist conditions, its methods are surely as limited as those of sexology in defining the complex mechanisms that generate erotic identifications. Neither theory can altogether elucidate how the family produces persons whose desires might not comply with celebrated heterosexual ideals.

So where else might theorists look for analytic models that will help explain the intense conflict between heterosexual dominance and homosexual dissidence? What other tools might there be to consider the conditions that give rise to many different sexual identities and behaviours? One of the most influential alternatives has been psychoanalysis, a critical method and clinical practice that examines many of the phenomena that fascinated the sexologists but which locates their origins in a previously unexplored domain: the unconscious mind. Invented by Freud and developed further by Lacan, psychoanalysis questions what sexology singularly fails to illuminate: how the psyche organizes the sexual drives, often in socially rebellious ways. The next chapter reveals how psychoanalytic research pioneered a distinctive ensemble of critical terms that enabled it to leave sexology well and truly behind.

2

PSYCHOANALYTIC DRIVES

FREUD'S COMPLEXES

'According to the prevailing view', wrote Sigmund Freud near the end of his career, 'sexual life consists essentially in an endeavour to bring one's own genitals into contact with those of someone of the opposite sex' (Freud 1964, XXIII: 152). Moreover, he states that the conventional 'prevailing view' assumes the desire for opposite-sex relations emerges at puberty and leads to its natural consequence: reproduction. But, as Freud proceeds to observe, there are 'certain facts' that 'do not fit into the narrow framework of this view'. He adds that, although heterosexual intercourse may appear to be the necessary result of normal development in human beings, three significant phenomena show that eroticism extends well beyond the scope of the reproductive capacities of sexually mature adults. First, there is the widespread existence of homosexuality. Second, there are people classified as 'perverts', whose desires 'behave exactly like sexual ones but who at the same time entirely disregard the sexual organs or their normal use'. And third, there is the question of why young children frequently take an interest in their genitals and experience excitation in them. Once these 'three neglected facts' have been taken into account, then the following findings become clear: (1) sexual life begins during infancy; (2) the 'sexual' and the 'genital' have separate meanings, since the 'sexual' encompasses many behaviours that are not 'genital' in character; and (3) sexual pleasure involves the development of erogenous zones, ones that may or may not lead to reproduction. These, in sum, are the decisively innovative findings of Freud's psychoanalytic investigations. Controversial from the outset, the critical repercussions of the models he used to theorize these insights can be felt to this day. This chapter shows why.

Dating from 1938, these summative remarks by Freud appear in 'An Outline of Psycho-Analysis', the unfinished manuscript where he brings together in concise and accessible form the fruits of his longstanding researches into the psychic life of the subject. Psychoanalysis, after all, had begun, more than half a century before, in the 1880s. Trained as a neuroscientist at the University of Vienna, Freud in his early work from that decade was devoted to medical issues such as motor paralyses. Included in these writings were studies of hypnotism and hysteria. The direction of his research changed dramatically during a period of study at La Salpêtrière clinic in Paris where he witnessed the distinguished physician Jean Martin Charcot (1825–93) employ hypnosis apparently to cure hysterical symptoms in women patients. Throughout the next ten years, much of his time was devoted to the study of hysteria, and he gradually dissented from Charcot's innovative belief that hysteria could be understood as a neurological disease. Drawing an entirely different conclusion, Freud produced a substantial work with his senior colleague, Josef Breuer (1842–1925), comprising five case histories which revealed why hysterical symptoms had their sources in conflicted sexual feelings. Published in 1895, *Studies in Hysteria* set the stage for Freud's deepening inquiries into the psychic realm he called the unconscious.

Freud's next major study, *The Interpretation of Dreams* (1900), makes a radical claim on the ways in which the unconscious exists in parallel with the conscious mind but operates according to a distinct logic of its own. Unlike the conscious mind, which functions under the rational orders demanded by culture, the unconscious is the psychic domain that has undergone the arduous but ineluctable process of repression. To ensure the subject can function as successfully as possible in the world, mechanisms of repression necessarily come into play. It is through repression that desires and wishes forbidden to consciousness are deposited in the unconscious. That is not to say, however, that the unconscious remains completely debarred from the conscious mind. To the contrary, the unconscious makes its presence frequently known through such phenomena as parapraxes or slips of the tongue (commonly termed 'Freudian slips'), memories of dreams (which enact unconscious wishfulfilments), and gestures (ones that betray what the conscious mind is obliged to repress). Psychoanalysis, both as a body of theory and a clinical practice, could not operate without placing these visual and corporeal signs under careful scrutiny, thereby gaining interpretative access to the remote but none the less decipherable activity of the unconscious.

This pathbreaking theory of the unconscious provides one of the main supports to the innovative account of sexuality Freud first elaborated in 1905, and which would absorb much of his attention for the remainder of his career. Published in that year, his *Three Essays on the Theory of Sexuality* discloses how the unconscious becomes the turbulent zone where diverse sexual drives have to be repressed so that the human subject maintains its identity. The first phase of this process occurs early in infantile life, its second phase during puberty, and between the two there is a period of latency. (Hence Freud calls this a *diphasic* model of sexual development.) But, as Freud repeatedly shows, the sexual identity initially taken up by the infant is the result of a far from easy process, since it refuses to obey any preordained path of development. Stressing continually how biological instincts cannot have exclusive rights in determining sexuality, Freud argues that the infant's body becomes sexualized through ambivalent psychic responses to the anatomical distinction between the sexes. To understand the complex identifications through which the infant must pass in the formation of sexuality, Freud theorized two interdependent structures: the Oedipus complex and the castration complex. Given greatest detail in several later papers, published during the 1920s and 1930s, these two complexes never ceased to stretch beyond Freud's formidable analytic reach. In many respects, the Oedipus and castration complexes became both his main preoccupation and his most enduring problem. Suggestive yet schematic, ingenious yet infuriating, they provide two of the main foundations to Freud's explorations of sexuality. Comprehending the implications of each complex, however, can prove difficult because they emerge in piecemeal fashion throughout his voluminous later writings, first in footnotes appended to four subsequent editions of the *Three Essays* (the last appearing in 1924), and then in scattered papers such as 'The Dissolution of Oedipus Complex' (1924) and 'Female Sexuality' (1931). So it is vital to remember that no single book or essay by Freud provides a total picture of his reflections on sexuality.

To appreciate exactly how Freud's work broke with earlier sexological models of desire and laid the foundations for the Oedipus and castration complexes, it is useful to look first of all at the innovative lines of inquiry he started to pursue in the *Three Essays*. The essays deal in turn with 'The Sexual Aberrations', 'Infantile Sexuality', and 'Transformations of Puberty'. In examining the 'sexual aberrations', Freud abstracts some overarching points about the case histories compiled by sexologists such as Havelock Ellis and Richard von Krafft-Ebing, particularly these researchers' analyses of sexual inversion or homosexuality (on both writers, see Chapter 1). Having summarized these sexologists' discoveries, Freud concludes that it is impossible to make hard and fast distinctions between 'congenital' and 'acquired' forms of inversion, since there are many sexual experiences shared by homosexuals and heterosexuals in early life. Similarly, he casts serious doubt on Karl Heinrich Ulrichs's belief that male inverts contained a female brain in a male body, remarking that science remains unsure about precisely what might constitute a 'feminine brain' (Freud 1953: VII, 142). That said, Freud entertains the idea – one that will become increasingly significant for him – that inversion might be a form of psychic bisexuality (that is, combining feminine and masculine attributes), largely because this concept accentuates a distinction between sexual *instinct* and sexual *object*. (At this point, it is worth noting that in the original German, Freud employs the word *Trieb* rather than *Instinkt*. *Trieb* roughly translates as *drive*, while *Instinkt* correlates with the biological sense of *instinct*. There are ongoing debates among students of Freud's work that focus on whether one should refer to sexual 'drives' or 'instincts', especially since his theory of sexuality sought to detach itself from biological determinism. [On this issue, see Bowie 1991: 161.]) 'It seems probable', writes Freud, 'that the sexual instinct is in the first instance independent of its object; nor is its origin likely to be due to its object's attraction' (Freud 1953: VII, 148). In other words, sexual inversion indicates that there might be arbitrary connections between initial erotic drives, on the one hand, and eventual libidinal attachments, on the other.

By way of clarifying this point, Freud explains how even 'normal sexual life' – namely, that which leads to heterosexual intercourse – involves behaviours that do not have a direct function in the reproductive process. Such 'preliminary' or 'intermediate' sexual aims, argues Freud, include touching and looking at the sexual object, leading to extremely pleasurable activities such as kissing. Seen in the cold light of dispassionate science, he states, kissing could well be viewed as a 'perversion'. Why? Because 'the parts of the body involved do not form part of the sexual apparatus but constitute the entrance to the digestive tract' (Freud

1953: VII, 150). On this basis, Freud finds it possible to substantiate the claim that many different parts of the body can become sites of intense sexual valuation. Even though disgust may interfere with a person's response to a specific body part (such as the mouth, the genitals, or the anus), it remains the case that the libido may well override the revulsion that convention often attributes to these somatic zones. To show what he means, Freud focuses on the customary abhorrence of the anus, the organ most frequently associated with male homosexuality. He indicates that the horror that anal intercourse often arouses in people is somewhat illogical. But as the following remarks reveal, in making this bold assertion Freud is not entirely averse to sexism:

> Where the anus is concerned it becomes still clearer that it is disgust which stamps that sexual aim as a perversion. I hope, however, I shall not be accused of partisanship when I assert that people who try to account for this disgust by saying that the organ in question serves the function of excretion and comes in contact with excrement – a thing which is disgusting in itself – are not much more to the point than hysterical girls who account for their disgust at the male genital by saying that it serves to void urine.
>
> (Freud 1953: VII, 152)

Each body part, therefore, can be interpreted in a striking variety of ways – even, it seems, by 'hysterical girls'. They can serve biological functions, become erogenous zones, and represent sites of disgust. From this perspective even the penis, that has a natural reproductive capacity, is potentially an object of revulsion. In sexual terms, then, the human body has many features that may be loved or loathed, esteemed or scorned, depending on the disposition of the subject.

But body parts, in all their multifariousness, are hardly the only objects onto which libidinal attachments are made. Freud promptly notes how fetishes – 'such as the foot or hair' or 'some inanimate object' – substitute for the sexual object, a point he embellishes much later in his paper titled 'Fetishism' (1927). Rather like kissing, which has no direct purpose in reproduction, fetishism is present in heterosexual love. To prove his point, Freud quotes the following lines from Goethe's *Faust* (1808–32): 'Get me a kerchief from her breast, / A garter that her knee has pressed' (Freud 1953: VII, 154). Likewise, there are other notable perversions that reveal how sexuality departs from the apparent biological imperative to reproduce. Just as the aforementioned aberrations disclose why the sexual instinct should be separated from the sexual object, so too do masochism and sadism enlarge our understanding of aggression in sexuality. 'Sadism and masochism', observes Freud, 'occupy a special position among the perversions, since the contrast between activity and passivity which lies behind them is among the universal characteristics of sexual life' (Freud 1953: VII, 159). In no way biologically functional, masochism and sadism push to an extreme familiar types of activity and passivity – and, correspondingly, masculinity and femininity – that are elsewhere normalized by convention in sexual relations between men and women. So rather than consign such perversions to types of illness or degeneracy, Freud contends these erotic behaviours and preferences have a constitutive role in all human sexuality, especially the reproductive heterosexuality that the sexologists were often at pains to differentiate from seemingly unnatural desires.

Consequently, Freud reaches two main conclusions in 'The Sexual Aberrations'. First, he insists that 'the sexual instinct has to struggle against certain mental forces which act as resistances', notably 'forces' such as shame and disgust. The subject, therefore, strives to regulate the sexual instinct through repression. Such regulation, however, is not always victorious in securing the development of 'normal' sexual life. Second, the perversions reveal that the sexual instinct has many discrete, if not disharmonious, sources. In other words, the perversions have 'a composite nature'. 'This gives us', writes Freud, 'a hint that perhaps the sexual instinct may be no simple thing, but put together from components which have come apart again in the perversions' (Freud 1953: VII, 162). Having drawn attention to these matters, Freud's task is to infer (1) how the subject labours to limit the sexual instinct, and (2) how the sexual instinct itself combines varying, and often conflicting, elements.

How, then, does Freud explore these two hypotheses? To answer this question, it is necessary to look first at some of the salient points made in the second of the *Three Essays*, 'Infantile Sexuality'. There Freud declares that 'germs of the sexual impulses are already present in the new-born child', and these shall go through the first of the two phases that organize human sexuality (Freud 1953: VII, 180). Especially significant is the creation of autoerotic pleasures that retrace the infant's earliest somatic comforts. To illustrate the child's incipient autoeroticism, Freud considers the infantile practice of thumb-sucking. This practice, he argues, involves re-enacting the joyous activity of breastfeeding. 'There is no question of the purpose of this procedure being the taking of nourishment', he remarks (Freud 1953: VII, 182). Serving no other function than physical comfort, thumb-sucking mimes a 'pleasure that has already been experienced' (Freud 1953: VII, 181). Subsequently, the lips and mucous membrane of the mouth become sites of somatic intensity. The same is true for any other organ of the body. In a footnote added in 1915, Freud remarked: 'I have been led to ascribe the quality of erotogenicity to all parts of the body and to all the internal organs' (Freud 1953: VII, 184). As Freud's remarkable case histories would show, many different areas of the body could become the focus of profound eroticism, neurosis, and perversion – the nose, the throat, the stomach, the anus, among them.

But even if Freud asserts that any bodily part has the potential to be eroticized, there are three zones in particular which absorb his attention. In analysing infantile sexuality, he concentrates on the mouth, the anus, and the genitals. Each of these areas, he argues, retains the capacity for intense erotogenicity. These somatic areas have an intimate connection with pleasures derived from biological functions. The anal sphincter, for example, becomes highly significant for the child, first when its diapers are changed and then when it learns to defecate at regular intervals. 'Children', writes Freud, 'who are making use of the susceptibility to erotogenic stimulation of the anal zone betray themselves by holding back their stool till its accumulation brings about violent muscular contractions and, as it passes through the anus, is able to produce powerful stimulation of the mucous membrane' (Freud 1953: VII, 186). In fact, the production of faeces may well take on an exceptional symbolic significance because it represents the infant's ability to negotiate its relationship with the world – to withhold or to give its faecal mass. Subsequent perversions, such as 'special scatalogical practices' or 'masturbatory stimulation of the anal zone by means of the finger', can be traced back to this acutely important episode in the infant's life (Freud 1953: VII, 187). Having shown how the infant must advance beyond first oral and then anal erotogenicity, Freud accentuates the infantile pleasure in genital masturbation. Like the anus, this sensitive area experiences heightened stimulation when rubbed during bathing and cleaning. Masturbation, which may or may not persist until puberty, substitutes for the pleasures derived from this early bodily pleasure. In sum, the erotogenic development of the oral and anal zones marks the 'pregenital' phase of infantile sexuality. Puberty, which witnesses the growth of the genitals, brings about the final phase through which sexuality should pass. Thus we have in place Freud's diphasic model for understanding how sexuality is organized.

In its earliest formation, however, sexuality does not depend solely on autoerotic stimulation of the oral, anal, and genital zones. In a section added to 'Infantile Sexuality' in 1915, Freud discusses how children begin their 'sexual researches' between the ages of three to five (Freud 1953: VII, 194). He argues that when children first examine their social worlds, they are preoccupied with only one question: Where do babies come from? This inquiry, we are told, precedes any interest a child might have in the division between the sexes. Yet as the child's 'researches' deepen, the whole issue of sexual difference becomes a source of considerable anxiety. It is at this point that Freud briefly sketches one of the two structures for which his work is notorious: the castration complex. Here is how Freud proposes what happens to boys and girls when they confront symbolic castration:

> It is self-evident to a male child that a genital like his own is to be attributed to everyone he knows, and he cannot make its absence tally with his picture of these other people.
>
> This conviction is energetically maintained by boys, is obstinately defended against the contradictions which soon result from observation, and is only abandoned after severe internal struggles (the castration complex). The substitutes for the penis which they feel is missing in women play a great part in determining the form taken by many perversions.
>
> The assumption that all human beings have the same (male) form of genital is the first of the many remarkable and momentous theories of children. It is of little use to a child that the science of biology justifies his prejudice and has been obliged to recognize the female clitoris as a true substitute for the penis.
>
> Little girls do not resort to denial of this kind when they see that boys' genitals are formed differently from their own. They are ready to recognize them immediately and overcome by envy for the penis – an envy culminating in the wish, which is so important in its consequences, to be boys themselves.
>
> (Freud 1953: VII, 195)

Presented in such summary form, the dynamics involved in the castration complex may well look doubtful. Why should the male child initially assume that everyone has a penis? Why should little girls envy this particular part of the male anatomy? And why should children of either sex experience fear at being robbed of this organ? It is frustrating to find that Freud does not supply ready answers. For no sooner have we read these paragraphs than he instantly moves to his next observation: how children witness and interpret scenes of sexual intercourse. It would take Freud at least another decade before he explored the consequences of the castration complex. And, even then, he often remained unclear about the exact role symbolic castration played in the formation of female sexuality – for reasons we shall examine shortly.

In the *Three Essays*, it remains unclear how the castration complex interacts with the Oedipus complex, even though the latter structure emerged as far back as 1897 during Freud's researches for *The Interpretation of Dreams*. One has to look at later works, such as *The Ego and the Id* (1923) and 'The Dissolution of the Oedipus Complex' (1924), to understand exactly how boys and girls supposedly follow divergent paths that involve conflicting loves and losses. In these writings, Freud characteristically pays greater attention to the tortuous route taken by the boy than that of the girl, as they head towards 'normal' heterosexuality. Undoubtedly, the boy undergoes a highly conflicted process before he becomes the active, masculine, heterosexual male that society wants him to be.

In theorizing the Oedipus complex, Freud abstracted his paradigm from the great classical tragedy by Sophocles (*c.* 494–06 BC). In this drama, the Greek hero kills his father and weds his mother. But Oedipus does so in ignorance. For the tragedy, of course, lies in how Oedipus does not know until after the event who his parents are. As in all tragedies, there are higher forces at work that determine the fatal path that Oedipus is compelled to take. How, then, does this tragic drama represent the sexual development of Freud's boy? First of all, the male infant discovers that his mother takes measures to inhibit his infantile masturbation. But it takes a while for the boy to understand the reality behind this symbolic castration. In *The Ego and the Id*, Freud explains how the boy must first of all pass through the deeply troubling Oedipus complex:

> At a very early age the little boy develops an object-cathexis [i.e. transfer of erotic energy on to an object] for his mother, which originally related to the mother's breast . . . ; the boy deals with his father by identifying himself with him. For a time these two relationships proceed side by side, until the boy's sexual wishes in regard to his mother become more intense and his father is perceived as an obstacle to them; from this the Oedipus complex originates. His identification with his father then takes on a hostile colouring and changes into a wish to get rid of his father in order to take his place with his mother. Henceforward his relation to his father is ambivalent; it seems as if this ambivalence inherent in the identification from the beginning had become manifest. An ambivalent attitude to his father and an object-relation of a solely affectionate kind to his mother make up the content of the simple positive Oedipus complex in the boy.
>
> Along with the demolition of the Oedipus complex, the boy's object-cathexis of the mother must be given up. Its place may be filled by one of two things: either an identification with his mother or an intensification of his identification with his father. We are accustomed to regard the latter outcome as the more normal; it permits the affectionate relation to the mother in a measure to be retained. In this way the dissolution of the Oedipus complex would consolidate the masculinity of the boy's character.
>
> (Freud 1961: XIX, 32)

Although for some time he enjoys his phallic phase, the boy soon realizes that he is his father's rival for his mother's love, thus inaugurating the Oedipus complex. This rivalrous structure places competing demands upon the boy: (1) to love his mother and to hate his father; (2) to relinquish his love for his mother and to identify with his father. If he negotiates the customary path towards heterosexuality, then the boy will retain an affection for his mother while identifying with his father. But in order to achieve this final step, a further stage in the drama must come to a head: the castration complex.

In 'The Dissolution of the Oedipus Complex', Freud insists it is the 'acceptance of the possibility of castration, his recognition that women were castrated' that enables the boy's Oedipus complex to come to a close. The castration complex has many implications for the boy: (1) he understands that his mother is not 'phallic' like himself; (2) he cannot love his mother, since that is his father's right; and (3) he must develop alternative libidinal attachments to a female object to secure his identity. Maintaining an identity, however, involves more than establishing the health of the ego, the term Freud uses to define the psychic agency that negotiates between the unconscious forces of the id and the pressures from the external world. Symbolic castration, which manifests itself culturally in the incest taboo, leads to the formation of the superego, the psychic agency that reaches deep into the id to act censoriously against the ego. The superego is where the subject internalizes cultural prohibitions, such as the interdiction against sexual relations between sons and mothers. If the boy eventually identifies with the authority of a paternal superego, then he will enter the period of latency in the years before puberty as a subject predisposed to heterosexual desire.

The picture, however, is markedly different when Freud attempts to explain how the castration and Oedipus complexes operate for girls. Although Freud remarks in *The Ego and the Id* that the Oedipus complex performs in 'a precisely analogous way' for girls (Freud 1961: XIX, 32), the following year in 'The Dissolution of the Oedipus Complex' the analogy is altogether less clear ('our material – for some incomprehensible reason –

becomes far more obscure and full of gaps' [Freud 1961: XIX, 177]). Only in 1925, in 'Some Psychical Consequences of the Anatomical Distinction between the Sexes', did Freud seek to untangle his views on how girls respond to the threat of castration. And it is here that we begin to see how boys and girls are hardly placed in a similar relation to the castration complex. For once Freud explains how a girl reacts to the threat of castration, it soon emerges that the absence of the penis marks, not the end, but the *beginning* of her Oedipus complex:

> A little girl behaves differently. She makes her judgement and her decision in a flash. She has seen it and knows that she is without it and wants to have it.
>
> Here what has been named the masculinity complex branches off. It may put great difficulties in the way of the regular development towards femininity, if it cannot be got over soon enough. The hope of some day obtaining a penis in spite of everything and so of becoming a man may persist to an incredibly late stage and may become a motive for strange and otherwise unaccountable actions. . . . Thus a girl may refuse to accept the fear of being castrated, may harden herself in the conviction that she *does* possess a penis, and may subsequently be compelled to behave as though she were a man. . . .
>
> After a woman has become aware of the wound to her narcissism, she develops, like a scar, a sense of inferiority. When she has passed beyond her first attempt at explaining her lack of a penis as being a punishment personal to herself and has realized that that sexual character is a universal one, she begins to share the contempt felt by men for a sex which is the lesser in so important a respect, and, at least in holding that opinion, insists on being like a man.
>
> (Freud 1961: XIX, 253)

Even though the boy must pass along a tormented route through what Freud frequently terms the 'positive' Oedipus complex towards 'normal' heterosexuality, the girl has to travel a much more arduous path towards the same destination. Indeed, in this essay, everything for the girl goes from bad to worse. The conflict she experiences comes about because of an imbalance between the masculine and feminine, active and passive, aspects to her psyche. By this point in his work, Freud is assured that in infancy all subjects have a bisexual disposition that permits the interplay between active and passive desires. If the girl's masculinity complex comes into its own, then she will not only hold her sex in contempt, but also discover great disappointment in the auto-erotic satisfactions derived from clitoral stimulation. How, then, will the girl get through this castration complex? What will lead her out of this drastic situation?

The answer, we are assured, is the Oedipus complex. But since the drama on which this complex was modelled involves a male protagonist, it may come as no surprise that Freud found it difficult to rework the Oedipal paradigm to explain the girl's sexual life. (Repeatedly, he repudiated the idea that one could dramatize the girl's experience in terms of a model drawn from an alternative Greek myth, the 'Electra complex'.) Committing himself to the explanatory power of Oedipus' tragedy, Freud finds it hard indeed to clarify the precise sequence that leads from the girl's masculinity to the feminine disposition required for heterosexual desire. Having wanted to be a man, claims Freud, the girl must accept that 'she cannot compete with boys and that it would therefore be best for her to give up the idea of doing so' (Freud 1961: XIX, 256). She becomes, in other words, resigned to her femininity, and thus discovers an appropriate substitute for the penis she has lost. How is this done? 'She gives up her wish for a penis and puts in place of it a wish for a child: and *with that purpose in view* she takes her father as a love-object'. Disillusioned with her clitoris, she focuses instead upon her vagina. With this somatic shift of interest, she can at last move out of her masculine phase to fulfil what is culturally expected of femininity.

But given that the Oedipus complex is now in place between herself and her father, nothing has been resolved for sure. In the case of girls, then, the Oedipal phase remains incomplete at best. All Freud can say about this unresolved state of affairs is that the 'Oedipus complex may persist far into women's normal life' (Freud 1961: XIX, 257). For some reason, the girl may well stubbornly refuse to break her libidinal attachments from the father, since it is he who promises the child that reinstates the lost penis. There is every possibility that her development shall be arrested at this stage. Later, he would reiterate this point in no uncertain terms. 'Girls', he remarks in 'Femininity' (1933), 'remain' in the Oedipus complex 'for an indeterminate length of time; they demolish it late and, even so, incompletely'. Left to linger in the Oedipal phase, the girl's superego may endure without 'the strength and independence which give it its cultural significance'. Recognizing the controversial implications of this assertion, Freud acknowledges how 'feminists are not pleased when we point out to them the effects of this factor upon the average feminine character' (Freud 1964: XXII, 129).

Freud was the first to admit that his twin complexes did not always serve femininity well, even though he steadfastly maintained his commitment to the analytic power of both models. In both 'Female Sexuality' (1931) and 'Femininity' (written two years later), he found it especially difficult to clear up the puzzling questions about female sexuality first raised in the paper he published in 1925. In 'Female Sexuality', two questions guide his discussion. 'How does she [the girl] find her way to her father? How, when and why does she detach herself from the mother?' (Freud 1961: XXI, 225). Having summarized more or less everything he said six years previously, Freud remains troubled by how and why the girl must turn against her mother, often in intensely hostile ways. His fascination lies in the girl's pre-Oedipal phase, a period he suggestively compares to 'the discovery, in another field, of Minoan–Mycenean civilization behind the civilization of

Greece' (Freud 1961: XXI, 226). This comparison implies that female sexuality has an archaic and inscrutable quality, rendering it only partly accessible to coherent analysis. Persistently, Freud searches for reasons that will account for the rupture with the mother that must occur in this early period of the girl's sexual life. 'What does the little girl require of her mother?' he asks. 'What is the nature of her sexual aims during the time of exclusive attachment to her mother?' (Freud 1961: XXI, 235).

By way of a response, Freud claims that the little girl experiences both active and passive drives, drawing attention once more to the bisexual disposition of infants. Take, for instance, being suckled. Where the child at first experiences the passive pleasure of being nourished from the breast, it will later enjoy active sucking. Here activity and passivity correspond with masculine and feminine impulses. To illustrate his point, Freud discusses how we might construe the pleasure girls often take in playing with dolls:

> We seldom hear of a little girl's wanting to wash or dress her mother, or tell her to perform her excretory functions. Sometimes, it is true, she says: 'Now let's play that I'm the mother and you're the child'; but generally she fulfils these active wishes in an indirect way, in her play with the doll, in which she represents the mother and the doll the child. The fondness girls have for playing with dolls, in contrast to boys, is commonly regarded as a sign of early awakened femininity. Not unjustly so; but we must not overlook the fact that what finds expression here is the *active* side of femininity, and that the little girl's preference for dolls is probably evidence of the exclusiveness of her attachment to her mother, with complete neglect of her father-object.
>
> (Freud 1961: XXI, 237)

In explaining the links between femininity, activity, and passivity, this intriguing example suggests some interesting complications in Freud's scheme. Although he frequently equates masculinity with activity, and femininity with passivity, here he asks us to bear in mind the '*active* side of femininity'. This formulation may, according to some of his principles, sound like a contradiction in terms, a contradiction to which he would return in his later lecture, 'Femininity', published in 1933 (see Freud 1964: XXII, 115). Yet no sooner has Freud shown how this active – and thus masculine – femininity reveals how the girl identifies with the mother's desires than he emphasizes a very different type of active behaviour that will gradually distance the girl from the mother. He believes that such distance is required so that the girl will at last become feminine at puberty. To strengthen this view, Freud reports how his female patients have at times divulged their phallic, and thus active, belligerence towards the maternal figure, often because these patients have revealed how in their infantile lives they lived in fear of being devoured by her. And when, according to Freud, the girl is not anxious about being consumed by the mother, then she fantasizes about eating up the maternal source of nourishment itself.

Keen to stress exactly why the 'turning-away from her mother is an extremely important step in the course of a little girl's development' (Freud 1961: XXI, 239), Freud puts pressure on how the girl experiences the sadistic–aggressive impulses of the phallic phase, impulses which culminate in infantile clitoral masturbation. Yet the active dimension to the phallic phase cannot have full rein if the girl is to achieve the culturally required norm of femininity. During this period, he claims, there are also passive drives that significantly accompany these distinctly active ones. 'In regard to the passive impulses', he remarks, 'it is noteworthy that girls regularly accuse their mother of seducing them' (Freud 1961: XXI, 238). Both here and elsewhere, Freud declares the fantasy of seduction arises because the mother stimulates the genitals while rubbing them clean. (Early in his career, Freud concluded that those of his patients who claimed to have been seduced by their parents in infancy were suffering from a commonplace fantasy that recalled the subject's enduringly difficult negotiation with the world. His decision to claim that seduction was an imagined event, not a real experience of abuse, remains a source of controversy. See, for example, Masson 1984.) Ultimately, passive trends such as the fantasy of seduction will remain sufficiently intact to enable the girl to convert her libidinal attachments to the father-object. For the girl eventually recognizes that her active desires simply cannot be realized. Even though the arrival of a newborn child in the family may suggest to the girl that she has given her mother a baby, she finally has to confront the fact that she cannot rival her father's phallic authority. So, once again, it is in a spirit of compromise that the girl's femininity falls into place. To comprehend female sexuality, therefore, Freud's readers have to bear in mind the following: (1) how the Oedipus complex succeeds the girl's castration complex; (2) how the phallic phase involves both active and passive impulses; and (3) how masculine trends must eventually flow into feminine channels. In the process, the femininity that is finally gained comes at a price, since 'a considerable portion of her sexual trends is permanently injured too' (Freud 1961: XXI, 239).

Freud's writings on femininity, if striving to maintain consistency within the terms of the castration and Oedipus complexes, are notable for what they refuse to entertain, as if they were acting out their own systematic repressions. To conclude this review of Freud's theoretical work on sexuality, it is useful to note how he selectively interprets female same-sex desire in a detailed case history published in 1920. In 'The Psychogenesis of a Case of Homosexuality in a Woman', Freud discusses how a 'beautiful and clever girl of eighteen' troubled her parents when they discovered she was consorting in public with an older woman known by many as a '*cocotte*' (Freud 1955: XVIII, 147). When her father accidentally met them in public and flashed them an angry glance, the young woman attempted suicide by flinging herself down an embankment next to a railway line. Six months later, she was placed in Freud's hands for treatment. During her analysis with Freud, the young woman revealed that at the age of thirteen or fourteen she became closely attached to young boy who was not quite three years old. Freud claims this relationship betokened her desire to be a mother and have a child of her own. But for some reason, she grew bored with the child, developing instead 'an interest in mature, but still youthful, women' (Freud 1955: XVIII, 156). We learn that this shift of attention occurred when her mother once again became pregnant. The young woman's third brother was born when she was about sixteen. Putting her dreams under scrutiny, Freud believed that this patient's 'lady-love was a substitute for – her mother'. Why should this be? Here is how Freud spells out his explanation:

> It was just when the girl was experiencing the revival of her infantile Oedipus complex at puberty that she suffered her greatest disappointment. She became keenly conscious of the wish to have a child, and a male one; that what she desired was her *father's* child and an image of *him*, her consciousness was not allowed to know. And what happened next? It was not *she* who bore the child, but her unconsciously hated rival, her mother. Furiously resentful and embittered, she turned away from her father and from men altogether. After this first great reverse she forswore her womanhood and sought another goal for her libido.
>
> (Freud 1955: XVIII, 157)

Having 'changed' – as Freud puts it – 'into a man' (Freud 1955: XVIII, 158), the young woman, we learn, intensified her libidinal choice when she realized the depth of her father's hostility. In fact, her homosexuality appeared to Freud as a protest against her father, who had won over her in their rivalry for the mother's affections. Indeed, Freud regards her behaviour as a form of 'revenge' against the paternal prerogative to love the mother (Freud 1955: XVIII, 160). So deep was her enmity towards her father that during the course of her analysis she 'transferred to [Freud] the sweeping repudiation of men which had dominated her ever since the disappointment she had suffered from her father' (Freud 1955: XVIII, 164). Given the force of this transference, Freud broke off the treatment, believing that only a woman analyst could complete the task successfully. To be sure, this intriguing text reveals that his analytic skills were pushed beyond their limit.

This richly detailed case history is fascinating because it shows how hard Freud tried and failed to resolve what faced him as the Sphinx-like 'riddle' or 'enigma' of femininity (Freud 1964: XXII, 113, 131). Repeatedly, this narrative yields insights into women's desires that Freud either could not or would not pursue. At the centre of the case there lies one interpretative crux that Freud fails to examine. It remains unclear whether the young woman's desire for another woman depends on (1) her identification with her father's privileged love for the mother, or (2) her reawakened pre-Oedipal attachment to the maternal body. Noticeably, both of her parents are, at different stages of the case history, her rivals. Yet they are, at the same time, figures with whom she identifies (to be a mother, to be a man).

Given the many possible identifications suggested by the scenario Freud depicts, Diana Fuss usefully raises the following questions:

> [W]hy is it presumed from the outset that desire for the mother is a displaced articulation of unfulfilled desire for the father, and not the other way around? Why is the daughter's 'disappointment' imagined to be provoked by her inability to have the father's baby and not her failure to give the mother one (a possibility Freud later allows for in 'Femininity' [Freud 1964: XXII, 112–35])? Why is the daughter's resentment and bitter-

ness surmised to be directed toward the mother as competitor for the father's affections and not toward the father as interloper into the mother–daughter relation? Why, in short, is the daughter's 'rivalry' assumed to be with the mother and not with the father?

(Fuss 1995: 63)

Why, indeed, does Freud favour one set of identifications over another? In this case history, no simple answer is forthcoming. Instead, it has been left to later analysts to reinterpret the materials Freud presents to us. 'A Case of Homosexuality in a Woman', like all of Freud's renowned cases, has attracted painstaking readings by critics such as Fuss who are adept at using Freudian concepts to question, redirect, even undermine Freud's own conclusions. So even if Freud's writings on sexuality may at times fail to acknowledge the full implications of their discoveries, they none the less remain an immensely fruitful resource for comprehending the intricate, if at times baffling, psychic processes that create masculine and feminine, heterosexual and homosexual, desires and identifications.

LACAN'S ORDERS

Towards the end of Freud's career, a young French psychiatrist began publishing papers that would eventually have a huge impact on how twentieth-century intellectuals contemplated subjectivity and sexuality. The work of Jacques Lacan, which came to prominence with the publication of his *Écrits* in France (1966), has for decades been notorious for its persistent inaccessibility. Faithful to Freud's exploration of the ego, the unconscious, and sexual desire, Lacan built up a distinctive theoretical framework that remains contentious to this day. Frequently decried for its inscrutability, Lacan's abstruse and elliptical style draws attention to the very material from which in his view the human subject must emerge: language itself. For Lacan's aim is to reveal how complex tensions within signification comprise the field where the subject must battle for its identity. Determined to eliminate any remaining traces of biological thought from Freud's enterprise, Lacan is decidedly anti-humanist in revealing how the 'I' is besieged, not by impulses and instincts, but signs and meanings. Identity, in Lacan's world, always remains precarious, and that is because the subject seeks to consolidate itself through processes of *mis*recognition. This structure forms the basis of Lacan's succeeding analyses of (1) how the subject emerges within the linguistic order, and (2) how the subject must take up a sexual position in relation to the primary signifier: the phallus. This part of the present chapter explores these concepts in turn.

Lacan introduces the fragile status of the 'I' in a brief but dense conference paper first delivered in Zürich in 1949, which returns to one of the concepts he presented to the same audience some thirteen years before. In 'The Mirror Stage as Formative of the Function of the I as Revealed in Psychoanalytic Experience', Lacan reports that his theory of the 'mirror stage' has been widely accepted by the French Freudians. Denoted in French as the *'stade du miroir'*, this 'stage' has a double meaning. At one and the same time, it signifies a phase of development *and* a type of spectacle. Moreover, when placed next to *'miroir'*, this 'stage' concerns both the *specular* and the *spectacular*. The very term condenses the complex features of this fundamental psychoanalytic concept. Bearing this double 'stage' in mind, the *stade du miroir* accounts for a formative experience that young children undergo between the ages of six and eighteen months. At that point, when placed in front of a mirror, the child will be able to recognize its own image. But rather than claim the child simply sees its own reflection, Lacan insists that this episode places the primordial 'I' in a 'fictional direction'. Why? This is how Lacan explains the 'fictional' quality to this *stade*:

The fact is that the total form of the body by which the subject anticipates in a mirage the maturation of his power is given him only as *Gestalt*, that is to say, in an exteriority in which this form is certainly more constituent than constituted, but in which it appears to him above all in a contrasting size (*un relief de stature*) that fixes it and in a symmetry that inverts it, in contrast with the turbulent movements that the subject feels are animating him. Thus, this *Gestalt* – whose pregnancy should be recognized as bound up with the species, though its motor cycle remains scarcely recognizable – by these two aspects of its appearance, symbolizes the mental permanence of the *I*, at the same time as it prefigures its alienating destination; it is still pregnant with the correspondences that unite the *I* with the statue in which man projects himself, with the phantoms that dominate him, or with the automaton in which, in an ambiguous relation, the world of his own making tends to find completion.

(Lacan 1977: 2–3)

This is a demanding paragraph to understand. But once we untangle its line of reasoning, we can see how the young child hardly finds *itself* in the mirror. For the *Gestalt* (or figure) that appears on the silvered surface is what grants the 'I' its identity. That is why the *Gestalt* is 'more constituent than constituted'. In reflecting the young child, the *Gestalt* offers an illusion. To begin with, it appears large and stands motionless, like a statue. In fact, this reflection resembles an automaton. So it is not surprising that Lacan regards this image as the 'alienating destination' of the 'I'. When the child discovers its 'I' in the mirror, that 'I' happens to be nothing more than a projection. On this model, the reflection is far from real. Instead, it is like a hallucination. But for the child to operate in the world, it requires a projected 'I' that will at least provide an image of coherence. Such an image permits the

'I' to come together from fragmentary parts, to gain some stability, no matter how imaginary, in its development.

Yet stability is not easily attained. From this moment on, the young child enters a structure of anticipation, since it projects the 'I' it believes itself to be. Given that the mirror stage inaugurates a temporal dimension, the 'I' enters history. Propelled into the historical process, the 'I' labours under an obligation to harden itself against the world, creating the belief that its completeness and wholeness are guaranteed by what is only a mere image set before it. 'The *mirror stage*', writes Lacan, 'is a drama whose internal thrust is precipitated from insufficiency to anticipation – and which manufactures for the subject, caught up in the lure of spatial identification, the succession of phantasies that extends from a fragmented body-image to a form of its totality'. Eventually, the 'I' adopts 'the armour of an alienating identity' (Lacan 1977: 4). In fact, the 'I' must defend itself well because its 'fictional direction' means it can never coincide with itself. In other words, the 'I' will always remain in an asymptotic relation to the subject. So in no respect can the 'I' be seen as self-sufficient. For the 'I' only comes into being in the field of the other: the statue-like *Gestalt* that the young child necessarily *mis*recognizes as itself.

Yet Lacan's theory of the 'I' does not rest at the mirror stage. Later, in papers delivered during the 1950s, he turns to linguistics to explain how his theory of the 'I' remodels the prevailing tradition of thought descending from René Descartes (1596–1650) that asserts '*cogito ergo sum*' ('I think, therefore I am'). The Cartesian paradigm, writes Lacan, wrongly assumes a 'link between the transparency of the transcendental subject and his existential affirmation' (Lacan 1977: 164). What, then, can shake the Cartesian conviction that the 'I' is transparently present to itself? One needs to look at how language splits the subject, fracturing the certainty that the 'I' that *thinks* remains the 'I' that *is*. Lacan sums up this particular question when he declares: 'It is not a question of knowing whether I speak of myself in a way that conforms to what I am, but rather of knowing whether I am the same as that of which I speak' (Lacan 1977: 165). There are, then, two separate aspects to the 'I' that situates the subject.

To comprehend the non-coincidence of the 'I' that is and the 'I' that speaks, Lacan forces attention on Freud's foundational work of psychoanalytic inquiry, *The Interpretation of Dreams* (1900). By devising techniques to unravel his patients' recollection of dreams, Freud discovered how the unconscious operated by its own organizational principles. These are principles that arrange meanings in a fashion that is initially incomprehensible to the conscious mind. In coming to terms with the peculiar structure of the unconscious, Freud detected two predominant tendencies: towards condensation, on the one hand, and towards displacement, on the other. Later, theorists working in the field of linguistics would elaborate how condensation equates with metaphor, and displacement with metonymy – although both metaphor and metonymy, like many rhetorical figures, have a tendency to flow into and merge with one another. Lacan takes the concept much further, by enumerating a great many of the tropes – or rhetorical figures – that fall under condensation and displacement:

> Ellipses and pleonasm, hyperbaton and syllepsis, repression, repetition, apposition – these are the syntactical displacements; metaphor, catachresis, autonomasis, allegory, metonymy, and synecdoche – these are the semantic condensations in which Freud teaches us to read the intentions – ostentatious or demonstrative, dissimulating or persuasive, retaliatory or seductive – out of which the subject modulates his oneiric discourse.
>
> (Lacan 1977: 58)

To Lacan, therefore, the unconscious that emerges from 'oneiric discourse' (the discourse of dreaming) is structured like a language. That is to say, the unconscious has its own combinatory powers, its own syntactical and semantic operations, piecing together bits of meaning in ways that may at first appear strange and unfamiliar, but which become lucid to a practised psychoanalytic eye. Lacan believes subjectivity depends on the separation between the peculiar field of meaning-production that inhabits the unconscious and the operation of language in the conscious mind. But that is not to claim that there is a neat division between these two fields of meaning.

Lacan extends his interest to the modes of signification structuring the field in which consciousness must operate, not just the revelations about repressive processes disclosed by dreams. Rather than assume that the subject has autonomous control over its expression as an 'I', Lacan insists that language subordinates the subject to its own orders: 'The form in which language is expressed itself defines subjectivity. Language says: "You will go here, and when you see this, you will turn off there"' (Lacan 1977: 85). Instead of asserting self-sufficiency, the 'I' within language can only know itself in terms of the other that recognizes the 'I'. Adopting a stance familiar to any reader of *The Phenomenology of Spirit* (1975 [1807]) by the philosopher G.W.F. Hegel (1770–1831), Lacan sketches the predicament of the 'I' in these terms:

> What I see in speech is the response of the other. What constitutes me as subject is my question. In order to be recognized by the other, I utter what was only in view of what will be. In order to find him, I call him by a name that he must assume or refuse in order to reply to me.
>
> I identify myself in language, but only by losing myself in it like an object. What is realized in my history is not the past definite of what was, since it is no more, or even the present

perfect of what has been in what I am, but the future anterior
of what I shall have been for what I am in the process of
becoming.

(Lacan 1977: 86)

These playful sentences, which accentuate Lacan's own linguistic
self-consciousness, draw attention to how the tense of the 'I' is
always in a process of deferred *becoming*. In other words, the 'I' can
only know of itself in terms of the other who shall offer a
response. But the response of the other cannot be known in
advance, thus placing the 'I' in a state of anticipation, if not ago-
nized suspension. For the subject remains, as he suggestively
remarks, in the condition of the 'future anterior': a projective
tense that looks in expectation to both the past and the future, to
what one *will have been* and to what one *is going to become*. It is, as
Samuel Weber remarks, a structure of *'anticipated belatedness'*
(Weber 1991: 9). Oscillating between anticipation and belatedness, Lacan's subject is by definition a subject of desire, constantly launching itself into the field of other where it seeks to know
what it might have become.

To explain how the subject is positioned within these fields of
signification, Lacan turns to the work of the early twentieth-
century Swiss linguist, Ferdinand de Saussure (1857–1913),
whose posthumously published *Course in General Linguistics*
(1915) brought together lectures delivered between 1906 and
1911. Saussure asserted that the linguistic sign could be divided
into two components: the signifier (the materiality of the sign)
and the signified (the meaning of the sign). The relation between
these two elements, Saussure insists, is arbitrary. Not only that,
the signifier cannot define the signified alone. For the production
of meaning depends on more and more signifiers that proliferate
along a chain. One signifier has to come to the aid of another signifier, in an unending process. They are, to cite Lacan's simile,
like 'rings of a necklace that is a ring around another necklace

made of rings' (Lacan 1977: 153). This image concisely represents the chain of signifiers as both a closed system and an infinite system, one in which the phonemes or units of sound are limited in number and yet whose combination remains innumerable.

Since the 'I' anticipates its own becoming within the signifying chain, and since it correspondingly seeks its meaning within the field of the other, Lacan devised three orders that explain the forces in which the subject finds itself caught. Just as Freud invented the terms id, ego, and superego to comprehend how the 'I' negotiated its place in the world, so too did Lacan construct his own tripartite scheme: the Symbolic, the Imaginary, and the Real. Using his own distinctive terminology, Lacan's three topoi bear a loose resemblance to Freud's already well-established categories.

In Lacanian theory, the Imaginary defines the realm of identificatory misrecognitions inaugurated at the mirror stage when the subject seeks to cohere its self-image. Throughout his later work, *The Four Fundamental Concepts of Psycho-Analysis* (1978 [1973]), Lacan repeatedly comments on the role played in the Imaginary by the *objet petit a*: an untranslatable term which captures the idea that the subject must project a little object into the field of the other (*autre*), so that it can recognize itself. In many respects, the *object petit a* stands for the subject's ambiguous relation to its specularized *Gestalt*. In order to maintain its identity, the subject must undergo the hallucinatory effort to pull its mirrored image together out of disparate parts. In the field of the Imaginary, the *objet petit a* marks the inevitable gap that the subject must constantly seal over in the process of recognizing its mirrored *Gestalt*. That is to say, the *objet petit a* arises from the contradictory moment when the subject situates itself in what remains an alienating specular realm. 'Through the function of the *objet a*', writes Lacan, 'the subject separates himself off, ceases to be linked to the vacillation of being, in the sense that it forms the essence of alienation' (Lacan 1978: 258).

Desperately seeking to find a place within the Imaginary, the subject is forever under siege from Lacan's second order, the Symbolic. Fluctuating, disjointed, heterogeneous, the Symbolic outdoes and overreaches the subject's desires to find a stable point for its identity in the Imaginary. For the Symbolic is shared by all subjects, providing the realm of signification where everyone has access to the pronoun 'I'. In his elegant introduction to Lacan's work, Malcolm Bowie characterizes this distinctly social and intersubjective field of signification in a particularly memorable way: 'It is a *res publica* that does not allow any one of its members to be himself, keep himself or recreate in his own image the things that lie beyond him' (Bowie 1991: 93).

The Real, by comparison, is harder to construe. It defines the zone that falls outside the domain of signification. It is where psychic materials remain unsymbolized, through processes such as trauma. In psychosis, for example, the subject collapses into the Real. So the Real, a profoundly threatening order, encompasses both the Imaginary and the Symbolic, and it puts immense pressure on both to keep their intersubjective processes at work. In many ways, one can view the Imaginary and Symbolic as fields that tensely rise up against each other, creating friction between opposing agencies that compete for meaning, forever fending off the field of non-meaning marked by the Real.

How, then, might Lacan's reflections on the split subject, the field of signification, and the domains of the Imaginary, Symbolic, and Real throw light on sexuality? To answer this question, more attention must be paid to Lacan's theory of desire. We have already noted that the Lacanian subject, which is always caught within a significatory process, is a subject of desire. Moreover, this subject is compelled to desire because it is by definition a subject of lack. For this subject has to enter the field of the other to discover what it may become. Lacan phrases 'that which structures desire' in the following way:

> Desire is that which is manifested in the interval that demand hollows within itself, in as much as the subject, in articulating the signifying chain, brings to light the want-to-be, together with the appeal to receive the complement from the Other, if the Other, the locus of speech, is also the locus of want, or lack.
>
> That which is thus given to the Other to fill, and which is strictly that which it does not have, since it, too, lacks being, is what is called love, but it is also hate and ignorance.
>
> (Lacan 1977: 263)

These sentences reveal that there is no neat reciprocity between the giving and receiving of love. Why? Because there is a necessary incommensuration between demand and need. On the one hand, the infant experiences need – for nourishment. On the other, the infant makes a demand – for love. But the two are not necessarily congruent. Opposing the subject's wishes, the other, after all, may well have its own perceptions about what constitutes need. Lacan remarks, for example, that the infant may feel overfed by the breast, the 'choking pap' that comes from the other. Such a situation results in a confusion between the satisfaction of need and the gift of love. That is why Lacan writes that 'desire is neither the appetite for satisfaction, nor the demand for love, but the difference that results from the subtraction of the first from the second, the phenomenon of their splitting (*Spaltung*)' (Lacan 1977: 287). Once again, therefore, we return to the idea that the desiring subject is split, this time because of the subtraction of need from demand, resulting in desire.

This *Spaltung* refers to the term on which Freud concentrates in one of his unfinished posthumous papers, 'Splitting of the Ego in the Process of Defence' (published in 1940). There Freud explains what happens when the child's 'ego is under the sway of a powerful instinctual demand which it is accustomed to satisfy' yet finds itself 'suddenly frightened by an experience which teaches it that the continuance of this satisfaction will result in an almost intolerable real danger' (Freud 1964: XXIII, 275). To Freud, the resulting *Spaltung* means that the ego must (1) refuse the threat of prohibition *and* (2) manage the fear in the form of a pathological symptom. In Lacanian terms, by comparison, this event marks the moment that structures desire, where need can never be met in terms of demand.

But this model still fails to account for how desire becomes focused on certain objects – what Freud calls sexual object-choices. In the process of having needs, making demands, and therefore becoming a desiring subject, the child will doubtless confront the crux that fascinates Freud: how the subject faces up to the anatomical distinction between the sexes. To explain how the subject becomes sexed, Lacan employs what is perhaps his most controversial theoretical device: the phallus. Dating from 1958, 'The Signification of the Phallus' emphasizes that the phallus 'is the signifier intended to designate as a whole the effects of the signified, in that the signifier conditions them by its presence as a signifier' (Lacan 1977: 285). If these words sound like a riddle, then his succeeding explanation looks even more perplexing:

> The phallus is the privileged signifier of that mark in which the role of the logos is joined with the advent of desire.
>
> It can be said that this signifer is chosen because it is the most tangible element in the realm of sexual copulation, and also the most symbolic in the literal (typographical) sense of the term, since it is equivalent there to the (logical) copula. It might be said that, by virtue of its turgidity, it is the image of the vital flow as it is transmitted in generation.
>
> All these propositions merely conceal the fact that it can play its role only when veiled, that is to say, as itself a sign of the latency which any signifiable is struck, when it is raised (*aufgehoben* [in the Hegelian sense]) to the function of the signifier.
>
> (Lacan 1977: 287–8)

This densely argued passage stakes several significant claims upon the phallus. First of all, the phallus enjoys the inviolable position of God's own word (the logos) in structuring the order of signification. Like Freud's anatomical penis, the phallus has a vivid role to play in how subjects negotiate both the castration and Oedipus complexes. But, given Lacan's aversion to biological systems of thinking, his phallus presents itself as a purely textual element – as the most crucial piece of significatory material within the chain of meaning. It has, for Lacan, rich connotations. Since the penis may be used for copulation, so the phallus may be seen as a linguistic copula: the verbal unit (enshrined in the verb 'to be') that yokes disparate elements together, securing the chain of shifting meanings. In all its mysterious primacy, the phallus remains forever veiled within signification. Since the phallus is always masked, it serves as a constant lure for desire. 'It is', writes Mikkel Borch-Jacobsen, 'the signifier that we seek through all other signifiers, all other objects' (Borch-Jacobsen 1991: 211). Through this ongoing search for the all-important but elusive signifier, sexuality emerges.

In the subject's desirous search for the phallus, two basic positions may be taken up. Returning to terms first used in Freud's *Group Psychology and the Analysis of the Ego* (1921), Lacan draws on the distinction between *being* and *having*. 'It is easy', writes Freud about the boy's Oedipus complex, 'to state in a formula the distinction between an identification with the father and the choice of the father as an object. In the first case one's father is what one would like to *be*, and in the second he is what one would like to *have*' (Freud 1955: XVIII, 106). Lacan appropriates this model to show how the phallus structures the relations between the sexes. The movement between *being* the phallus for another, and *having* the phallus for oneself creates the dialectic of desire. The Lacanian subject has to discover, like Freud's boy and girl, that the mother does not have the phallus. Likewise, this subject may well seek to be the phallus when returning the mother's desire. Sexual identifications, therefore, are arranged around this primary signifier. Elsewhere, Lacan styles its significatory power in slightly different terms. He remarks that this signifier represents the 'father, the Name-of-the-father' which 'sustains the structure of desire with the structure of the law' (Lacan 1978: 34). Like an omnipotent phantom or all-presiding deity, the phallic symbol of paternal authority retains is pre-eminence by hiding within the structures it governs.

What, then, are the implications of the veiled phallus for the two sexes? What are the consequences for either *being* or *having* the primary signifier whose hidden position creates the lure of desire? Lacan stresses that the anatomical distinction between the sexes provides the cultural form through which subjects come to recognize their position on either the male or female side of sexual difference. Repeatedly, Lacan's exegetes stress that, for him, anatomy is not destiny. Instead, the imagined presence or absence of the penis provides the acknowledged framework in which subjects seek – but necessarily fail – to adopt a settled position on either side of the sexual divide. That is why Lacan insists that any attempt either to *be* or to *have* the phallus rests on an imposture. Given that the Lacanian subject desires precisely because of lack, it can never remain complete in the sexually differentiated position it strives to take up. Even if the male side may provide the illusion that masculinity *has* the phallus, it only does so by covering over the male subject's constitutive lack. Conversely, if the female side may suggest that femininity can *be* the phallus, then it does so only in the form of a 'masquerade'. Considering how women are under pressure to make themselves into desirable objects, Lacan argues that, in the process, femininity has to reject 'an essential part' of itself: 'It is for that which she is not that she wishes to be desired as well as loved' (Lacan 1977: 290).

But in Lacan's later writings, femininity is not always subjected to the 'masquerade' demanded by the reigning phallus. To show that femininity might elude phallic law, he returned in the mid-1970s to aspects of the vexed debate on femininity that absorbed Freud's attention some fifty years before, and which has remained a source of critical interest to modern feminist theory. In the essays by Lacan and his students brought together in *Feminine Sexuality: Jacques Lacan and the école freudienne* (Mitchell and Rose 1982), there are several statements that indicate how the phallus might not have complete dominance over all aspects of sexual difference. This collection features one of the most thought-provoking seminars on female sexuality that Lacan published in *Encore* (1975). In 'God and ~~the~~ *Jouissance* of The Woman' – renowned for both its density of reference and its linguistic provocations – Lacan returns our attention to the notorious difficulties into which Freud ran when attempting to settle the 'riddle' of femininity. So fraught has this longstanding controversy been that 'petty considerations', claims Lacan, 'have caused havoc' (Mitchell and Rose 1982: 145). In this seminar, Lacan aims to explain how and why the phallus erects itself on a fantasy of woman, or – more vividly – 'The Woman'. To expose how 'The Woman' is a myth, Lacan deletes the definite article in both the title and text of his seminar. Instead of 'The Woman', he explores the *jouissance* of '~~the~~ woman', a phenomenon that confounds, defies, and exceeds the phallic order. Such *jouissance* – a word which remains extremely hard to paraphrase in English – captures the exhilarating bliss and intensity of sexual experience.

In the brief preface to her translation of this seminar, Jacqueline Rose remarks that here Lacan 'underline[s] the problem which has dominated the psychoanalytic debate on feminine sexuality to date: how to hold on to Freud's most radical insight that sexual difference is a symbolic construct; how to retrieve femininity from a total subordination to the effects of that construct' (Mitchell and Rose 1982: 137–8). To tackle this issue, Lacan declares that, since he was twenty, he has been a student of Western love, and his researches into its history have revealed the significance of female mystics, such as Hadewijch d'Anvers (fl.

early thirteenth century) and Saint Theresa of Avila (1515–82). Commenting on the well-known Roman sculpture 'Saint Theresa in Ecstasy' (*c.* 1665) by Giovanni Lorenzo Bernini (1598–1680), Lacan asks: 'what is her *jouissance*, her [sexual] *coming* from?' 'It is clear', he adds, 'that the essential testimony of the mystics is that they are experiencing it but know nothing about it' (Mitchell and Rose 1982: 147). Rather than assert that such ecstasy is about 'fucking', Lacan claims this experience is *'something more'*: 'that which puts us on the path of ex-istence'. Such 'ex-istence' is literally the *ex stasis* encrypted in 'ecstasy': an intensely pleasurable out-of-body state that, as these puns vividly dramatize, cannot be contained. Indeed, such feminine *jouissance* cannot be captured by the 'God' in his title. What, then, does this 'God' signify? In his highly attentive reading of this seminar, Bowie remarks that it refers to two structures. The first is '"the One" that male sexuality ordains, and that psychoanalysis, in temporary partnership with Christian theology, is able to unmask in an indefinite variety of human contexts'. The second is 'the Other': the 'impediment . . . that comes between partners in the well-known [loving] arrangement', an arrangement Lacan reminds us we are 'not strictly entitled to call "a sexual relationship"' (Bowie 1991: 154). And why cannot we speak of 'a sexual relationship'? Because a third party – the other's Other, so to speak – always interrupts the subject's desire. That is to say, a subject never obtains complete reciprocity from its beloved other, since both parties are displaced, if not torn apart, by the chain of signifiers where all desires circulate. Saint Theresa's mystical experience, therefore, represents a *jouissance* that evades 'the One' and 'the Other', both of them 'Gods'.

Yet in her defiance of such omniscient authority, Saint Theresa's apparent orgasmic 'ex-istence' certainly gives one pause. What really is at stake in removing 'The Woman' by putting the 'the woman' under typographical erasure? Is it really the case that *jouissance* marks the only moment in which femininity subverts phallic authority? Although Lacan wants us to see how Saint Theresa's autoeroticism confounds the phallic signifier, we might be tempted to conclude that his appeal to this female mystic represents yet another mystification of femininity – femininity *as* mystification perhaps. Is Lacan's critique necessarily distinct from widespread stereotypes that appeal to the eternal mystery of femininity? Here, I think, we come up against a notable instance of how psychoanalytic theory may be reinscribing the sexual myths it ostensibly strives to overturn. Understandably, this type of double bind has prompted many searching feminist investigations into the sexist assumptions upon which psychoanalysis would appear to be based.

FEMINIST INTERVENTIONS

It scarcely needs stating that psychoanalysis has, since its inception, been the subject of highly contentious debate. Even though psychoanalytic methods have gained ascendancy in some disciplines such as film studies, many areas of academic research remain firmly unpersuaded by its claims, and it is worth briefly summarizing some general objections. Critics hostile to the critical work of Freud and Lacan frequently raise the following (often related) points:

1 psychoanalysis fails to address the historical specificity of the structures and narratives it explores, by seeking to pass off its findings as timeless and universal;
2 psychoanalysis conspires with the phallic authority it strives to analyse, by refusing to propose models that could or would remove the penis or phallus from its omnipotent place;
3 psychoanalysis is preposterously based on an epistemological impossibility, by professing to interpret what it cannot by definition understand, since the unconscious is not immediately accessible to knowledge;

4   psychoanalysis lays far too much emphasis on the conserva-
    tive nature of sexual identifications, by presuming that eroti-
    cism can only be understood by returning it to foundational
    events that occurred extremely early in childhood, and which
    supposedly determine all succeeding relations;
5   psychoanalysis purports, but does not manage, to resist bio-
    logical assumptions, by reducing its critique of sexuality to
    questions of anatomy.

These are only some of the remonstrations made against psychoanalysis, both as a clinical practice and a field of academic
research.

If one area of inquiry has explored these criticisms in strenuous
detail, then it is assuredly feminist theory. That is why the final
section of this chapter summarizes the divided positions feminists
have adopted in relation to psychoanalysis. It is important to note
that late twentieth-century feminist engagements with Freud
reactivated a much earlier discussion involving many different
women analysts who extensively critiqued his work in the late
1920s, particularly in relation to his studies of femininity. In
'Female Sexuality', Freud engages with the writings of a number
of psychoanalysts, including Helen Deutsch (1884–1982), Karen
Horney (1885–1952), and Melanie Klein (1882–1960), who varied in their viewpoints on how the girl acquires femininity.
Deutsch generally supported Freud's positions, while Horney
contended that his theory of penis-envy was mistaken, emphasizing instead how men were both envious and fearful of the
woman's capacity to reproduce. Klein, by comparison, drew
increasing attention to the crises children undergo in the pre-
Oedipal phase; her work explores how the infant projects parts of
its emerging ego on to the mother's body, a topic pursued by later
psychoanalysts, such as Julia Kristeva. Even if Freud's women
contemporaries were not uniformly sympathetic to feminism,
their powerful interventions made it clear that his models of

female sexuality could be revised along several different lines of psychic identification. In addition, it is worth observing that no matter how masculinist one might think Freud and Lacan, women therapists and theorists have maintained a prominent place in the development of psychoanalytic thought. (On the latter point, see Sayers 1991.)

In the English-speaking world, the vigorous feminist discussion of Freud's writings emerged once again in the late 1960s, when the renewal of campaigns for women's rights during that decade initially looked most unfavourably on his theory of penis-envy. In the 1970s, however, the controversy changed direction with the gradual appearance of books and essays that claimed Freud's writing could be interpreted in a critically advantageous way for feminism. By the 1980s, Lacan's difficult and demanding texts were widely circulating in English, and these too prompted significant questions for feminists seeking theoretical tools that would illuminate the psychic and social formation of femininity within a patriarchal culture. It Britain, the journal *m/f* became one of the most significant forums for considering how and why psychoanalysis might be used to feminist ends. Published between 1978 and 1986, this periodical brought together some of the most pioneering work in this field, and many of its notable contributions are collected in a volume titled *The Woman in Question* (Adams and Cowie 1990). Subsequent feminist research in this vein unfolded rapidly, as *Feminism and Psychoanalysis: A Critical Dictionary* (Wright 1992) comprehensively reveals.

Simply to sketch the main areas of contention between feminism and psychoanalysis, let me begin with Kate Millett's notorious polemic against penis-envy in *Sexual Politics* (1970), before examining some rather different feminist approaches to Freud and Lacan. A landmark study for its time, Millett's *Sexual Politics* provides an immensely ambitious analysis of patriarchal culture in both the Victorian and modern periods. On the whole, Millett's discussion focuses on male literary figures such as D.H.

Lawrence (1885–1930) and Henry Miller (1891–1980), in a series of chapters examining the development of sexist thinking from the Victorian epoch to the sexual revolution of the 1960s. Freud's work features in Millett's central chapter, 'The Counterrevolution, 1930–1960'. To Millett, these three counter-revolutionary decades mark an era that quelled the advanced sexual views pioneered in writings by Henrik Ibsen (1828–1906), George Bernard Shaw (1856–1950), and Oscar Wilde, all of whom came to prominence during the *fin de siècle*. Protesting against the 'habitual masculine bias of Freud's own terms and diction', Millett rebuts Freud's castration complex on the basis that he makes no distinction between 'fact' and 'fantasy' (Millett 1970: 182–3). 'It is interesting', she notes parenthetically, 'that Freud should imagine the young female's fears centre about castration rather than rape – a phenomenon which girls are in fact, and with reason, in dread of, since it happens to them and castration does not' (Millett 1970: 184). But even if this observation points to a prejudice in Freud's choice of terms, it remains hard to see how he ever passed off the castration complex in girls as 'fact' rather than 'fantasy'. Millett contends that Freud's theories collapse culture into nature, the social into the biological – and with devastating consequences:

> Freud had spurned an excellent opportunity to open the door to hundreds of enlightening studies on the effect of male-supremacist culture on the ego development of the young female, preferring instead to sanctify her oppression in terms of the inevitable law of 'biology'. The theory of penis envy has so effectively obfuscated understanding that all psychology has done since has not yet unravelled this matter of social causation. If, as seems unlikely, penis envy can mean anything at all, it is productive only within the total cultural context of sex. And here it would seem that girls are fully cognizant of male supremacy long before they see their brother's

> penis. . . . Confronted with so much concrete evidence of the
> male's superior status, sensing on all sides the depreciation in
> which they are held, girls envy not the penis, but only what the
> penis gives one social pretensions to.
>
> (Millett 1970: 187)

For several years, Millett's rhetorically assured polemic exerted influence over some sections of the Women's Liberation Movement. But, as later writers would stress, the very arguments Millett angles at Freud's exploration of penis-envy are to a degree answered by Freud himself. One possibility which Millett flatly refuses to entertain is that Freud regards the castration complex as a moment which symbolizes precisely the sexual antagonism at work within 'the total context'. Perhaps if Millett reflected for a moment, penis-envy might appear as a consequence, rather than a cause, of what it means to find one's place on either side of the sexual divide.

Following the empowering rise of the Women's Liberation Movement, the study that most sharply contested Millett's claims was Juliet Mitchell's *Psychoanalysis and Feminism: Freud, Reich, Laing and Women* (1974), an imposing volume of considerable scope and foresight whose impact on feminist theory cannot be underestimated. On the very first page, Mitchell declares: 'psychoanalysis is not a recommendation *for* a patriarchal society, but an analysis *of* one' (Mitchell 1974: xiii). It is with this principle in mind that Mitchell rounds on the work of several feminist contemporaries, notably Betty Friedan, Shulamith Firestone, Eva Figes, and – most incisively – Millett herself. Criticizing the 'realist' empiricism of *Sexual Politics*, Mitchell shows how Millett wrongly assumes that the female infant remains a psychologically rational subject that envies the penis in a wholly knowing manner. 'Desire, phantasy, the laws of the unconscious or even unconsciousness', remarks Mitchell, 'are absent from [Millett's] social realism' (Mitchell 1970: 354). Repeatedly, Mitchell insists that

Freud's inquiries are definitely not rooted in biological thought – a point, it is worth noting, disputed by a later monumental study, *Freud, Biologist of the Mind: Beyond the Psychoanalytic Legend* by Frank J. Sulloway (1983 [1980]), and one scrutinized by Jean Laplanche, a writer faithful to Freud's project (Laplanche 1989). 'To Freud', writes Mitchell, 'society demands of the psychological bisexuality of both sexes that one sex attain a preponderance of femininity, the other of masculinity: man and woman are *made* in culture' (Mitchell 1974: 131).

Yet, despite the force of such criticism, Mitchell's own study would in turn become the subject of further feminist critique. In a book whose title echoes Mitchell's, *Feminism and Psychoanalysis: The Daughter's Seduction* (1982), Jane Gallop finds the conclusion to Mitchell's work just as 'realist' in its assumptions as those of feminist writers, such as Millett, whose arguments Mitchell does not hesitate to castigate in precisely those terms. In her final chapter Mitchell makes a rallying-cry to overthrow the patriarchal order, as if a 'realist' approach to this matter would achieve this end. Here is how Mitchell stakes her claim on the sexual revolution that must come:

> Under patriarchal order women are oppressed in their very psychologies of femininity; once this order is retained only in a highly contradictory manner this oppression manifests itself. Women have to organize themselves as a group to effect a change in the basic ideology of human society. To be effective, this can be no righteous challenge to the simple domination of men (though this plays a tactical part), but a struggle based on a theory of the social non-necessity at this stage of development of the laws instituted by patriarchy.
>
> (Mitchell 1974: 414)

The trouble with this position, as Gallop sees it, is that it removes exactly the emphasis that Mitchell elsewhere puts on the significance of desire, fantasy, and the unconscious that a 'realist' such as Millett has been criticized for counting out of her analysis. Little wonder Gallop is led to scrutinize the logic of Mitchell's claim: 'If women "can organize themselves as a group to effect a change in the basic ideology of human society" and "can insist on the birth" of "new structures" in the unconscious, then somehow they transcend the non-contingent fact that human beings, subject to the unconscious, are fated not to be rational' (Gallop 1982: 13). Gallop's comment drives at the centre of one of the most enduring conflicts in feminist engagements with psychoanalysis. To what extent does psychoanalysis provide feminism with a model of social, if not psychic, change? Do its findings suggest that women are inevitably 'fated' by certain determinations? Or does this body of theory demand a 'rational' analysis that helps us to understand more clearly the arbitrary process of how we become sexed subjects? What restrictions does psychoanalysis force upon concepts of sex and gender? And what freedoms from social and sexual hierarchies does it enable us to imagine?

It is instructive to see how this conflict of interests emerges in two significant essays published by the British journal *Feminist Review* in the early 1980s. In 'Psychoanalysis: Psychic Law and Order?' (1981), Elizabeth Wilson reflects on some of Freud's best-known passages that explain the castration and Oedipus complexes. Wilson finds that Freud inconsistently veers between nature and culture, between what is biologically determined and what is socially constructed – a point that should become quickly apparent to anyone reading his work for the first time. 'Sometimes', claims Wilson, 'he seems to be addressing the problem of the psychological consequences of biology and how the psyche of the individual is built on a biological base; at others he seems rather to use biological analogies and metaphors' (Wilson 1981: 67). Wilson points to a similar contradiction in Mitchell's analysis. On this view, although Mitchell suppresses the 'biological' side of Freud, privileging that aspect which shows how 'man and woman are made in culture', at times her positive reading of Freud risks duplicating his biases. For example, after she has discussed Freud's analysis of the girl's Oedipus complex in 'Femininity', Mitchell concludes: 'The woman's task is to *reproduce* society, the man's to go on and *produce* new developments. There is an obvious link between the security of Oedipal father-love and the happy hearth and home of later years' (Mitchell 1974: 118). From Wilson's perspective, this is a lamentable conviction to hold because it indicates that 'the sexual division of labour as we know it in an industrial capitalist society has some *permanent* correspondence with the creation of "masculinity" and "femininity"' (Wilson 1981: 69). Wilson contends that, even if psychoanalysis offers a theory of how women have been psychically subordinated under patriarchy, such theoretical speculations remain a political distraction. So she insists that campaigns to 'change the conditions of work – in the world and in the home – might do more for our psyches as well as for our pockets than an endless contemplation of how we came to be chained' (Wilson 1981: 76).

Jacqueline Rose's 'Femininity and Its Discontents' (1983) is in part a studied reply to Wilson's essay. More generally, however, Rose's discussion provides a painstaking account of why psychoanalysis retains such a contentious position in feminist theory. Rose confronts the belief held by many left-wing intellectuals, such as Wilson, that psychoanalytic thought does not provide an adequate model of social change. She observes how the work of Freud and Lacan has been regularly accused of 'functionalism', the consequences of which she spells out as follows:

> [Psychoanalysis] is accepted as a theory of how women are psychically 'induced' into femininity by a patriarchal culture, and is then accused of perpetuating that process, either though a practice assumed to be *prescriptive* about women's role (that is what women *should* do), or because the very

effectiveness of the account as a *description* (that is what is demanded of women, what they are *expected* to do) leaves no possibility of change.

(Rose 1983: 8)

There is no doubt that many feminists have claimed that psycho-analysis simply offers yet another bleak account for women's inevitable socialization in a male-dominated society. Confronting attacks on psychoanalytic 'functionalism', Rose argues that there is much to be learned from the way Freud's work reveals how femininity is 'induced' by the patriarchal order. In her view, there are distinct limitations to criticizing Freud and Lacan for produc-ing a theory that supposedly shows how women are psychically conditioned into femininity. If, Rose claims, one censures Freud and Lacan for producing theories that steadfastly uphold the Name-of-the-Father, then '[p]sychoanalysis is drawn in the direc-tion of a general theory of culture or a sociological account of gender because these seem to lay greater emphasis on the pres-sures of the "outside" world'. But, as she adds, 'it is this very pulling away from the psychoanalytic stress on the "internal" complexity and difficulty of psychic life which produces the func-tionalism which is then criticized' (Rose 1983: 10). That is to say, feminist opponents of psychoanalysis misguidedly assume that sexual inequality can more fruitfully be tackled by appealing purely to the external world. It is precisely that assumption, Rose suggests, which comes at an extremely high theoretical cost to feminism. She firmly believes feminist politics has much to gain from understanding how psychoanalysis 'allows into the political arena problems of subjectivity (subjectivity *as* a problem) which tend to be suppressed from other forms of political debate'. So, by drawing attention to the vexed question of subjectivity, psycho-analysis 'may also help us to open the space between different notions of political identity – between the idea of a political iden-tity for feminism (what women require) and that of a feminine identity for women (what women are or should be)' (Rose 1983: 19).

In making these remarks, Rose is largely challenging the traditional Marxist insensitivity to 'subjectivity *as* a problem'. In the past, Marxist thought often believed that concentrating on subjective needs led to a narrow individualism: a preoccupation that revolutionaries regard as extremely hazardous when attention should be paid instead to collective struggles for political change. Rose's point is that, once we consider the conflicted condition of our gendered subjectivities, it might become possible to comprehend why there may well be fraught divisions within the very collectivities that seek to work together in the name of emancipation. In the light of Rose's comments, it could be fairly claimed that the feminist engagement with psychoanalytic thought has made a significant contribution to the larger debate about 'difference' that preoccupied many feminist theorists in the 1980s. In focusing on 'difference', feminists were increasingly questioning, not only how one thought about the difference between women and men, but also how one considered the many differences – including those of age, class, ethnicity, and sexuality – that at times came between women seeking liberation from patriarchal oppression.

Rose's influential essay stresses that feminist explorations of psychic processes need not defend Freud and Lacan to the letter. It is indeed the case that Freud's and Lacan's respective works have provided feminism with the opportunity to revise psychoanalytic models that explain how subjectivity develops. The theorist who has become most notable for modifying the phallocentric paradigms of psychoanalysis to feminist ends is Julia Kristeva. From the outset of her career, Kristeva has been preoccupied with the processes that bring the subject into the domain of language. Trained as a linguist and semiotician, Kristeva's earliest research redefined the Lacanian distinction between the Imaginary and the Symbolic. She elaborates three orders – the semiotic, the thetic, and the symbolic – to explain the intricate stages through which the subject comes to represent itself to itself. Since her research concentrates on the channelling of the drives, Kristeva consequently has much to say about sexuality.

Kristeva details her three orders in *Revolution in Poetic Language*, first published in France in 1974. There she explains how the semiotic refers to its Greek etymology, where the word means 'distinctive mark, trace, index, precursory sign, proof, engraved or written sign, imprint, trace, figuration' (Kristeva 1984: 25). Since the word implies '*distinctiveness*', it helps to identify 'a precise modality in the signifying process': that is, the process that sustains the subject. Like Freud and Lacan, Kristeva wants to define how the infant's multiple drives are manipulated and directed by its encounters with both its body and its environment:

> Discrete quantities of energy move through the body of the subject who is not yet constituted as such and, in the course of his development, they are arranged according to the various constraints imposed on this body – always already in the semiotic process – by family and social structures. In this way the drives, which are 'energy' charges as well as 'psychical' marks, articulate what we call a *chora*: a nonexpressive totality formed by the drives and their stases in a motility that is as full of movement as it is regulated.
>
> (Kristeva 1984: 25)

Adapted from the cosmology detailed in Plato's *Timaeus*, the *chora* denotes 'an essentially mobile and extremely provisional articulation constituted by movement and their ephemeral stases'. Not yet related to the signifying chain, the *chora* is a pre-symbolic realm that provides the dual rhythms of freedom and constraint from which a relation to signification will gradually emerge. The *chora* represents the pre-linguistic moment where the child remains unable to differentiate itself from the maternal body.

But, unlike Freud and Lacan, Kristeva remarks that this stage involves, not random polymorphous perversity, but a space in which perceptions and sensations are taking on some semblance of organization.

Following the semiotic comes the rupture marked by the thetic: 'a break in the signifying process, establishing the *identification* of the subject and its object as preconditions of propositionality' (Kristeva 1984: 43). 'All enunciation', Kristeva adds, 'is thetic'. So the creation of a word or sentence is based on 'propositionality': that is, a proposing of meaning. Placed on the 'threshold of language', the thetic is where symbolization can begin. The thetic stage combines both the Lacanian mirror stage and Freud's established model of castration. It marks the moment where subjectivity necessarily emerges through imaginary misrecognition and through a relation to the primary but veiled signifier: the phallus.

The third and final order is called the symbolic, and it bears some resemblance to the field of signification to which Lacan gave the same name. Here is how Kristeva outlines how and why the symbolic eventually must intervene: 'Dependence on the mother is severed, and transformed into a symbolic relation to an other; the constitution of the Other is indispensable for communicating with an other'. Entry into the symbolic marks 'the first social censorship' because the subject, as it propels its image of itself into the world, meets with symbolic castration (Kristeva 1984: 48). But for Kristeva the subject never quite deserts the semiotic. Certain types of avant-garde literary writing – especially by French *Symbolistes*, such as Stéphane Mallarmé (1842–98), as well as Irish modernists like James Joyce (1882–1941) – reveal '"distortions" of the signifying chain'. Such works, argues Kristeva, disclose 'those drives that the thetic phase was not able to sublate [*relever*, *aufgehoben* – the concept is a Hegelian one] by linking them into signifier and signified' (Kristeva 1984: 49). From this perspective, art enacts the 'semiotization of the symbolic', and in doing so 'represents the flow of *jouissance* into language' (Kristeva 1984: 79).

Kristeva's later work, *Powers of Horror: An Essay on Abjection* (1980), makes it clear that her concern with the semiotic *chora* means that sexual desire refers as much to the maternal body as it does to the phallic signifier that constitutes the subject's lack. What she calls the 'abject' marks 'our earliest attempts to release the hold of the *maternal* entity even before ex-isting outside of her'. This 'abject-ing', argues Kristeva, consitutes a 'violent, clumsy breaking away' that carries the 'risk of falling back under the sway of a power as securing as it is stifling' (Kristeva 1982: 13). To be sure, this focus on the significance of the '*maternal* entity' to the inchoate human subject provides a counterweight to the phallocentrism of Freud's and Lacan's paradigms. Yet it is worth bearing in mind that, in examining how the sign 'represses the *chora* and its eternal return', Kristeva may well be in danger of rewriting an antiquated sexist myth herself (Kristeva 1982: 14). For Kristeva, in associating the maternal body with pre-Oedipality, suggests that the feminine remains to some degree passive, if not primitive. After all, even if the semiotic is always ready to rise up against symbolic constraints, it plays a muted, intermittent, and contained role beneath the inevitable gover-nance of the phallus.

The avant-garde writings of French philosopher and psychoan-alyst Luce Irigaray provide a striking contrast to Kristeva's modi-fication of psychoanalytic orthodoxies. In Irigaray's exuberant work, she refutes the unquestionable phallic dominance of Freudian theory so that an alternative feminine economy arises in its stead. On the opening page of *Speculum of the Other Woman* (1985a [1974]), Irigaray quotes the infamous passage where Freud declares femininity is a 'riddle'. 'Through history', remarks Freud in 'Femininity', 'people have knocked their heads against the riddle of the nature of femininity'. Pursuing its Sphinx-like status, he adds: 'Nor will *you* have escaped worrying over this problem – those of you who are men; to those of you who are women this will not apply – you are yourselves the problem' (Freud 1964: XXII, 113). Responding to Freud's apparent condescension, Irigaray exclaims: 'So it would be a case of you men speaking among yourselves about woman, who cannot be involved in hearing or producing a discourse about the *riddle* . . . she represents for you' (Irigaray 1985a: 13). Interlarding many quotations from Freud's writings on sexuality into her vigorously questioning prose, Irigaray seeks to expose how his '"differentiation" into two sexes derives from the *a priori* assumption that the little girl is, must become a man minus certain attributes whose paradigm is morphological – attributes capable of determining, of assuring, the reproduction-specularization of the same' (Irigaray 1985a: 27). From her perspective, the Freudian model reproduces sexual difference through reflection (or specularization), thus creating a self-monumentalizing and repetitive structure of *sameness*.

But Irigaray's relentless and thorough criticism of Freud's work does not result in a wholehearted rejection of psychic models for comprehending female sexuality. Indeed, much of Irigaray's polemic examines the psychic and somatic dimensions to women's desires that Freud's work tellingly excludes or suppresses. Noting how Freud insists that 'woman devotes . . . very little cathexis to auto-erotism, auto-representation, auto-reproduction, even in homosexuality', Irigaray celebrates instead 'the pleasure of caresses, words, representations of representations that remind woman of her sex, her sex organs, her sexes' (Irigaray 1985a: 103). It is precisely towards the realm of autoeroticism and homosexuality that Irigaray turns, so that a domain of pleasures can be sustained without being subordinated to the Freudian penis or the Lacanian phallus. In 'This Sex Which Is Not One', Irigaray finds delightful eroticism in exactly the somatic zone in which Freud detects such castratory lack: the female genitals. Declaring that 'woman's autoeroticism is very different from man's' because he 'needs an instrument: his hand', she insists that 'woman . . . touches herself in and of herself without any need for mediation, and before there is any way to distinguish activitity from passivity'. Why? Because 'her genitals are formed by two lips in continuous contact'. So, Irigaray continues, 'she is already two − but not divisible into one(s) − that caress each other' (Irigaray 1985b: 24). Free from the phallomorphic logic of the 'same', unfettered by the dictates of another party, woman emerges not as 'one' sex, nor does she belong to a neatly sequential logic where $1 + 1 = 2$. Defying both unitary and binary calculations, Irigaray's vision of woman claims femininity is at once multiple yet inseparable, plural yet autonomous.

Such assertions have proved highly debatable among feminist readers. Diana Fuss explores how and why feminist critics have often taken Irigaray to task for promoting an essentialist vision of the female body, one that reduces femininity, in much the same way as Freud had done, to a matter of anatomy. Even when construed as a metaphor, Irigaray's celebration of the 'two lips' may well appear to imply that women only speak through their bodies, not their minds. Yet, as Fuss argues, it is possible to produce a sympathetic reading that reveals how Irigaray's 'language of essence' remains 'a politically strategic gesture of displacement'. Why should this be? Because Irigaray's work exposes exactly how, in the Western philosophical tradition descending from Aristotle, 'woman' has remained an enduring 'site of contradiction': 'on the one hand, woman is asserted to have an essence which defines her as woman [designated through qualities such as weakness, passivity, receptivity, and emotion] and yet, on the other hand, woman is relegated to the status of matter and can have no access to essence (the most she can do is to facilitate man's actualizing of his inner potential)' (Fuss 1989: 72). On this basis, Irigaray may be thought to undo women's essential lack, so to speak, through a tactical discourse that mimes only to subvert the contradictory location that the feminine has occupied in Western metaphysics.

Hélène Cixous's 'Sorties' (1986 [1975]) bears comparison with Irigaray's work, since it, too, focuses on the masculinist logic of the 'same': a rigid system of reasoning that Cixous memorably names 'the Empire of the Selfsame'. In Cixous's view, the masculinist imperialism of the 'Selfsame' violently enacts an ongoing 'story of phallocentrism'. This is a phallic narrative that 'keeps the movement toward the other staged in a patriarchal production, under Man's law' (Cixous 1986: 79). Faced with the aggrandizements of the triumphal 'Selfsame', Cixous longs to liberate women's *jouissance*. Such feminine *jouissance*, she claims, belongs to an 'instinctual economy' that 'cannot be identified by a man or referred to the masculine economy' (Cixous 1986: 82). Similar to Kristeva's *chora*, Cixous's feminine economy of desire asserts that woman 'has never ceased to hear what-comes-before-language reverberating' (Cixous 1986: 88). But although one may feel carried away by the poetic vitality of Cixous's prose, here too we might wonder if this suppressed feminine *jouissance* really poses an alternative to the binary logic of gender upheld by the phallocratic patriarchy. In this respect, the sexual logic celebrated by her *écriture féminine* – or feminine writing practice – may be somewhat more traditional than it appears. 'Let masculine sexuality', declares Cixous, 'gravitate around the penis, engendering this centralized body . . . under the party dictatorship'. 'Woman', she argues, 'does not perform on herself this regionalization that profits the couple head-sex', and she adds this eloquent sentence whose breathless phrasing dramatizes her concept of feminine sexuality:

> Her libido is cosmic, just as her unconscious is worldwide: her writing can also go on and on, without ever inscribing or distinguishing contours, daring these dizzying passages in other, fleeting, and passionate dwellings within him, within the hims

and hers whom she inhabits just long enough to watch them, as close as possible to the unconscious from the moment they arise; to love them, as close as possible to instinctual drives, and then, further, all filled with these brief identifying hugs and kisses, she goes on and on infinitely.

(Cixous 1986: 88)

Against the fierce limits set by masculine desire, claims Cixous, feminine *jouissance* remains unbounded: it reaches into the unconscious of both sexes because it represents the traces of all the bodily pleasures that have been repressed from the moment the infant must submit to the symbolic phallus. But, once again, it is worth asking if Cixous's model of feminine sexuality does not reduce women to precisely those qualities that have long been stigmatized in a patriarchal order. Consigned to the unconscious, to instinct, to the body, even to irrationality, this feminine libidinal economy bears an uncanny resemblance to familiar stereotypes of women. That said, such writing surely solicits an affirmative interpretation as well. Cixous's *écriture feminine* clearly demands to be understood as a strategic writing practice, one that seizes on exactly the terms used by the patriarchy to demean women and subversively transform them into celebratory qualities of feminist strength.

Taken together, the works of Kristeva, Irigaray, and Cixous dramatize some of the contradictions that emerge when feminists seek to free women's desires from the structures erected by psychoanalytic phallicism. What is more, their writing forces attention on how sexuality can only be comprehended once we examine the economic principles which inform differing masculine and feminine desires. Their work forms part of a wide-ranging series of theoretical debates about the hoarding, circulation, and expenditure of sexual energies and flows. Throughout the twentieth century, many theorists have grappled with the view that sexuality brings together life-giving and death-dealing forces, often in extremely violent unions. The next chapter considers why sexuality has repeatedly been viewed in a volatile life-and-death struggle that will lead to either emancipation or destruction.

3

LIBIDINAL ECONOMIES

(DE)GENERATING PLEASURES

To show how sexuality has often been thought to exist in a life-and-death struggle, let me begin this chapter with a familiar literary example. Anyone acquainted with *Songs and Sonnets* by the English Renaissance poet John Donne (1572–1631) is more than likely to recall his provocative play on the word 'die'. Collected posthumously in 1633, his erotically charged poem 'The Canonization' is arguably his most memorable work that exploits this verb to show how death haunts sexual desire. In the third and fourth stanzas, the male speaker boldly challenges his implicitly hostile listeners to recognize the depth of his passion. Once he finishes reproving them by making it plain that his love shall cause injury to no one, he promptly conjures a striking image that vivifies this intense emotion. 'Call her one, me another flye', he proclaims, 'We'are Tapers too, and at our owne cost die' (Donne 1985: 58). In this deft conceit, the lovers figure as both the lit taper and the hapless fly that rushes madly into its flame. Such is the burning power of the libido that both lovers must 'die' – in several senses of the word. For the verb to 'die', in this context, draws on sexual slang to indicate that these lovers shall reach orgasm. What is more, this punning death occurs at a considerable 'cost' because, according to the Renaissance mind, it ultimately shortens one's life. So in enjoying sex, the lovers not only 'die' as they climax, they also bring actual death closer through this pleasurable practice. In other words, they experience the 'little death' whose transitoriness paradoxically lets love thrive. Thus Donne's persona declares: 'Wee can dye by it, if not live by love'. Little wonder 'The Canonization' views this contradiction like the 'Phoenix ridle'. Just as the mythical bird takes flight from its ashes, so too must love 'prove / Mysterious'.

Donne's poetry, of course, predates the modern discourse of sexuality by more than three centuries. But the mystery he identifies through his unforgettable sexual pun has never ceased to obsess Western accounts of sexual desire. Rarely, however, have modern inquiries into the sexual struggles between life and death displayed the teasing wit of Donne's poetry. For the evident 'cost' of this libidinal economy has been a frequent preoccupation among modern theorists precisely because it involves, not only the 'little death', but also – most troublingly – the erotic impulse to take life. To be sure, many literary and film genres have gone to great lengths in manipulating this potentially terrifying idea, all the way from the libertine narratives of the Marquis de Sade (1740–1814) to contemporary horror and 'slasher' movies. If one style of modern writing has insistently detailed the potency of deathly desire, then it is surely the Gothic (see Botting 1995). So pervasive has this belief in the deathliness of sex become throughout many areas of twentieth-century cultural production that some critics have gone so far as to insist that certain desires, especially male ones, are in themselves murderous. In this respect, one of the most turbulent debates in recent decades focuses on how pornographic representation either leads to sexual crimes or liberates suppressed eroticism. The large markets for films and magazines that feature scenes of abuse, humiliation, even simulated death emblematize a widespread interest in sexual violence. Such materials, which are mainly but not exclusively aimed at male consumers, constantly provoke debates about their precise role in psychic fantasy and in homicidal reality. So what is it that has induced Western culture to believe that sexuality wages an ongoing battle between life and death? Is desire aroused by death-dealing impulses or is it driven by intense forces that emancipate body and mind?

To answer these and related questions, the first part of the present chapter investigates why many theorists concur that sexuality remains caught within what might be called a conflicted system of (de)generating pleasures. Beginning with the economic principles governing Freud's influential model of the death drive, I proceed to subsequent critical works that struggle to define the volatile energies comprising the libido. The psychic and somatic antagonism between productive and unproductive, life-giving and death-driven energies certainly materializes in the realm of pornography, a hugely profitable commodity that encourages us to reflect carefully on the political and moral connections between libidinal and economic principles. In the second part of this chapter, I consider why pornography, more than any other erotic product, has been such a focus of concern for the contending harms and joys of sexuality. Since feminist commentators have explored this field of inquiry in much greater detail than anyone else, my discussion concentrates principally on their work.

Freud's *Beyond the Pleasure Principle* (1920) certainly sets the agenda for many subsequent theoretical studies that examine the antagonistic drives that mobilize sexual desire. This study counts as one of his greatest speculative inquiries into how male and female subjects psychically manage the libido. Here, for the first time, Freud draws attention to what his translators initially called the 'death instinct', and which later commentators would more frequently term the death drive. (On the debate concerning the appropriate use of 'instinct' and 'drive' when discussing Freudian theory, see p. 68.) In this absorbing meditative account of psychic conflict, Freud declares that his psychoanalytic inquiry will pursue the 'economic' factor that regulates the subject's experiences of pleasure and unpleasure. It is the latter quality, he remarks, that interests him most. He wants to discover precisely which mechanisms come into play so that the subject avoids pleasure. At this stage of his research, one of these mechanisms is plain to see, since '[u]nder the influence of the ego's instincts of self-preservations, the pleasure principle is replaced by the *reality principle*' (Freud 1955: XVIII, 10). That is to say, the ego – which always strives, as best it can, for homeostasis – must at times face up to realities that threaten the subject's immediate demands for pleasure. The pleasure principle, Freud adds, appears to be closely associated with the 'sexual instincts, which are so hard to "educate"'. Consequently, the pleasure principle 'often succeeds in overcoming the reality principle, to the detriment of the organism as a whole'. So he feels confident in asserting that this is a wholly explicable tension between two psychic operations, one demanding pleasure, the other allowing unpleasure to arise in the face of prohibitive reality.

Yet, having established this point, Freud is left with a vexed issue to resolve. By his own admission, the tension he has identified is certainly not the only psychic operation that permits the release of unpleasure. Something else, he suspects, is at work within the psyche, and he wants to know what it is. In a highly self-reflective manner, Freud observes how his researches have shown that 'individual instincts or parts of instincts turn out to be incompatible with their aims or demands with the remaining ones, which are able to combine into the inclusive unity of the ego' (Freud 1955: XVIII, 11). These 'incompatible' instincts, he claims, are split off from the ego through repression and thus severed from pleasurable satisfaction. But repressed elements, as Freud frequently notes, often return 'by roundabout paths', resulting in an experience that the ego can only recognize as unpleasure. For the moment, he cannot comprehend how these 'incompatible' instincts or drives undergo such transformation from pleasure to unpleasure. Puzzled by this phenomenon, he devotes the rest of *Beyond the Pleasure Principle* to finding an explanation for it.

Drawing on many observations from contemporary experiments in zoology, Freud concludes that at a certain point of development all organisms experience a compulsion to repeat. He observes that, although adults quickly lose interest in reading a novel for a second time, children often adore having stories told to them again and again. It may well be the case, he suggests, that adulthood should free one from such obsessive, if not regressive, childish desires. But Freud's point is that repetition-compulsion, under specific stressful conditions, can still erupt in adult life. Early in this study, he remarks how countless cases of shell-shock after the First World War of 1914–18 bring into stark relief the nature of traumatic neurosis, revealing how the subject under severe pressure cannot help repeating frightening episodes. Such cases prompt him to think that there might be an aspect to the instincts or drives that has little or no relation to the pleasure principle. Focusing on repetition-compulsion, he entertains the idea that '*an instinct is an urge inherent in organic life to restore an earlier state of things*' (Freud 1955: XVIII, 36). He openly acknowledges that this observation appears rather strange, since until this point psychoanalysis has always assumed that the instincts or drives follow paths of change and development. What, then, should Freud make of what he calls 'the *conservative* nature of living substance'? What is it that impels the organism to return to the 'quiescence of the inorganic world' (Freud 1955: XVIII, 62)?

Reflecting on this matter, Freud advances the view that the organism's instincts or drives would seem to travel in two directions at once. Pulled between change and development, on the one hand, and conserving an 'earlier state', on the other, the subject's psychic energies move with a 'vacillating rhythm'. 'One group of instincts', writes Freud, 'rushes forward so as to reach the final aim of life as quickly as possible; but when a particular stage in the advance has been reached, the other group jerks back to a certain point to make a fresh start and so prolong the journey' (Freud 1955: XVIII, 41). That is to say, the instincts or drives that lead to reproduction ('the final aim of life') are challenged by ones that insist on returning to an earlier phase ('to make a fresh start'). Contemplating this double movement, Freud realizes that the very project of life is necessarily burdened by the prospect of death. To Freud, these two competing forces converge most powerfully in heterosexual copulation:

> We have all experienced how the greatest pleasure attainable by us, that of the sexual act, is associated with a momentary extinction of a highly intensified excitation. The binding of an instinctual impulse would be a preliminary function designed to prepare the excitation for its final elimination in the pleasure of discharge.
>
> (Freud 1955: XVIII, 62)

These sentences unravel the enigma he has been pursuing all along. Instead of releasing the life instincts, the exquisitely pleasurable moment of orgasm (which may lead to reproduction) involves extinction. The perpetuation of life, therefore, rests upon a momentary death – the 'little death', no less.

Three years later, in *The Ego and the Id*, Freud would once again remark how the 'discharge of the sexual substances' derives from the way the psyche deals with 'libidinal tensions' (Freud 1961: XIX, 47). Here, however, he considers this question in relation to the fraught relationship between the two opposing psychic agencies he calls the ego and the id. Since the ego always demands constancy, he argues that its function is to desexualize the libidinal energies rising up from the unconscious depths of the id. At the same time, he observes, the ego's impulse towards constant self-preservation actually endangers it. Since the ego demands not to be disturbed by sexual tensions, its homeostatic imperative means that it is forever losing energy. The ego remains, in Freud's words, on 'a continuous descent towards death'. To combat this potentially entropic state, the id must keep fighting back. Orgasm, he argues, is the only act that can bring together the desexualizing descent towards death and the libidinal excitation for life. Hence we can grasp 'the likeness of the condition that follows complete sexual satisfaction to dying, and . . . the fact that death coincides with the act of copulation in some of the lower animals' (Freud 1961: XIX, 47). In their ecstatic convergence, therefore, both sets of instincts resolve the widely acknowledged paradox of how death inhabits sex. But succeeding investigations by later theorists would cast doubt on the seemingly magical resolution of Eros (life instincts) and Thanatos (death instincts) in the orgasmic moment reached in heterosexual copulation.

Some three decades afterwards, French cultural theorist, novelist, and sometime surrealist Georges Bataille produced his own distinctive model to comprehend the battle fought between prohibitive reality and the inflammatory death drive. In *Eroticism* (1962 [1957]), he examines how and why 'tenderness has no effect on the interaction between eroticism and death'. To uphold this claim, Bataille situates the disruptive nature of the death drive in systems of economic circulation. In his view, sexuality involves disorderly and anti-rationalistic experiences that are by turns excessive, wasteful, ruinous, even murderous. Although he does not follow Freud in theorizing the psychical organization of the instincts or drives, Bataille readily writes of 'contagious impulses' that impel eroticism on its (de)generating path (Bataille 1962: 41). He states that sexuality must discharge its deathly energy at all costs:

> Erotic conduct is the opposite of normal conduct as spending is the opposite of getting. If we follow the dictates of reason

we try to acquire all kinds of goods, we work in order to increase the sum of our possessions or of our knowledge, we use all means to get richer and to possess more. Our status in the social order is based on this sort of behaviour. But when the fever of sex seizes us we behave in the opposite way. We recklessly draw on our strength and sometimes in the violence of passion we squander considerable resources to no real purpose. Pleasure is so close to ruinous waste that we refer to the moment of climax as a 'little death'. Consequently anything that suggests erotic excess always implies disorder.

(Bataille 1962: 170)

So great can this 'rising tide of excess' become that Bataille observes how '[b]rutality and murder are further steps in the same direction'. The most intense pleasures, he claims, arise from this ruinous squandering of resources, as they expend themselves in symbolic death. The remainder of *Eroticism* sets out to prove why this should be the case.

Early in his book, Bataille declares that 'eroticism is assenting to life even in death' (Bataille 1962: 11). *Eroticism* comprises a series of short overlapping studies that throw into relief Bataille's main conviction that symbolic death paradoxically guarantees the continuation of life. In his view, the sexual act dramatizes a deathly moment when human subjects experience what is denied elsewhere in their lives: a loss of self. The problem for humanity, he claims, is that we are all *'discontinuous* beings' (Bataille 1962: 12). Since we are *'discontinuous'* individuals, Bataille asserts that there remain inescapable gulfs between each and every one of us. In other words, '[i]f you die, it is not my death'. Inevitably isolated, individuals can only eradicate the fundamental divides between the self and the other by entering into vertiginous experiences whose breathtaking dizziness provides exactly the continuity demanded by death. Bataille largely derives this dialectic between continuity and discontinuity from the Enlightenment philosopher G.W.F. Hegel, who explores the distinction between identity and difference throughout the *Phenomenology of Spirit* (1807). Unlike Hegel, however, Bataille is very much a twentieth-century thinker in locating this dialectic of desire, not just in the divide between the self and other, but in the erotic mechanisms that generate the tension between the two. Just as Freud believed that heterosexual copulation brought together contending psychic energies of life and death, so too does Bataille draw parallels with biological reproduction to disclose how these rivalrous forces converge. Bataille remarks that, although the '[s]perm and ovum are to begin with discontinuous entities', they may well *'unite'*, enabling 'a new entity' to come 'into existence' from 'the death and disappearance of the separate beings' (Bataille 1962: 14). On this basis, he examines types of physical, emotional, and ritualized eroticism which provide 'a feeling of profound continuity' in a world where each human being otherwise remains agonisingly alone (Bataille 1962: 15).

Bataille brings the systematic antagonisms between desire and death most clearly into focus by exploring two related structures common to prehistoric, classical, and modern cultures: first, the significance of taboos and transgression; and second, the intimate friction between the sacred and the profane. Having absorbed the anthropological researches of Marcel Mauss (1872–1950), Bataille remarks that taboos ostensibly serve to eliminate violence from society. In many civilizations, he observes, there are systematic taboos on murder, rape, incest, and adultery. But such taboos can only function successfully when individuals recognize that these prohibitions demand to be transgressed. Solely by being broken can the taboo remain in place. Although Bataille is not especially interested in elaborating a model of Freudian repression, his view of culture partly follows the theoretical contours of Freud's turbulent id by insisting that 'man's natural impulses to violence' must eventually rebel against the restrictions laid down by custom (Bataille 1962: 69). Time and again, he insists that taboos inten-

sify erotic rebellion, since they solicit precisely the symbolic
death they outlaw. Not only that, taboos often signify that sexual
pleasure is dirty, shameful, sinful, and unclean. Such is Bataille's
faith in this dynamic that he makes the following polemical
statement: 'Many women cannot reach their climax without pre-
tending to themselves that they are being raped' (Bataille 1962:
107). Consumed by transgressive violence, therefore, eroticism
ultimately involves a symbolic death that secures the life of the
taboo.

To accentuate the contradictory movement between taboo and
transgression, Bataille frequently forces attention on how this
structure is clearly evident in the ways past civilizations organized the sacred and the profane. He claims that ritual sacrifice
enables us to see how cultures elevate acts that are at all other
times outlawed. Bataille observes that, in ritually sacrificing animals or people, a culture killed what it managed to hoard, and
thus made a gift from that acquired surplus. In effect, this type of
sacrifice brought 'life and death into harmony', giving 'death the
upsurge of life', and 'life the momentousness and the vertigo of
death opening on to the unknown' (Bataille 1962: 91). Modern
culture, however, finds it hard to grasp this dynamic. Why? The
answer, as he sees it, lies in Christian ritual. Christianity, he contends, has made it expressly difficult for modern Western culture
to comprehend how and why eroticism is closely connected with
rites of transgression, since this anti-pagan religion elevates sacrifice on to a wholly symbolic plane. 'However obsessive we find
the symbol of the Cross', he writes, 'the [Christian] mass is not
readily identified with the bloody sacrifice' (Bataille 1962: 89).
Rarely, if ever, do practising Christians admit that the celebration
of the Eucharist bears the traces of earlier pagan feasts involving
ceremonial cannibalism and the shedding of blood. Bataille notes
that the Crucifixion, which stands at the focus of the Christian
mass, can itself be viewed as the violation of a taboo that seeks to
harmonize the sacred and the profane. Yet Christianity does its

utmost to dissociate its interpretation of the Crucifixion from pagan traditions. Although Christian liturgy describes the murder of the Saviour as *'felix culpa'* (the 'happy fault'), it strips away the erotic investment in the sacrificial breaking of the taboo. The Christian treatment of sacrifice thus points to two related issues: (1) how the Christian mass absorbs and neutralizes the pagan practices it wholeheartedly condemns; and (2) how Christian teaching severs the link between eroticism and divinity. So, if Christianity symbolically brings the sacred and the profane together, then it does so only by sundering religion and desire from each other. Piety alone, not eroticism, is what leads the Christian towards the continuity promised by the infinite. Not surprisingly, Bataille believes this emphasis on piety has particularly damaging consequences for the way modern culture perceives the tormented relations between sexuality and death.

According to Bataille, the Christian attitude has convinced us that the lost continuity for which we yearn lies only in the immortal afterlife promised to those who are pious. But Christian piety, as Bataille observes, simply could not manage to embrace all desires for continuity. Although it undertook the rigorous repression of unclean practices deriving from pagan times, Christianity failed to purify all aspects of humanity. Given its excessiveness, libidinal energy could not be accommodated by the Christian emphasis on symbolic transgression alone. As a result, this form of institutionalized religion 'deepened the degree of sensual disturbance by forbidding organized transgression' (Bataille 1962: 127). Put another way, the more Christianity sought to purge the world of sin, the greater pressure there was on the deathly power of sexual desire to transgress. In sum, Bataille believes Christianity bears the burden of responsibility for why sexuality has been associated with shame, filth, and even hatred.

Under these appalling conditions, Bataille argues, it is no surprise that women become the most reviled and thus eroticized objects of desire. Although in making such claims Bataille often appears to be replicating the prejudices of a patriarchal culture, he notes that it 'would be quite wrong to say that women are more beautiful or even more desirable than men' (Bataille 1962: 131). This comment indicates that Bataille is aware of how cultures construct arbitrary values of beauty and ugliness. At the same time, however, his sensitivity to the contingency of cultural values never leads him to focus on what the male eroticization of female beauty might imply for women's own desires. In this respect, the masculinist bias of his discussion becomes evident when he examines 'low prostitution' (rather than the work performed by the well-paid courtesan) (Bataille 1962: 134). In turning to the indecency, degradation, and sordidness associated with 'low' prostitutes, Bataille asserts that it is exactly these qualities that provide men with the pathway that leads to deathly continuity. He observes that the female sex worker serves a paradoxical function: she is the *erotic object* that 'implies the abolition of the limits of all objects' (Bataille 1962: 130). On this view, male heterosexuality requires a female sexual object, not to fuse with a woman, but to fuse with death. In the process, the female sexual object is negated. From the man's perspective, therefore, the 'low' prostitute becomes the symbolic embodiment of death.

By now it should be clear that Bataille's largely anthropological account of desire operates within a system of accumulation and expenditure, where life and death are opposing forces structured around a system of taboos and trangressions. Even though Bataille only minimally acknowledges the Freudian concern with the economic return of repressed psychic energies, his writing in large part shares the strong interest psychoanalysis has in the withholding and unleashing of sexual forces. Chapter 2 has already explained in some detail how psychoanalytic theory, through the work of Lacan, pursues the idea that desire arises from a sense of lack that yearns for completion, only to discover that such longing can never be fulfilled. But the libidinal economies structured by each model have struck a number of subsequent theorists to be entirely wrongheaded. Several later writers contest the belief that sexuality is built upon either deficiencies that require energetic compensation or cultural prohibitions that must be ritually violated. Several works appearing in France throughout the 1970s seriously question Freud's, Lacan's, and Bataille's respective propositions. Each study in turn seeks to create alternative frameworks for considering the economic principles animating sexual desire.

Perhaps the most polemical challenge to earlier theories that posited desire in relation to lack emerges in Gilles Deleuze and Félix Guattari's *Anti-Oedipus: Capitalism and Schizophrenia* (1984 [1972]). Infuriated by the Freudian death-drive, Deleuze and Guattari declare that it is a principle that supports the oppressive myth of Oedipus central to psychoanalysis. The Freudian death drive, they claim, exists within a closed circuit that entraps the subject. 'If Freud needs death as a principle', they write, 'this is by virtue of the requirements of the dualism that maintains the qualitative opposition between the drives (you will not escape the conflict)' (Deleuze and Guattari 1984: 332). They continually insist that Freud's theorization of the Oedipus complex remains complicit with the capitalist structures that demand the maintenance of the nuclear family. Rather than provide an account of how to emancipate sexual desires, in their view psychoanalysis submits eroticism to the punishing cultural laws: 'instead of participating in an undertaking that will bring about genuine liberation, psychoanalysis is taking part in the work of bourgeois repression at its most far-reaching level, that is to say, keeping European humanity harnessed to the yoke of daddy-mommy and *making no effort to do away with this problem once and for all*' (Deleuze and Guattari 1984: 50). They believe that Freudian and Lacanian thought, in proclaiming that the child must pass through the Oedipal conflict to become a fully operative subject, refuses to explore possible desires that might bring about the downfall of the imprisoning Oedipal triad of 'daddy, mommy, and me' (Deleuze and Guattari 1984: 101). The Oedipal drama, they write, is an indisputable form of 'blackmail': 'either you recognize the Oedipal character of infantile sexuality, or you abandon all positions of sexuality' (Deleuze and Guattari 1984: 100). How, then, do Deleuze and Guattari propose to obviate the incarcerating designs of Oedipus?

The project of *Anti-Oedipus* is to turn completely upside-down all theoretical models that claim desire is predicated on lack. Close to the start of their defiant analysis, they make the sweeping declaration that '[t]he traditional logic of desire is all wrong from the outset' (Deleuze and Guattari 1984: 25). From the moment the West engaged with the 'Platonic logic of desire', so they say, a decidedly mistaken choice was made between *production* and *acquisition*. Ever since Plato committed this grave error, it seems, desire has been erroneously placed on the side of acquisition, misguidedly forcing us to think that it is lack that spurs desire. Although they concede that an alternative perspective can be found in the writings of Enlightenment philosopher Immanuel Kant (1724–1804), Deleuze and Guattari insist that almost all theoretical positions to date assume that desire means 'the lack of a real object'. Reading this strand of Western thought against the grain, they set out to demonstrate that desire is an explicitly productive principle. Even on the level of psychic fantasy, they maintain, desire appears to be immensely capable of producing objects to satisfy wishfulfilments. Pursuing this point, Deleuze and Guattari contend that, since desire manages to produce so many objects for itself, it can hardly be understood as lacking anything at all. In fact, the problem with psychoanalysis, as they see it, lies in the fallacious view that there is indeed a given subject from which desire must proceed as lack. To their minds, desire proliferates innumerable objects for itself precisely because it has no subject. 'Desire does not lack anything', they observe, 'it does not lack its object. It is, rather, the *subject* that is missing in desire, or desire that lacks a fixed subject' (Deleuze and Guattari 1984: 26). *Anti-Oedipus* urges us to acknowledge that the illusion of a fixed subject only comes into being through the repressive law enshrined in Oedipus. If, they argue, one does away with Oedipus, then at last one can see how desire is fundamentally *productive*, rather than lacking. Moreover, they state that desire produces *real objects*, not phantasmatic ones. Throughout its sprawling discussion, *Anti-Oedipus* remains true to its theory by generating a voluminous amount of often repetitious text to explain how and why desire attaches to all relations of social production. In this way, they seek to bind the material world and the libido into one and the same form.

To capture the explicitly productive power of desire, Deleuze and Guattari argue that we need to detach libidinal energies from the subject and think instead of 'desiring-machines', an anti-humanist metaphor that strategically prevents them from fastening their idea to a traditional notion of the bounded organic body. Recognized as an unstoppable flow (whose source they never question), desire remains for Deleuze and Guattari in perpetual movement, following diverse channels, proliferating and multiplying, fragmenting and reconfiguring, forever adopting unforeseen shapes and forms. 'Desire', they declare, 'constantly couples continuous flows and partial objects that are by nature fragmentary and fragmented' (Deleuze and Guattari 1984: 5). Missing a subject rather than an object, desire impersonally connects one erotic machine with another, continually devising innovative circuits through which it can whirl. On one page after another, Deleuze and Guattari figure this process as a matter of 'plugging in'. Like the cables and sockets that carry electricity, desire for them moves in too many pleasurable networks to be contained by either Freud's myth of Oedipus or Bataille's sacrificial breaking of taboos: 'The satisfaction the handyman experiences when he plugs something into an electric socket or diverts a stream of water can scarcely be explained in terms of "playing

mommy and daddy", or by the pleasure of violating a taboo'
(Deleuze and Guattari 1984: 7). In their view, 'plugging in' permits desire to flow in unanticipated ways. Yet the concept of
'plugging in' may well appear to subvert their concern with the
manifold operations of desire. Even if Deleuze and Guattari are
frequently provocative in their use of metaphor, the connection
they want to illustrate through plugs and sockets surely discloses
more than a residual phallicism in their thought. Such 'plugging
in', however, is not a ceaseless process. They argue that desire
does not move entirely without interruption. The further we
travel into *Anti-Oedipus* the clearer it becomes that there is a force
countering the desiring-machine's intensely productive energies.

They name the force that resists the compulsive stamina of
desiring-machines the 'body without organs'. This is an organless
'body' that can take many different manifestations, in variably
full or empty, intense or exhausted forms. In explaining what
they mean by this paradoxical term, Deleuze and Guattari
describe the body without organs as distinctly non-productive.
Repudiating Lacanian accounts of the body as 'an original noth-
ingness' that comes into its own only as an imaginary 'projection', they insist that the body without organs exists 'without an
image' (Deleuze and Guattari 1984: 8). They contend that the
body without organs repulses the desiring-machines, since it aims
at stasis, rather than flow. Unlike a human subject, the organless
body refers to any phenomenon that arrests or impedes desire.
Their cardinal example is capitalism. 'Capital', they claim, 'is
indeed the body without organs of the capitalist, or rather of the
capitalist being' (Deleuze and Guattari 1984: 10). In other
words, capital appropriates the productive power of desire on to
its surface, and it is so successful in absorbing these energies that
it miraculously presents itself as the origin of production. In
commandeering desire to its own arrogant ends, capital suggests
that it, and not the desire that fuels the energy of labour, is the
only productive power. Psychoanalysis, they believe, does much

the same. Just as capital takes over and hardens the desirous flows of human toil, so too does the human subject in Freud's Oedipal scheme become resistant to the multiplicitous movements of libidinal energy. 'The full body without organs', they write, 'is produced as antiproduction, that is to say it intervenes within the process as such for the sole purpose of rejecting any attempt to impose on it any sort of [Oedipal] triangulation implying that it was produced by its parents' (Deleuze and Guattari 1984: 15). Since the Oedipus complex involves rejecting desires for one's parents, Deleuze and Guattari assert that the Freudian subject creates the terrible delusion that it has freed itself at last from the machines that keep the circuits of desire in motion. Even though they concede that Freud's myth of Oedipus at least has the virtue of glimpsing the many psychic conflicts that energize the desiring-machines, Deleuze and Guattari imply that his theory is ultimately another body without organs, since it impedes and resists the anarchic libidinal movements of desire evident everywhere in the world. In fact, for them there is one figure in particular that makes the limitations to Oedipus abundantly clear. The figure in question is the schizophrenic.

Emerging in many ways from the anti-psychiatry movement of the 1960s, Deleuze and Guattari's work celebrates the schizophrenic's ability to *scramble all the codes* (Deleuze and Guattari 1984: 15). 'A schizophrenic out for a walk', they memorably remark, 'is a better model than a neurotic on the analyst's couch' (Deleuze and Guattari 1984: 2). By forever connecting with the outside world, the figure they abbreviate as the 'schizo' accomplishes exactly what the Oedipalized subject cannot. This is, to say the least, an unorthodox position to adopt in relation to schizophrenia. Yet it is because they take such a counterintuitive viewpoint on mental illness that Deleuze and Guattari feel free to unfold how the 'schizo' represents the emancipation of desire:

How is it possible that the schizo was conceived of as the

autistic rag – separated from the real and cut off from life – that he is so often thought to be? Worse still: how can psychiatric practice have made him this sort of rag, how can it have reduced him to this state of a body without organs that has become a dead thing – this schizo who sought to remain at that unbearable point where the mind touches matter and lives its every intensity, consumes it?

(Deleuze and Guattari 1984: 20)

Rather than consign the 'schizo' to 'another world', they uphold this figure as 'a free man, irresponsible, solitary, and joyous, finally able to say and do something simple in his own name, without asking permission' (Deleuze and Guattari 1984: 131). The 'schizo' expresses a desire 'lacking nothing'. And so they conclude: 'He has simply ceased being afraid of becoming mad'.

In their companion work, *A Thousand Plateaus: Capitalism and Schizophrenia* (1987 [1980]), Deleuze and Guattari turn once again to the liberatory power of the desiring 'schizo', this time focusing on the need for 'schizoanalysis', as opposed to psychoanalysis. Whereas Freudian psychoanalysis 'bases its own dictatorial power upon a dictatorial conception of the unconscious', schizoanalysis 'treats the unconscious as an acentered system' (Deleuze and Guattari 1987: 18). By way of elaborating the 'acentered' disposition of the unconscious and desirous 'machinic network', they employ yet another metaphor that captures the productive multivalency of libidinal energy. The metaphor in question is the 'rhizome'. A root with filaments moving in all directions, the rhizome serves them as a figuration that subverts the vertical 'arborescent' structures they believe have damagingly prevailed over Western thought, especially Freudian psychoanalysis. 'We're tired of trees', they declare. 'We should stop believing in trees, roots, and radicles. They've made us suffer too much' (Deleuze and Guattari 1987: 15). 'Arborescent systems', we are told, 'are hierarchical systems with centres of significance and subjectification' (Deleuze and Guattari 1987: 16). Although they argue that the rhizome is not entirely antithetical to the tree ('[t]here are knots of arborescence in rhizomes, and rhizomatic offshoots in roots'), the rhizome remains unfettered by the top-down despotism they attribute to the root-tree model. Having neither a beginning nor an end, the rhizome is perhaps best seen as a suspended middle, with 'linear multiplicities' (Deleuze and Guattari 1987: 20–21). Operating by 'variation, expansion, conquest, capture, offshoots', the rhizome's unpredictable lines of flight are intimately connected with sexuality. In their theory, the rhizome represents how desire thrives on a plateau of intensity: the horizontal plane without a centre upon which sexuality produces its innumerable aleatoric movements.

It may well seem that 'schizoanalysis' and 'rhizomatics' operate at such a high level of abstraction that readers can only wonder at the cognitive or political reach either concept might have. But Deleuze and Guattari's influential work has been of some interest to feminist theorists seeking alternatives to the 'arborescent' phallicism inscribed in Freud's Oedipus and castration complexes and the Lacanian 'Name-of-the-Father'. Elizabeth Grosz remarks that, for some time, Deleuze and Guattari had little appeal to feminist inquiry, since *Anti-Oedipus* celebrates the arguably sexist writings of D.H. Lawrence and Henry Miller to support this machinic model of desire. (The works of both Miller and Lawrence, it is important to note, are subject to severe criticism for their unremitting sexism in Kate Millett's influential feminist polemic, *Sexual Politics*, published in 1970.) Yet, as Grosz observes, Deleuze and Guattari's work bears some similarities with the project of French feminist theorist Luce Irigaray (see pp. 110–13), a writer who has persistently sought to undo the phallic logic of Freudian thought. Grosz maintains that Deleuze and Guattari count among the few analysts of sexuality to follow the seventeenth-century philosopher Baruch Spinoza (1632–1677) in not taking the body for granted as the locus of a conscious subject. It is, indeed, by reconceptualizing the relation between bodies and desires that Deleuze and Guattari provide feminism with the opportunity to imagine corporeality anew:

> Deleuze and Guattari's notion of the body as a discontinuous, nontotalized series of processes, organs, flows, energies, corporeal substances and incorporeal events, intensities, and durations may be of great relevance to those feminists attempting to reconceive bodies, especially women's bodies, outside of the binary polarizations imposed on the body by the mind/body, nature/culture, subject/object, and interior/exterior oppositions.
>
> (Grosz 1994: 193–4)

Especially significant to Grosz are the central sections of *A Thousand Plateaus*, devoted to the concept of 'becoming-woman'. Rather than confine the concept of 'woman' to a sexed body that defines a female subject, Deleuze and Guattari elaborate two of their leading analytic terms to explain how the most dispersed libidinal energies are 'molecular' while the ones that strive to aggregate into totalities are 'molar'. In the context of 'becoming-woman', they suggest that molecular energies might be labelled 'microfemininities', since these atomized intensities rhizomatically circulate across the social field. Molar formations, by comparison, are ones that define 'woman by her form, endowed with organs and functions and assigned as a subject' (Deleuze and Guattari 1987: 275–6). The point, however, is that there is no hard and fast distinction between molecular and molar, since their energies infract each other. 'Doubtless', they note, 'the girl becomes a woman in the molar or organic sense'. But, at the same time, 'girls do not belong to an age group, sex, order, or kingdom: they slip in everywhere, between orders, acts, ages, sexes' (Deleuze and Guattari 1987: 276–7). So even if, in the molar sense, girls shall become women, the feminine forces witnessed in 'becoming-woman' produce their molecular powers in all areas of culture. In reviewing this dialectic between molar and molecular conceptions of femininity, Grosz suggests that it faces feminist theory with a dilemma. On the one hand, experimental thinking of this kind has the virtue of releasing the category of 'woman' from a question of anatomical sexing. Yet on the other, it frees femininity into such a state of scattered or formless 'becoming' that this idea could simply serve to obliterate or marginalize women's struggles. In many respects, Deleuze and Guattari are so adamant in dismantling 'arborescent' and 'molar' structures that enjoy such dominance in the world that it becomes hard to see exactly how political campaigns might be run along 'rhizomatic' and 'schizoanalytic' lines. The sceptical reader will no doubt think that *Anti-Oedipus* and *A Thousand Plateaus* are simply idealistic libertarian tracts that, no matter how much they address capitalism, have lost all contact with pragmatic action and the material world.

A similar charge could be brought against *Libidinal Economy* by Jean-François Lyotard, an experimental work that strongly echoes *Anti-Oedipus*, and which gained notoriety when it first appeared in 1974 for its discussion of how Marx's writings failed to analyse their own libidinal investments. Lyotard reformulates the Freudian opposition between the death drive and the pleasure principle, thus bringing into focus once more the topic that absorbs the authors of *Anti-Oedipus*: the mechanisms that raise and lower intensities of sexual force. Although much of *Libidinal Economy* assumes its readers already possess a working knowledge of Bataille, Freud, Lacan, and Marx, among other theorists, there are sections of this frenetically written and far from user-friendly book that make Lyotard's densely allusive project plain. Following Deleuze and Guattari, Lyotard refuses to take for granted the enduring psychoanalytic association between desire and lack. Instead of imagining a subject that must always submit to the lack he satirically personifies as the 'great Zero', Lyotard recommends that we first of all consider desire travelling the one-sided but ever-moving Moebius band. This suggestive metaphor gives Lyotard the scope to realize desire outside the binary frame of reference that keeps desire and lack locked in opposition. The Moebius band, after all, has the virtue of making it hard to tell which is the outside part and which is the inside. Through this thought-provoking metaphor, we can glimpse the infinite dimensions to this 'immense membrane of the libidinal "body"':

> It is made from the most heterogeneous textures, bone, epithelium, sheets to write on, charged atmospheres, swords, glass cases, people, grasses, canvases to paint. All these zones are joined end to end in a band which has no back to it, a Moebius band which interests us not because it is closed, but because it is one-sided, a Moebian skin which, rather than being smooth, is on the contrary (is this topologically possible?) covered with roughness, corners, creases, cavities which when it passes on the 'first' turn will be cavities, but perhaps on the 'second', lumps. But as for what turn the band is on, no-one knows nor will know, in the eternal turn.
>
> (Lyotard 1993: 203)

Here Lyotard advances the idea of a boundless 'membrane' whose capacity for shape-changing has to some extent a precedent in Deleuze and Guattari's desiring-machines. But the more one looks at how he is trying to map out a terrain for comprehending the ceaseless permutations of desire, the more it seems he is constructing a topography whose 'cavities' and 'lumps' do not conform to the endlessly productive principle celebrated in *Anti-Oedipus*. Instead, Lyotard's libidinal 'body' – we should note his hesitant inverted commas – spreads out all its infinite metamorphoses in an 'eternal turn', almost suggesting it has a spiritual, sublime, or even trascendent quality. This emphasis on eternity implies that, if Lyotard severs the connection between desire and lack, then he fuses the libido with everlasting life. 'The libido', he insists, 'never fails to invest regions, and it doesn't invest under the rubric of lack and appropriation. It invests without condition' (Lyotard 1993: 4). Perhaps, like a free spirit, the libido refuses to be wholly bound to mortal corporeality.

But even if it seems to come from a transcendental realm, in Lyotard's scheme the libido nevertheless does not always invest its energies at a continually high level of exuberant intensity. To indicate how desire must at times slow down, he turns to the concept of the theatre: a metaphor, which he elaborates elsewhere in his work, that provides him with a means of discriminating between separable phenomena, such as stage and audience, that are none the less bound within the same structure. At such moments of what he calls 'theatricization', the bar that keeps whirling the Moebian band has to decelerate, making it possible to see a tenuous distinction between exterior and interior, between one side and another, between what he emphatically identifies as '*this*' and '*not-this*':

> [E]very intensity, scorching or remote, is always *this and not-this*, not at all through the effect of castration, of repression, of ambivalence, of tragedy due to the great Zero [i.e. lack], but because intensity pertains to an asynthetic movement, more or less complex, but in any event so rapid that the surface engendered by it is, at each of its points, at the same time *this and not-this*. Of no point, of no region, however small, can one say what either is, because this region or this point has not only already disappeared when one claims to speak of it, but, in the singular or atemporal instant of intense passage, either the point or the region has been invested in from both sides at once.
>
> (Lyotard 1993: 15)

Given the speed at which desire raises and lowers its intensities, it is perhaps not surprising that this passage faces us with a paradox. Here Lyotard declares that, at the very moment '*this*' separates from '*not-this*', it remains cognitively impossible to tell that this process has in fact occurred. For no sooner has one sought to discern the distinction between the two than they collapse back into each other, reinvesting their energies elsewhere.

How, then, can we know that '*this*' and '*not-this*' ever managed a momentary differentiation in the first place? This kind of question really does not interest Lyotard, and for good reason. 'Why does the movement of the bar slow down?' (Lyotard 1993: 25). His answer is ingenious. 'We turn this question around, we say: when it is turning intensely, no why; your why itself results from it turning less strenuously, it is recuperative and nostalgic. The movement of the bar slows down *because*, and then this *because . . .* is intensified'. In other words, theoretical inquiry in itself arrests libidinal intensity because it creates the 'theatre' where concepts and structures of representation thrive, struggling to discern what is '*this*' and '*not-this*'. He calls such an endeavour 'nihilism'. Examining this and related passages from *Libidinal Economy*, Geoffrey Bennington observes that Lyotard is developing a theory that openly raises the question of its own legitimacy:

> [T]he primary process, the libidinal band, the death drive, are not representable insofar as they exceed and precede the whole representational set-up. And insofar as *Economie Libidinale* [*Libidinal Economy*] is concerned to talk of singularities (events), and insofar as language is the domain of generality, then it cannot deliver its objects as concepts without betraying them.
>
> (Bennington 1988: 28)

Bennington claims that the playful and flamboyant '*dandyesque*' style of *Libidinal Economy* dramatizes how 'there can be no direct presentation of libido and the death drive' in any theroetical endeavour (Bennington 1988: 29–30). So this extraordinary work strives as much as it can against precisely the 'theatre' that its own theoretical labour must inevitably construct. Lyotard, then, cannot escape betraying the rapid movements of libidinal energy by inhibiting them in static concepts and solidifying representations.

Lyotard's critique of the 'nihilism' involved in trying theoretically to separate '*this*' from '*not-this*' gains special power when he turns the spotlight on Freud's *Beyond the Pleasure Principle*. Constantly provoked by this work, Lyotard asks: 'why and how can the two principles, of life and death, be assumed if they cannot be discerned through their two functions, if bound wholes can be as congenial to life (organisms, statues, institutions, memories of all kinds) as to death (neuroses and psychoses, paranoiac confinements, lethal stable disorders of organic functions)?' (Lyotard 1993: 29). His parenthetically listed examples suggest that the distinction between qualities attributed to life and to death respectively are not only arbitrary, but also infused in each other. Like most structures of binary thinking, this type of opposition has a tendency, when put under scrutiny, to merge and dissolve its purported contraries, suggesting that ostensibly fixed antitheses are precarious at best. 'Freud', observes Lyotard, 'was well aware of these formal demands'. Like all theorists, Freud wanted 'order' in the face of libidinal disorder. Freud's mistake, it seems, was to build a theoretical system that imposed categorical divisions where there were infinite libidinal amalgamations. To Lyotard, the Freudian project is altogether too large in its ambitions, constructing an edifice that misguidedly generalizes formations of desire, thus losing contact with the ever-varying pulsions of desire. By way of correcting Freud, Lyotard claims the best method for analysing desire lies in 'examining a particular effect with patient, almost infinite care' (Lyotard 1993: 30). The painstaking descriptions to be found in the fiction of French novelist Marcel Proust (1871–1922) suggest to Lyotard a model for this type of microanalytical attentiveness.

Everywhere we look in modern French theories of desire, the question of thinking about the libido in economic terms throws increasing light on how the grand designs of any theoretical system will ultimately be defeated by desire. This point becomes evident in Jean Baudrillard's *Seduction*. Published in 1979, this work has clearly absorbed the 'molecular' revolution of Deleuze and Guattari's thought. But whereas *Anti-Oedipus* claims that libidinal energy is ceaselessly productive, Baudrillard attempts to go one better by declaring that it is precisely the *productive* nature of sex that deludes us. In the place of production, Baudrillard advances the significance of *seduction*:

> One may catch a glimpse of another, parallel universe (the two never meet) with the decline of psychoanalysis and sexuality as strong structures, and their cleansing with a *psy* and molecular universe (that of their final liberation). A universe that can no longer be interpreted in terms of psychic or psychological relations, nor those of repression and the unconscious, but must be interpreted in the terms of play, challenges, duels, the strategy of appearances – that is, the terms of seduction.
>
> (Baudrillard 1990: 7)

How, then, might we conceptualize the 'play' of seduction? To answer this query, Baudrillard makes a rather contradictory response to feminist politics. To begin with, he claims that Freud was right in viewing sexuality as phallic; its masculinism cannot be denied. Women's lives, argues Baudrillard, are constantly threatened by the phallic order. This view leads him to emphasize how, in women's struggles for liberation, the 'danger . . . for the female is that she will be enclosed within a structure that condemns her to either discrimination when the structure is strong, or a derisory triumph within a weakened structure' (Baudrillard 1990: 6). In other words, women cannot benefit from gaining an equal place in a phallic order, since to do so would plainly perpetuate a patriarchal system. (He seems to be unaware how feminism has for decades reflected carefully on this problem.) Yet rather than suggest how women's liberation might transform the patriarchal hegemony, Baudrillard bemoans the fact that feminists seem uninterested in what he feels is the most subversive quality attributed to femininity: seduction. So he is led to assert, somewhat condescendingly, that the women's movement does 'not understand *that seduction represents mastery over the symbolic universe, while power represents only mastery of the real universe*' (Baudrillard 1990: 8). For the moment, it almost sounds as if Baudrillard is advising feminists to adopt the role of those *femmes fatales* and seductive temptresses familiar to many narrative and film genres.

Baudrillard is certainly aware of the sexist implications to the stereotypical way he is gendering seduction. But he declares that, even if 'one calls the sovereignty of seduction feminine by convention' (Baudrillard 1990: 7), femininity none the less retains the monopoly on artifice, appearances, illusions. Not for a moment will Baudrillard entertain either Irigaray's appeal to the non-phallic libidinal economy of the female body or Deleuze and Guattari's metaphor of the body without organs. From his perspective, each of these writers reduces desire – either literally or figuratively – to a question of anatomy. An altogether more helpful way of thinking about the symbolic power exerted by feminine seduction lies for him in a famous essay by Joan Riviere first published in 1929. In 'Womanliness as a Masquerade', Riviere influentially observes the conflicts that arise when professional women assume and wear womanliness 'as a mask' to secure their place in a male-dominated world. Riviere believes that this 'masquerade' of femininity, even if compromised in the face of male authority, can allow the intellectual woman 'both to hide the possession of masculinity and to avert the reprisals expected if she was found to possess it – much as a thief will turn out his pockets and ask to be searched to prove that he has not stolen the goods' (Riviere 1986: 38). Idealizing feminine 'masquerade', Baudrillard observes how masculinity, by contrast, aggrandizes itself on the dangerous pretence that it 'possesses unfailing powers of discrimination and absolute criteria for pronouncing the truth'. He finds femininity altogether preferable because it blurs the distinction between 'authenticity and artifice', thus manipulating the seductive realm of 'simulation': a term that absorbs many of his studies devoted to the symbolic regimes that govern the current postmodern world (Baudrillard 1990: 10–11). It is as if Baudrillard himself were seduced by a highly uncritical notion of feminine seduction.

But why should the symbolic seductiveness of the feminine be elevated over and above the masculinist imperative to claim truth and certainty? What precisely is at stake for Baudrillard in identifying these gendered contraries? The answer returns us, as it does in both *Anti-Oedipus* and *Libidinal Economy*, to capitalism. He maintains that just as capitalist economies stress production, so too do modern understandings of sex proceed with this relentlessly productive logic in mind. Although one wonders to what degree Baudrillard believes that capitalism shapes and determines modern understandings of sex, his argument gains some plausibility if we consider for a moment how in Victorian Britain the verb 'to spend' was sexual slang for male ejaculation. Even today in the pornography industry, 'cum' scenes are frequently known as 'money shots'. With these points in mind, let us look at how Baudrillard pieces sex and capital together:

> Ours is a culture of premature ejaculation. Increasingly, all seduction, all manner of enticement – which is always a highly *ritualized* process – is effaced behind a *naturalized* sexual imperative, behind the immediate and imperative realization of desire. Our centre of gravity has been displaced towards a libidinal economy concerned with only the naturalization of desire, a desire dedicated to drives, or to a machine-like functioning. . . . This pressure towards liquidity, flux and the accelerated articulation of the sexual, psychic and physical body is an exact replica of that which regulates exchange value: capital must circulate, there must no longer be any fixed point, investments must be ceaselessly renewed, value must radiate

> without respite – this is the form of value's present realization,
> and sexuality, the sexual *model*, is simply its mode of appear-
> ance at the level of the body.
>
> (Baudrillard 1990: 38)

Here Baudrillard proposes that sexuality turns the body over into the service of capital, making it a value-producing machine which must continually reinvest its energies to keep the system going. It is as if the libido paralleled labour-power, and the regime of sexuality resembled the capitalist eager to seize on the surplus-value that accrues. To Baudrillard, sex is like human labour because it is a natural energy that Western culture demands should be treated in an entrepreneurial spirit. Even if this correlation between sex and capital might not hold up to much further scrutiny, it is intriguing to see how Baudrillard is led to observe that 'sexuality, desire and pleasure are *subaltern* values' (Baudrillard 1990: 39). In using the epithet '*subaltern*', he is referring to values associated with subjected groups that embody a fundamental energy which capitalism seeks to harness. He notes that, when they first appeared in the West, sexuality, desire and pleasure were viewed as 'fallen' values, in so far as they made a striking contrast with the 'aristocratic values of birth and blood, valour and seduction, or the collective values of religion and sacrifice' (Baudrillard 1990: 39). At this point, it becomes clear that he feels seduction is not only the province of femininity, but also a structure that belongs to the *ancien régime*. Seduction, therefore, begins to sounds as if it is feminine, simulational, and archaic all at once. In the meantime, sexuality, desire, and pleasure would appear to stem from the productive labour of the insurgent *nouveaux riches*, whose masculinist desire to conquer the real world shall continue into the foreseeable future.

The distinctly modern masculinism of desire emerges for Baudrillard most forcefully in pornography. In this genre of sexual representation, he argues, there is a lamentable 'excess of "reality"' (Baudrillard 1990: 28). Although he claims we may be tempted to believe along psychoanalytic lines that pornography presents a phantasmatic regime in which various fetishes and perversions are put into play, the only illusion it upholds is paradoxically a fantasy of the real: a 'hyperreality' in which any distinction between representation and the actual world collapses altogether. So Baudrillard charges pornography for having a 'sham vision', such is its pretence to reality (Baudrillard 1990: 31). Instead of providing a seductive world of rituals and apparitions that sustain the endless pleasures of seduction, all pornography can do is act out the deadening machinations of capital. He bluntly sums up this malaise in the following bleak equation: 'The realist corruption of sex, the productivist corruption of labour – same symptoms, same combat'.

But if pornography, according to Baudrillard, provides an example of 'reality' taken to a higher inflated power, then he assures us that seduction has not entirely departed from the world. Although he feels we may continue to struggle beneath the yoke of 'productivist corruption', seduction has none the less found its way into other areas of our lives, most evidently across the endless interfaces with computer and information technology. Yet he is quick to point out that our experiences at the interface are hardly seductive in the playful, artificial, feminine sense with which he began his study, and which wields symbolic power. Instead, the technological manipulation of simulated images comprises nothing more than a *cold seduction*': 'the "narcissistic" spell of electronic and information systems, the cold attraction of the terminals and mediums that we have become, surrounded as we are by consoles, isolated and seduced by their manipulation' (Baudrillard 1990: 162). In techno-simulation, then, we experience seduction in its 'disenchanted form' (Baudrillard 1990: 180). But since seduction, for Baudrillard, has the capacity to elude production, it may well turn out that it will never be fully absorbed by the technologies that render it 'cold'. His book leaves us on a suspended note, wondering how indeed seduction will outlast the productivist imperative, and how it might regain its charming feminine illusoriness. Given the rise of phone sex, pornography on the internet, and other sexual services involving computer technology, one wonders if this realm of simulation really retains, as Baudrillard suggests, even the '*cold seduction*' of artifice. Possibly this world of technological simulation belongs to the same arena of pornographic 'hyperreality': a field of vision in which actual and virtual at times become inseparable. (Some might argue, however, that it is precisely this realm of electronic 'hyperreality' that permits unrealized erotic desires to be liberated into cyberspace, leaving our experience of technological seduction anything but 'cold'.)

French cultural critic Roland Barthes (1915–1980) largely shares Baudrillard's despondent view of pornography. Throughout *The Pleasure of the Text* (1975 [1973]), Barthes draws thoughtful aperçus of how the greatest pleasures emerge from the '*unpredictability* of bliss' (Barthes 1975: 4). Maybe like Baudrillard's seduction, such bliss or *jouissance* can never be known in advance. Barthes emphasizes how 'corporeal striptease' and 'narrative suspense' are limited pleasures, since they simply cannot compare with 'perversion', which he equates with 'intermittence': 'skin flashing between two articles of clothing' (Barthes 1975: 10). It is, he claims, this intermittent 'flash itself which seduces, or rather: the staging of an appearance-as-disappearance'. Here, then, we have the pleasure of revelation and concealment, laid bare and covered in a movement that always remains in process. Turn, however, to modern pornography, and one quickly sees the level of disaffection with its limited eroticism. Since pornography is designed to lead its consumers towards an orgasmic climax, it must ultimately terminate desire:

> So-called 'erotic' books (one must add: of recent vintage, in order to except Sade and a few others) *represent* not so much

the erotic scene as the expectation of it, the preparation for it, its ascent; that is what makes them 'exciting'; and even when the scene occurs, naturally there is disappointment, deflation.

(Barthes 1975: 58)

Since it is frequently used for masturbation, pornography promises much excitement. But pornography ultimately proves dissatisfying, since the desire on which it draws must hurl itself headlong towards the 'little death'. That is why Barthes argues that so-called 'erotic' books represent '[p]leasure *as seen by psychoanalysis*', by which he probably means a model of desire built upon the psychic competition between Eros and Thanatos dramatized in Freud's *Beyond the Pleasure Principle*. Both forces, after all, converge in heterosexual orgasm, and thus come to an abrupt end. In pornography, therefore, modern cultural theorists come up against the constraining limits of what it means to imagine sexuality as a phenomenon driven by rivalrous energies of life and death.

There is no doubt that pornography has faced modern culture with extremely difficult questions about the ways in which sexuality appears uncontrollably to surge forth only to encounter its 'little death'. More than any other type of sexual representation, pornography has frequently focused deep-seated cultural anxieties about the (de)generating pleasures that arise from the conflicted libido. These anxieties about the pains and pleasures of eroticism emerge most clearly in the vigorous, if acutely divided, feminist discussion of pornography. Developing in the 1970s and persisting to this day, this significant debate opens up a wide range of perspectives on how we can best approach the moral and political dimensions to the volatile sexual energies that Freud identified many decades before.

PORNOGRAPHIC MATERIALS

'Pornography is the theory, and rape the practice', wrote radical feminist Robin Morgan in 1980 (Morgan 1980: 139). This memorable slogan has certainly left its imprint on feminist discussions about the links between pornography and sexual violence against women. This debate absorbed much feminist energy in the mid-1970s and 1980s. In many respects, this is still a decidedly controversial topic that divides activists and intellectuals working for women's liberation. Radical feminists (stressing a woman-centered analysis of culture) and socialist feminists (emphasizing women's struggles as an oppressed class) have often differed in their understandings of pornography.

Until radical feminists such as Morgan asserted that rape resulted from pornographic representation, the polemic about sexually explicit materials had largely been conducted in terms of how the law regulated obscenity. Even then, it needs to be borne in mind, legislation dealing with obscene and indecent materials did not always focus on what twentieth-century culture has come to regard as pornography. In England and Wales, for example, the Obscene Publications Act (1857) was used in the Victorian period to outlaw the publication of birth-control pamphlets by free-thinkers and feminists. Perhaps it is no accident that in the same year, according to the *Oxford English Dictionary*, the word pornography itself entered the English language. Unquestionably, by the mid-nineteenth century there was a regime of sexual representation that bears striking resemblance to the visual systems that would be currently classed as pornography. But the point is that it was only then that this identifiable genre was associated exclusively with eroticism. 'In early modern Europe, that is, between 1500 and 1800', observes Lynn Hunt, what would become known as 'pornography was most often a vehicle for using the shock of sex to criticize religious and political authorities' (Hunt 1993: 10). Hunt comments that between the sixteenth and eighteenth centuries, satirical and seditious writings that exploited sexual imagery circulated only among an educated elite. Following the illuminating researches of Walter Kendrick (Kendrick 1987), Hunt remarks that it was through the subsequent rise of literacy, the extension of print culture, and the gradual commodification of erotic representations in the Victorian era that pornography as we now perceive it came into its own (Hunt 1993: 12–13). Ever since this moment in history, competing defences, definitions, and denunciations of pornography have provided a testing-ground for ethical, moral, and social values. So what exactly encouraged radical feminists to break with the long-standing belief that pornography was an issue about obscenity? What led radical feminism to consider pornography as the cause of violent sex crimes such as rape?

It is sometimes asserted that pornography became an urgent campaigning issue because it gave the Women's Liberation Movement a common purpose at a time when the political direction of feminism was internally under factional strain. Rather than adopt the traditional standpoint on whether pornographic representation broke the law on the grounds of obscenity, radical feminists attacked pornography because they felt it starkly dramatized the systematic subordination of women. Whereas established debates about obscenity focused on how the subject consuming pornographic materials might become morally degenerate, radical feminist analyses stressed how pornography degraded women as sexual objects. Susanne Kappeler clarifies this distinction when she writes:

> Feminist critique is concerned with sexism, not with indecency or obscenity. The values of 'obscene' and 'indecent' change with changing mores; in particular, they are middle-class values of proven duplicity. They are part of the make-up of the society's constructed self-image. The setters of standards *to whom* indecencies and obscenities are offensive do

> not seem to share the values of women to whom pornogra-
> phy is offensive.
>
> (Kappeler 1986: 25)

Concentrating on sexism, rather than obscenity, radical feminism
claimed that hard-core pornography in particular led to the most
appalling forms of sexual abuse, both within the industry that
produced this commodity and at the hands of the ever-growing
market of largely male consumers. If pornography was the theory
that led to rape, then it was patently instrumental in many bar-
barous sex crimes committed by men.

The radical feminist position on graphic sexual materials
inspired several notable writers to adopt an immensely powerful
rhetoric to further its leading claims. In the same collection that
features Morgan's famous motto, the American essayist, novelist,
and political campaigner Andrea Dworkin takes her epigraphs
from the Old Testament to underscore the prophetic biblical tone
of her offensive against so-called 'radical' men's failures to reject
pornography:

> Men love death. In everything they make, they hollow out a
> central place for death, let its rancid smell contaminate every
> dimension of whatever still survives. Men especially love mur-
> der. In art they celebrate it, and in life they commit it. They
> embrace murder as if life would be devoid of passion, mean-
> ing, and action, as if murder were solace, stilling their sobs as
> they mourn the emptiness and alienation of their lives.
>
> (Dworkin 1980: 148)

Reading this series of proclamations, one would imagine that
male sexuality was indeed driven solely and utterly by a murderous instinct. Dworkin suggests that even politically 'radical' men
find in pornography an ideal means of regaining the virility that
has for some time been waning in the United States. She identifies two main reasons for this weakening of masculine potency.

One is the castratory impact of the military fiascos that sustained the Vietnam War (1955–75), while the other is 'the revolutionary militance of the women' during the same period (Dworkin 1980: 153). Between military incompetence and militant feminism, Dworkin states, a whole generation of men was left in a dilemma. 'The sons, dispossessed, did have a choice: to bond with the fathers to crush the women or to ally themselves with the women against the tyranny of all phallic power, including their own' (Dworkin 1980: 153). But rather than unite with feminists, these 'sons' turned to pornography instead, striving to maintain the supremacy of the penis. Having spelt out the violence of pornography in her own decisive chapter and verse, Dworkin's numerous later writings specify exactly why sexually explicit materials are such a source of moral outrage to feminism.

Throughout her polemical full-length study, *Pornography: Men Possessing Women* (1989 [1979]), Dworkin describes in overwhelming detail a great many scenes from pornographic publications, each of which in her view make hatred of women glaringly evident. Discussing a picture titled 'Beaver Hunters' from the avowedly misogynist magazine *Hustler*, Dworkin carefully details the sexual violence staged in this scene:

> Two white men, dressed as hunters, sit in a black Jeep. The Jeep occupies almost the whole frame of the picture. The two men carry rifles. The rifles extend above the frame of the photograph in the white space surrounding it. The men and the Jeep face into the camera. Tied onto the hood of the black Jeep is a white woman. She is tied with thick rope. She is spread-eagle. Her pubic hair and crotch are the dead centre of the car hood and the photograph. Her head is turned to one side, tied down by rope that is pulled taut across her neck, extended to and wrapped several times around her wrists.
>
> (Dworkin 1989: 26)

Dworkin's description continues by itemizing exactly which other parts of the woman's body in this bondage scene are tied by the endless length of criss-crossing rope. She draws attention to how a bumper sticker is placed between the woman's legs. Alluding to the brother of US President Jimmy Carter, the sticker reads: 'I brake for Billy Carter'. (This is a cultural reference whose meaning Dworkin does not explain.) To complete the picture, *Hustler* furnishes three contemptuous sentences that summarize the drama depicted here: 'Western sportsmen report beaver hunting was particularly good through the Rocky Mountain region during the past season. These two hunters easily bagged their limit in the high country. They told HUSTLER that they stuffed and mounted their trophy as soon as they got her home'. To Dworkin, this repugnant picture directly communicates the idea that men are hunters (they wield phallic guns) while women are to be treated as nothing more than captured animals (a 'beaver' is American sexual slang for a woman's crotch). 'Terror', writes Dworkin, 'is finally the content of the photograph, and it is also its effect on the female observer' (Dworkin 1989: 27). Since, from Dworkin's perspective, this image has special appeal to woman-hating men, she claims it will doubtless 'evoke fear' in the female spectator, 'unless she entirely dissociates herself from the photograph: refuses to believe or understand that real persons posed for it, refuses to see the bound person as a woman like herself' (Dworkin 1989: 27). It proves impossible for Dworkin herself to view 'Beaver Hunters' as anything other than a brutal reality. Recoiling from this picture, Dworkin professes this shocking image relays how the 'power of sex is ultimately defined as the power of conquest' (Dworkin 1989: 30). Not only does the picture display 'the nonconsensual character of the event', it also implies how the 'power of sex, in male terms, is also funereal'. 'Death permeates it', states Dworkin.

By regarding such pornography as the ultimate testament of men's deathly misogyny, Dworkin worked together with a distinguished law professor, Catharine A. MacKinnon, on a widely publicized campaign that aimed to shield women from the assumed harms that stemmed from the violent sexual fantasies represented in the pages of *Hustler* and similar magazines and films. In 1983, Dworkin and MacKinnon formulated a Minneapolis city ordinance that both defined the production, sale, display, and circulation of pornography and allowed victims of sexual violence attributable to such material to claim damages. This city ordinance was based on a platform of civil rights whose goal was to protect two groups: (1) those who have been violently exploited within the pornography industry, and (2) those who have been subject to abuse by its consumers. In the same spirit as Dworkin, MacKinnon claims that pornography 'institutionalizes the sexuality of male supremacy, fusing the eroticization of domination and submission with the social construction of male and female' (MacKinnon 1992: 462). Contrary to earlier analyses, such as Susan Sontag's, that stress the varying styles and genres of pornography (Sontag 1969), MacKinnon flatly declares that this form of eroticism 'is not a distortion, reflection, projection, expression, fantasy, representation or symbol either'. 'It is', MacKinnon insists, 'a sexual reality' (MacKinnon 1992: 462). In a later essay, MacKinnon underscores this point: 'Pornography does not simply express or interpret experience; it substitutes for it' (MacKinnon 1993: 25).

Since both Dworkin and MacKinnon lay such a complete emphasis on the *reality* presented by what others might perceive as a *representational* domain, they regard pornography as the lived world in which terrifying sexual inequalities persist. 'Pornography', writes MacKinnon, 'defines women by how we look according to how we can be sexually used' (MacKinnon 1992: 463). In almost identical terms, Dworkin sees the definitional power that pornography cruelly exerts over women's lives. But she takes the logic of this claim to its absolute limit:

> At the heart of the female condition is pornography: it is the ideology that is the source of all the rest; it truly defines what women are in this system – and how women are treated issues from what women *are*. Pornography is not a metaphor for what women are; it is what women are in theory and in practice.
>
> (Dworkin 1983: 223)

According to this argument, pornography must be viewed as an *action* that keeps women locked in a vicious all-encompassing system. Dworkin believes pornography presents *both the cause and the effect* of women's sexual subordination. So only by abolishing pornography can the liberation of women truly begin.

To counter the violence they attribute to pornography, Dworkin and MacKinnon produced a comprehensive definition of such material for the ordinance they presented to the city of Minneapolis in 1983, and which was passed by the City Council the following year. It is worth quoting this definition in full, since it spells out in precise terms exactly what constitutes their understanding of the systematic *dehumanization* and *objectification* evident in *Hustler* and its ilk:

> Pornography means the graphic sexually explicit subordination of women through pictures and/or words that also includes one or more of the following: (i) women are presented dehumanized as sexual objects, things, or commodities; or (ii) women are presented as sexual objects who enjoy humiliation or pain; or (iii) women are presented as sexual objects experiencing pleasure in rape, incest or other sexual assault; or (iv) women are presented as sexual objects tied up, cut up or mutilated or bruised or physically hurt; or (v) women are presented in postures or positions of sexual submission, servility, or display; or (vi) women's body parts – including but not limited to vaginas, breasts, or buttocks – are exhibited such that women are reduced to those parts; or (vii) women are presented being

penetrated by objects and animals; or (viii) women are presented in scenarios of degradation, humiliation, injury, torture,
shown as filthy or inferior, bleeding, bruised, or hurt in a context that makes these conditions sexual.

(Itzin 1992a: 435–6)

On no account does this highly inclusive definition admit that
scenes involving domination and submission, bondage, or other
styles of 'humiliation' or 'degradation' may have been either con-
tractually agreed or staged in a non-injurious manner. Dworkin
and MacKinnon's point is that such depictions enact harmful
types of conduct that frighten, offend, and even seriously endan-
ger women. Even though Dworkin and MacKinnon state categor-
ically that this exhaustive definition must be detached from
conventional views of obscenity, the ordinance itself was championed by moralistic conservatives who wished to see pornography
outlawed on traditional grounds of indecency. This victory was
short-lived. No sooner had this alliance between radical feminists
and the Moral Right persuaded the City Council that pornography affronted civil rights than the mayor vetoed the ordinance.
When a redrafted version of the document was subsequently
adopted by Indianapolis City Council, it was declared unconstitu-
tional because it violated the First Amendment of the United
States Constitution – namely, the amendment that protects free
speech. Although these ordinances proved unsuccessful in the
United States, campaigns were organized to ensure that similar
legislation would be implemented in Britain. (No such legislation has yet been passed in the UK.)

Sharing Dworkin and MacKinnon's political agenda, Catherine
Itzin published an imposing collection of essays that aim to show
how pornography lies at the root of child sexual abuse, sexual
addiction, and pathological erotic behaviour. In one of these articles, Diana E.H. Russell highlights psychological experiments
conducted with male students which repeatedly reveal that

increasing exposure to pornography result in an escalating 'proclivity to rape' (Russell 1992: 313). Scientific experiments have been conducted in laboratory conditions to measure the degree of penile tumescence that men experience when viewing pornographic scenes of rape. As part of the test, male subjects are asked to report on the fantasies they had when watching such material. Taken together, the results from these laboratory trials suggest to Russell that the majority 'of male students – not the most violent subpopulation in US culture – admit there is some likelihood that they would rape or sexually assault a woman if they could be assured of getting away with it' (Russell 1992: 326). Shocked by these responses, Russell concludes that *most men have at least some predisposition to rape women*. By any account, this is a drastic inference to make. Faced with such frightening data, Itzin finds it hard to believe that anyone could object to legislation modelled on the Minneapolis ordinance. She observes that lesbian and gay activists were severely critical of the original ordinance because it included within its definition a clause stating that 'the use of men . . . or transsexuals in the place of women is also pornography' (Itzin 1992a: 443). Given that same-sex desire remains oppressed and stigmatized at many levels of society, many lesbian and gay campaigners understandably feared that any appeal to the law would simply extend the power of the state to persecute sexual minorities. In 1985, for example, the London Metropolitan Police conducted a raid on Gay's the Word Bookshop, seizing over a thousand sundry titles, including classic works of literature, gay erotica, and life-saving information about safer sex. This police raid certainly accentuated the vexed question of what materials count as 'pornographic' in the eyes of the law. Similarly, gay male practitioners of consensual sadomasochism (SM) in the UK have been particularly vulnerable to state violence in recent years. In 1990, after the police seized a video tape made for private circulation among a group engaging in consensual SM, the Director of Public Prosecutions brought charges that resulted in prison sentences. But Itzin will have no truck with defences made in the name of oppressed sexual communities in the light of such events. 'These gays and lesbians', she writes, 'apparently believe their right to use sadistic pornography takes precedence over considerations of sexual violence to women and sex discrimination' (Itzin 1992a: 444). From what Itzin says, it would appear that the battle lines in this debate are drawn up between lesbian and gay libertarians, on the one hand, and feminist supporters of women's civil rights, on the other.

This, however, is a distorted picture. If Dworkin and MacKinnon's ordinance has been loudly contested by any political movement, then that challenge has come from another wing of feminism – a feminism which claims that such legislation will only worsen women's lives, especially by appealing to legal institutions that have traditionally paid little respect towards women's sexual freedoms. By implying that her work speaks on behalf of all feminists, therefore, Itzin fails to represent the views of women committed to an altogether different model of civil liberties and sexual emancipation. So at this juncture we need to examine briefly those feminist positions that contest the belief that 'pornography is the theory, rape the practice'.

In their lucid pamphlet, *Pornography and Feminism* (1991), the British collective Feminists against Censorship argue that Dworkin and MacKinnon stand at the vanguard of a movement that seriously fails to question the cause-and-effect model that supposedly explains what pornography is and does. Although they unquestionably accept that pornography causes considerable offence to many women, Feminists against Censorship observe that it is misguided to assert that graphic sexual images necessarily encourage male consumers to perform violent sexual assaults. The problem, as they see it, lies in the way supporters of the Dworkin–MacKinnon ordinance maintain two erroneous beliefs. The first is that society constructs gender differences in bleakly dualistic terms, making men into active abusers and women passive victims. The second is that pornography brainwashes men. Both beliefs, claim Feminists against Censorship, assume the same deterministic logic. What is more, they state that each of these beliefs betrays a naïve behaviourism. 'Behaviourists', the collective notes, 'believe that attitudes and responses are the result of "conditioning" or education'. In this respect, one might reflect for a moment on Itzin's approach to sexual 'conditioning': 'Women are coercively and painfully socialized into femininity'. Likewise, Itzin argues: 'Women are conditioned to conform to the stereotyped images of femininity and womanhood in such a way that they are often unaware that they are misrepresented and mistreated' (Itzin 1992b: 61–2).

Confronting such 'behaviourist' psychology, Feminists against Censorship accept that 'it is true that we *learn* to behave in certain ways'. Yet they add a crucial caveat by stressing how 'behaviourists miss out the vital element of self-consciousness, reflective and reasoning power *and* emotional response' (Feminists against Censorship 1991: 34–5). Their scepticism towards behaviourism means that they seriously doubt the findings that Itzin and Russell garner to support the view that pornography creates a 'proclivity to rape'. 'The evidence from psychological experiments', write Feminists against Censorship, 'is conflicting and unsatisfactory'. Noting that this type of laboratory-based research 'must be treated with caution', the collective identifies three main limitations to these psychological inquiries.

1   These experiments pay little attention to the fact that the interviews are full of leading questions: 'The subjects may "report" what they think the experimenter wants to hear'.
2   These reports do not indicate whether non-pornographic violence causes arousal.
3   The studies are conducted in entirely artificial conditions, failing to reveal where pornography fits into men's everyday lives.

Furthermore, these scientific investigations do not entertain the idea that 'pornography offers a form of release to those who might *otherwise* commit acts of violence' (Feminists against Censorship 1991: 53).

What action, then, do Feminists against Censorship feel should be taken on pornography? Having questioned the fundamental behaviourist assumptions underpinning the belief that 'pornography is the theory, rape the practice', they conclude that Dworkin 'has got the problem turned upside down' (Feminists against Censorship 1991: 67). 'Pornography', they state, 'may mirror the sexism of society but did not create it'. From their point of view, if feminists use legislation to protect women from pornography, then the consequences for the free expression of women's sexuality could be considerable. To their minds, just at the point when women are beginning to take greater control of their sexual lives, attacks on pornography threaten to restrict even further sexually explicit materials that adult women may themselves enjoy. 'Many women', they contend, 'are taking risks to produce feminist sexual images, images which do not exploit either the viewer or the producer' (Feminists against Censorship 1991: 74). Consequently, they regard pornography as completely the wrong target for feminist campaigns against patriarchal dominance. Demanding greater freedom of expression in all areas of society, Feminists against Censorship urge that 'the real battle is elsewhere: it is the battle against public and private violence, against unequal pay structures, against a lack of opportunities for girls and women' (Feminists against Censorship 1991: 75).

Set side by side, the Dworkin–MacKinnon ordinance and the pamphlet by Feminists against Censorship bring into very sharp focus contrasting approaches to pornography and its complicated relations to both sexual inequality and sexual desire. Some feminist critics, however, have been troubled by the polarized nature of this debate, and have therefore sought to establish a middle ground that accepts aspects of both the anti-pornography and anti-censorship viewpoints. One writer who mediates between these antithetical positions is Drucilla Cornell, an American legal theorist. Cornell argues that all human subjects should have the right to an 'imaginary domain' in which they can operate on a day-to-day basis without being systematically oppressed because of their class, race, gender or any other perceived mark of difference. In developing this concept of an 'imaginary domain', Cornell draws on Lacanian psychoanalytic thought to emphasize the struggles each and every one of us endures in our search for a coherent and sustaining self-image. She contends that, when pornography is displayed in the public sphere, it makes for 'enforced viewing' that wrongly encroaches both 'on psychic space and on bodily integrity' (Cornell 1995: 104–5). In Cornell's view, this is a rather different argument from saying that pornography is basically offensive to women. Instead, her discussion concentrates on types of regulation that permit free access to pornography, if restricting it from emblazoning its images within the public realm. Cornell recommends the practice of 'zoning', a practice which outlaws the imposition of graphic sexual representation on the streets and in the workplace, but which does not prevent retailers from selling erotic materials behind closed doors:

> The type of zoning that I advocate does protect the imaginary domain of each one of us, including those of us who wish to have easy access to pornographic materials. It is important to stress that the justification does not turn on the concept that these materials are offensive. I am more than sympathetic that these materials, even as they present the mainstream heterosexual scene, can be used by viewers in different ways to explore aspects of their sexuality that go way beyond the scene as it is rigidly played out.
>
> (Cornell 1995: 162)

Through this type of 'zoning', Cornell believes that everyone has the maximum opportunity to develop his or her 'imaginary domain'.

Like Feminists against Censorship, Cornell strongly disputes the belief that pornography actualizes or enacts the *real* conditions of women's subordination. Rather, Cornell claims that sexually explicit materials inhabit a realm of *representation*. If we attend closely to the representational qualities of pornography, then it becomes possible to imagine that its graphic erotic content produces, not a literal reality, but a wholesale myth. If this is indeed the case, then could it be that magazines like *Hustler* represent violence against women precisely because men feel anxious and defensive about their own sexualities? Contemplating this question, Cornell turns to psychoanalysis to explain how pornography, especially in its most frenzied forms, obsessively returns heterosexual men to an event that scarred their unconscious at an early age: the traumatic Oedipal discovery that the mother is castrated. 'The pornographic scene', argues Cornell, 'has to be repeated because the Phallic Mother, pushed under, dismembered, ripped apart, will always return on the level of the unconscious' (Cornell 1995: 130). Since, on this view, some heterosexual men still find it psychically difficult to imagine that the mother is not phallic, pornography exploits this fantasy by reactivating an erotic rage that reduces what was once a source of unconditional maternal love to a distressing site of castratory absence.

Cornell is hardly alone in maintaining this psychoanalytic viewpoint. English writer Angela Carter (1940–1992) takes a similar critical approach to the psychic anguish men experience when consuming violent pornography: 'The whippings, the beatings, the gougings, the stabbings of erotic violence reawaken the memory of the social fiction of the female wound, the bleeding scar left by her castration, which is a psychic fiction as deeply at the heart of Western culture as the myth of Oedipus, to which it is related in the complex dialectic of imagination and reality that produces culture' (Carter 1979: 23). Seen from this Freudian position, the Oedipal rage against the mother also involves the boy's anxiety about his own symbolic castration: the loss of the vital organ that represents the privilege of male power. Bearing this point in mind, Lynne Segal remarks that, when using pornography, men are probably in 'need of reassurance through fantasies of control over others' (Segal 1992: 77). She maintains that, in arguing '[a]gainst feminist anti-pornography discourse on the power and danger of male sexual domination, it is crucial to emphasize how the phallus as a symbol functions primarily to hide, as well as to create and sustain, the severe anxieties and fears attaching to the penis' (Segal 1992: 83). She implies that there is much to be gained politically by demystifying the conflicted relationship between the penis and phallus. In other words, there needs to be a developed discussion of how and why the male sexual organ will never measure up to the mythical power accorded to it.

Pursuing a similar insight, Linda Williams suggests that pornographic films, rather than displaying a sexual reality, frequently strive to represent erotic acts that are by definition impossible to visualize. The author of a comprehensive study of different genres of hard-core pornography, Williams observes that, if there was one moment that hard-core genres seek to capture, then it is 'the climactic "it" of ultimate pleasure': the ejaculating penis caught in the 'money shot' (Williams 1992: 242). But these films reveal that the pinnacle of pleasure represented by the 'money shot' is 'a paradoxical confession'. Reflecting on the way countless works of this kind stage the highly prized 'money shot', Williams contends:

> For while it ['the money shot'] afforded a perfect vision and knowledge of one genital organ's pleasure, the climax and achievement of a final sexual aim, this aim quite literally missed its mark: the genitals of its object. In fact, the 'object'

of masculine desire and pleasure is often missing altogether
as a visual representation in the frame.

(Williams 1992: 242)

In making this comment, Williams encourages us to think twice
about what might be the precise appeal of pornography to male
heterosexual consumers. On the one hand, this type of sexual representation leads towards the orgasmic penetration of the
woman's genitals. But, on the other, since it is by definition
impossible to bring the man's ejaculatory experience during penetration within the visual field, the 'money shot' is often staged
in incredibly elaborate ways – including the use of slow motion
and multiple angles – to compensate, as much as possible, for
what simply cannot be seen. What is more, the repeated emphasis on male ejaculation in these films surely raises questions about
what the male spectator should feel is the precise object of desire.
Does the man's ejaculation provide the climactic moment when
the male viewer *identifies with* the symbolic superiority of the
phallus? Or does the 'money shot' suggest that this same viewer
desires the penis more than the woman's body? Given how pornographic films devise special techniques for restaging the 'money
shot', it proves difficult to give a definite answer to either question. Since the 'money shot' appears as such a 'paradoxical confession', Williams declares that it animates 'the frenzy of the
visible', the urgency with which pornography struggles to glorify
an ecstatic moment that cannot be captured on film. In her view,
the 'money shot' stands as a perverse substitution which, like
Freud's conception of the fetish, seeks to sustain a desire in the
face of castratory loss. Such, we might think, are the lengths to
which pornography will go when trying to withstand the treacherous 'little death'.

Throughout her full-length study, *Hard Core* (1989), Williams
shows how various cinematic devices routinely employed in
pornographic films follow the elaborate substitutive pattern of

the 'money shot'. Here one might compare the so-called 'meat shot'. This type of shot ushers the camera as far as it can towards the female genitals, attempting to display the woman's sexual pleasure in the closest possible detail. But like the 'money shot', too, this complex visual technique faces a preposterous task. In the 'meat shot', the camera may at times supplant the penis that must be obligingly withdrawn for the purpose of this scene. On other occasions, the camera may give way to someone else's penis penetrating the woman. These multiple substitutions once more accelerate the 'frenzy of the visible':

> [W]e can see that it [the 'meat shot'] oscillates restlessly between genital show and genital event, sometimes signifying climax, culmination, possession, other times signifying the undeniable fact that the 'scopic regime' of cinema cannot depict such climax, culmination, possession, simply because the event of climactic pleasure cannot be shown. Thus we begin to see as well the dynamic of change that the cinematic process of compensation/disavowal involves: since he cannot touch the woman, the spectator gets to see more of her; but seeing more means confronting the hidden 'wonders' of sexual difference, which in turn may create the further need to prove masculinity by watching someone else going *inside*.
>
> (Williams 1989: 83)

Seeing and not seeing, penetrating and withdrawing, compensating and disavowing: these are the contradictory structures that, for Williams, generate ever insatiable but always dissatisfied desires of various pornographic genres. Having viewed many different types of pornographic film, Williams concludes: 'pornography, in formulating sexual pleasure as a problem, with solutions involving the need for further sex and further speculation about sex, begets pornography' (Williams 1989: 276). So, in aiming to ascertain the ultimate truth of sex, pornography only uncovers interminable erotic mysteries it feels driven to explore.

Given that pornography has an exceptional capacity to produce 'further speculation about sex', its investigatory impulses understandably extend well beyond the libidinal circuit where 'money shots' and 'meat shots' are routinely displayed for male heterosexual consumption. In its restless pursuit of sexual knowledge, pornography reaches out towards many other bodily zones and somatic pleasures. Some pornographic films, Williams emphasizes, are not compulsively drawn to the genitals. Films featuring SM, for example, focus more on structures of domination and submission than genital pleasure. In depicting active and passive erotic role-playing, SM pornography frequently represents a 'performance of perverse desires which do not follow the expected routes of sexual identity (hetero or homo) or gender (male or female) that keeps the viewer and protagonists guessing about desires and pleasures that take surprising twists and turns' (Williams 1992: 250–1). Such films, argues Williams, clearly require a comprehensive analysis that shows exactly why pornography enables sexual fantasy to fluctuate between a range of identificatory positions. She states that Jean Laplanche and Jean-Bertrand Pontalis' well-known essay, 'Fantasy and the Origins of Sexuality' (1986 [1964]), provides a useful paradigm for thinking about how all phantasmatic projections involve rapid movements between the subject and object, between the self and other. 'Fantasy', argue Laplanche and Pontalis, 'is not the object of desire, but its setting. In fantasy the subject does not pursue the object or its signs: he appears caught up in the sequences of images' (Laplanche and Pontalis 1986: 26). In other words, this psychoanalytic model suggests that in fantasy the subject may, as it were, experience the pleasures of being 'desubjectivized'.

Since the huge market for pornography widens well beyond the heterosexual 'stag film', Williams suggests that erotic representations such as 'bi' and 'sadie-max' (SM) pornography open up innovative possibilities for people of many different sexualities to enjoy desires not forever beholden to the phallus. Although she feels it might be rather utopian to believe that pornography will necessarily serve as an instrument of sexual liberation, it remains the case that a company led by women, such as Femme Productions, was established '[b]ecause heterosexual women wanted better sexual fantasies' than the ones previously available in the 'males-only' genre (Williams 1992: 283). In putting forward these arguments, Williams is clearly building on advances made in film theory set within a psychoanalytic framework. By employing some of Freud's and Lacan's leading concepts, Williams maintains that the field of pornographic representation remains full of identificatory conflicts, preventing the straight male viewer from adopting a singular perspective on the imaginary spectacle set before him.

But in explaining the visually frenzied condition of sexual fantasy, Williams also alludes to a body of theoretical inquiry that would contest many of the assumptions made by psychoanalytic criticism. Her powerful idea that pornography strives to produce ever-increasing amounts of knowledge to discover the 'truth' of sex owes much to the work of Michel Foucault. Repeatedly, Foucault argues that Freudian paradigms merely describe and thereby perpetuate the sexual desires they seek to understand. Hardly convinced that psychoanalysis is a radical critical method, Foucault urges us to demystify the categories – such as the Oedipus and castration complexes – through which we have come to comprehend desire. If we do so, he argues, then we can at last break free from the despotic 'agency of sex' (Foucault 1978: 157). Rather than accept that sexuality is in any way based on the conflicted libidinal forces, Foucault asks why the West has associated sexual desire with the system of (de)generating pleasures I have been tracing here, all the way from John Donne to contemporary feminism. In his far-reaching work, Foucault invites us to think hard about the ways in which 'sex', 'sexuality', and 'pornography' emerged in the first place, about the interests they have served, and about the kinds of power they continue to relay. Above all, he demands that we consider the discursive operations that shape and mould contemporary perceptions of sexuality as a site of repression and liberation. The next chapter examines Foucault's supreme scepticism towards sexuality as a matter of life and death.

4

DISCURSIVE DESIRES

FOUCAULT'S BODIES

Ever since its original publication in France as *La volonté de savoir* (*The Will to Knowledge*), the introductory volume to *The History of Sexuality* (1978 [1976]) by Michel Foucault has been a source of highly contentious debate. This remarkable book contests established theoretical orthodoxies about social control and repression developed by widely differing schools of Marxist and psychoanalytic thought. Little wonder, then, that Foucault's writing remains troubling to many intellectuals, since he refuses either to employ the dialectical materialism of Marx or to affirm the psychical realities elaborated by Freud. Neither class struggle nor the unconscious has a fundamental role to play in Foucault's assiduous critique of eroticism in the West. It is his goal to reveal how analyses of the class struggle and the unconscious, dear to Marxism and Freudianism respectively, are enmeshed in the very systems of power they seek to explain. In Foucault's work, therefore, the term sexuality provides the focus for indicating why Marx and Freud fail to see the ways in which their respective works re-impose the cultural laws they are striving to analyse.

Not surprisingly, Foucault has made a great many intellectual enemies. Yet even his harshest critics would hardly deny that his pathbreaking inquiry into the emergence and mobilization of the nineteenth-century term sexuality has completely transformed how we might think about the meaning of desire. It is fair to claim that Foucault, who completed three volumes of *The History of Sexuality* before his untimely death in 1984, was the first modern intellectual to present a critical paradigm that broke decisively with the sexological and subsequent psychoanalytic models that assumed dominance in both academic and popular cultures. Few disciplines have remained untouched by his inventive reflections on sexuality, and the ideas concisely sketched in his fascinating introductory volume have prompted productive exchanges between theorists working in fields as diverse as literary studies and political science. For it is in his introduction to *The History of Sexuality* that Foucault's arguments ask us to contemplate, not only why sexuality became such a focus of concern in the past hundred years, but also how sexuality concentrated extremely potent transfers of power that have exerted considerable influence on the regulation of the social order.

By emphasizing issues of power in his introduction to *The History of Sexuality*, Foucault extends his longstanding concern with the means through which institutions produce strategic methods of control to induce docility in the social body. Among his distinguished earlier writings is *The Birth of the Clinic: An Archaeology of Medical Perception* (1963), a study that examines how the medical gaze exerts specific forms of power over the human body. More than twenty years later, Foucault pursued this line of thinking in relation to the incarcerating designs of social institutions. Throughout *Discipline and Punish: The Birth of the Prison* (1977a [1975]), he asks us to consider how 'prisons resemble factories, schools, barracks, hospitals, which all resemble prisons' (Foucault 1977a: 228). Employing a theoretical vocabulary already brought into sharp focus in his methodological study, *The Archaeology of Knowledge* (1972 [1971]), Foucault's *The History of Sexuality* explains for the first time in some detail how power circulates within the social order through *discourse*. By employing such terms as discourse, discursive formation, and discursive regime, Foucault is alluding to historically variable ways of speaking, talking, and writing that function systematically – if, at times, contradictorily – to articulate what is desirable and undesirable, legitimate and illegitimate, within a culture.

To show the distinguishing features of Foucault's leading claims about the expressly discursive condition of desire, this chapter explores the principal arguments he makes against Marxism and psychoanalysis in his introduction to *The History of Sexuality*. Since Foucault's fascination with the links between discourse, knowledge, and power has scarcely passed without serious criticism, the central section of the present discussion surveys several Marxist, feminist, and post-colonial objections to his highly disputed model of domination, subordination, and resistance. But even if Foucault's writing remains polemical because of its supposed failure to ground his analysis in traditional categories of class, gender, and race, his writings have none the less powerfully shaped the critical work of contemporary sex radicals who have traced the institutional strategies, discursive formations, and structures of power/knowledge that maintain the dominance of heterosexuality. If *The History of Sexuality* has been instrumental in shaping any field of inquiry, then its presence is assuredly most visible in queer theory, a field of study that has flourished since the early 1990s, and which takes Foucault's lead in resisting the naturalizing assumptions that undergird normative sexual behaviours. There is no doubt that Foucault's significance for queer theory lies in the particular emphasis he puts on the discursive construction of eroticism, especially how and why desire has been damagingly constrained by the ways in which we have come to talk and think about a late nineteenth-century word, sexuality, particularly in its limited dualistic 'homo-' and 'hetero-' forms.

So how might we begin to approach Foucault's innovative

model of sexuality? A handful of selected passages in *The History of Sexuality* clarifies his leading claims. Roughly two-thirds of the way through his succinct introductory study, Foucault explicitly states his view of sexuality:

> Sexuality must not be described as a stubborn drive, by nature alien and of necessity disobedient to a power which exhausts itself trying to subdue it and often fails to control it entirely. It appears rather as an especially dense transfer point for relations of power: between men and women, young people and old people, parents and offspring, teachers and students, priests and laity, an administration and a population. Sexuality is not the most intractable element in power relations, but rather one of those endowed with the greatest instrumentality: useful for the greatest number of manoeuvres and capable of serving as a point of support, as a linchpin, for the most varied strategies.
>
> There is no single, all-encompassing strategy, valid for all of society and uniformly bearing on all the manifestations of sex. For example, the idea that there have been repeated attempts, by various means, to reduce all of sex to its reproductive function, its heterosexual and adult form, and its matrimonial legitimacy fails to take into account the manifold objectives aimed for, the manifold means employed in the different sexual politics concerned with the two sexes, the different age groups and social classes.
>
> (Foucault 1978: 103)

Rather than assume, as sexology and psychoanalysis do, that sexuality is a surging hydraulic force that Western culture struggles to repress, Foucault exposes what this particular belief about eroticism tells us of the ways power is distributed, mediated, and produced within modern culture. That is why Foucault wishes to situate sexuality as a concept that serves as a 'dense transfer point for relations of power'.

Foucault, therefore, demonstrates how and why eroticism is bound into structures of inequality. But lest we think these relations of power involve a static disparity between those who rule and those who are subordinated in an assortment of institutional settings, Foucault is quick to add that beliefs about sexuality do not necessarily produce decisive and unchangeable inequalities between groups of individuals. He states it is inadvisable to attribute the dominance of a sexual institution such as heterosexual marriage to one all-determining source, such as the belief that opposite-sex relations gained hegemony in Western society simply because of a cultural imperative to reproduce. There are, as Foucault insists, adjacent reasons for the privilege accorded to this organized form of sexuality, reasons that point to the cultural management of differences between men and women, between generations, and between classes. Foucault's point becomes clear if we trace the transformation of the family from the Renaissance to the present. The history of the Western family reveals that contemporary ideals of the companionate marriage based on romantic love began in the eighteenth century to supersede earlier familial models that placed greater stress on extensive ties of kinship and economic exchange. Any discussion of heterosexual marriage consequently entails a wide variety of considerations about where relations of power reside, depending on the epoch in which such relations emerge. Viewed through this interpretative lens, the concept of sexuality crystallizes the idea that there are indeed precise – if historically contingent – divisions that separate the sexes, generations, and classes from one another. But given the complex manner in which these differentials of power may intersect only to contradict one another, the relations in question remain in a dynamic and active condition. Hence Foucault argues that critical inquiries into sexuality must be sensitive to the non-uniformity between miscellaneous types of privilege and deprivation. Class, generation, race, and sex – just to give some of the main categories for mapping understandings of sexuality – are factors that can complicate our knowledge of how power is distributed in the West. Therefore it becomes possible to grasp exceptionally complex reconfigurations of dominance and subordination when we explore the interfaces between these multiple coordinates of power. Such a model, he claims, has a distinct advantage over one that appeals to the vertical binary of an inert, 'top-down' hierarchy neatly split between mastery and subordination.

Foucault elaborates this analysis to bear out his basic premise: that sex, far from having been silenced from the Middle Ages onwards through Christian imperatives to purge sinful fleshliness, has been the subject of an overwhelming explosion of discourse. Much as we might like to believe that a prudish Victorian culture did everything it could to silence sexuality (from devising techniques to prohibit masturbation in women and children to putting draperies to hide the sexual suggestiveness of piano legs), Foucault shatters the illusion that this wholehearted effort aimed to repress volatile desires. Instead, he claims that sexuality was in that period the subject of an immense verbosity, so that the desire to silence sex itself paradoxically became an almost unstoppable discourse. Focusing on this intriguing contradiction, Foucault states that the desire to speak about the repressed nature of sex participates in the very structure it is seeking to decipher. Here is how he elucidates what he calls this 'incitement to discourse':

> Rather than the uniform concern to hide sex, rather than a general prudishness of language, what distinguishes these last three centuries is the variety, the wide dispersion of devices that were invented for speaking about it, for having it be spoken about, for inducing it to speak of itself, for listening, recording, transcribing, and redistributing what is said about it: around sex, a whole network of varying, specific, and coercive transpositions into discourse. Rather than a massive censorship, beginning with the verbal properties imposed by the

> Age of Reason, what was involved was a regulated and poly-
> morphous incitement to discourse.
>
> (Foucault 1978: 34)

These comments pinpoint an acute tension in the manner in
which sex has been discussed in the West for the past 150 years.
The more modern Western culture devised methods for speaking
about the unspeakability of sex, the more sex itself became a type
of open secret, ushering into the public domain a scandal that
had to be masked. Such a view shows that censorship may in
some respects achieve the reverse of its aims. Not only does censorship condemn sexuality to silence, it must also articulate precisely what it subjugates to the rule of law. This is one of the
ruses that affects many legal pronouncements which are obliged
to give voice to locutions considered unlawful. Take, for instance,
how in the United States members of the military in the mid-
1990s can lose their jobs for uttering the words 'I am homosexual'. The law that censures this disclosure must itself articulate the
words 'I am homosexual' in order to denounce them. On this
model, sexuality becomes the site on which contradictory transfers of power occur, whereby the court that holds the power of the
law must, at least in theory, commit the crime it condemns. It
should be clear, then, that Foucault has no patience at all with
what he names the 'repressive hypothesis'. How could a society be
sexually repressed when there has been such an 'incitement to
discourse' on this very belief?

To support this overarching argument, Foucault examines
four nineteenth-century phenomena that fix attention on how
the exercise of power operates through complex discourses surrounding sexuality. In discussing these examples, he claims we
see clear manifestations of an 'era of "biopower"', an era when
there was 'an explosion of numerous and diverse techniques for
achieving the subjugation of bodies and the control of popula-
tions' (Foucault 1978: 140). First, he observes how the 'feminine

body was analyzed – qualified and disqualified – as being thoroughly saturated with sexuality' – a point that has already become apparent to us through the discussion of several late-Victorian sexological tracts in Chapter 1. This 'hysterization of women's bodies' served multiple but related functions: the maintenance of an 'organic communication' with the social body, with the family, and with children. To sustain each respective sphere, women's bodies were placed under careful scrutiny, ensuring their reproductive capacity, fitness as wives, and healthiness as mothers. In a similar vein, Foucault recognizes how transfers of power were especially active in what he calls the 'pedagogization of children's sex': that is, placing the child's body under surveillance to create the contradictory knowledge that, even though it was the case that children would masturbate as a matter of course, such behaviour was at the same time deemed contrary to nature, and thus had to be stopped. Not only parents and families intervened on this subject to educate the child's desires, but also doctors, psychologists, and teachers would develop disapproving views on the topic. Children's sexuality, therefore, presented itself as a threat that had to be contained. Third, a 'socialization of procreative behaviour' came into operation to ensure that heterosexual intercourse was increasingly bound to discourses espousing moral responsibility: following the lead of the theorist of population control, Thomas Malthus (1766–1834), society increasingly encouraged parents to produce children in appropriate circumstances. This Malthusian logic persisted into the twentieth century as married couples came under growing pressure to employ various types of birth-control (condoms, the oestrogen pill, spermicides, and vasectomy, among many others). Lastly, Foucault identifies a 'psychiatrization of perverse pleasure', whereby sexual instinct was granted an autonomous status, leading to research that sought to separate its healthy manifestations from distinctly pathological ones. On this basis, then, 'the hysterical woman, the masturbating child, the Malthusian couple, and the perverse adult' serve as the prominent formations where sexuality emerges as a technique of control in the nineteenth century (Foucault 1978: 104–5).

Read in isolation from the rest of his study, Foucault's enumeration of these four figures of sexuality may imply exactly the kind of functionalism that his theory of power wishes to debunk. It is not unfair to claim that his emphasis on how each sexual type was used as an instrument of state control and institutional manipulation could all too readily suggest that these bodies were completely in thrall to the law that kept them under close observation. To make sure that his work does not fall foul of this mistaken criticism, Foucault devotes a great part of his inquiry to explaining why the forms of power he is analysing are certainly not founded on a top-down model of subjection where law – either in cultural or statist forms – always succeeds in imposing authority from above. Instead, he insists that power is a distinctly *productive* relation, one that creates resistance in the same moment as it exerts force:

> Power comes from below; that is, there is no binary and all-encompassing opposition between rulers' and ruled at the root of power relations, and serving as a general matrix – no such duality extending from the top down and reacting on more and more limited groups to the very depths of the social body. One must suppose rather that the manifold relationships of force that take shape and come into play in the machinery of production, in families, limited groups, and institutions, are the basis for wide-ranging effects of cleavage that run through the social body as a whole.
>
> (Foucault 1978: 94)

This passage makes one point clear. If we believed that power managed to contain its subjects on a purely top-down basis, then we would have a remarkably monolithic understanding of how certain ideological forces gained ascendancy and managed to subdue opposing forces. Instead, Foucault argues for a nuanced comprehension of how contradictions fracture oppressors and oppressed, not in an us-versus-them dialectic, but in their 'strictly relational character'. In his view, the existence of power relations depends on 'a multiplicity of points of resistance':

> [T]hese play the role of adversary, target, support, or handle in power relations. These points of resistance are present everywhere in the power network. Hence there is no single locus of great Refusal, no soul of revolt, source of all rebellions, or pure law of the revolutionary. Instead there is a plurality of resistances, each of them a special case: resistances that are possible, necessary, improbable; others that are spontaneous, savage, solitary, concerted, rampant, or violent; still others that are quick to compromise, interested, or sacrificial; by definition, they can only exist in the strategic field of power relations. But this does not mean that they are only a reaction or rebound, forming with respect to the basic domination an underside that is in the end always passive, doomed to perpetual defeat.

> (Foucault 1978: 96)

In detailing this structure, Foucault implicitly condemns earlier political models that pitted the slave against the master (as in Hegel's *Phenomenology of Spirit* [1807]), and the proletariat against the capitalists (as in the *Communist Manifesto* [1848] by Friedrich Engels [1820–1895] and Marx). From his perspective, Hegel's and Marx's binarized methods for examining power can only fail to comprehend the complexity of a phenomenon such as sexuality.

How, then, might we grasp the intricate 'relational character of power relationships' in the context of sexuality? One of the most famous examples from the first volume of *The History of Sexuality* should make Foucault's distinctive perspective on power clear. In the chapter titled 'The Deployment of Sexuality', Foucault identifies several 'rules' or 'cautionary prescriptions' alerting us to how sexuality has served as a locus for the exercise of power. One of these 'rules' refers to the 'tactical polyvalence of discourses'. This heading points to the ways in which 'discourse can be both an instrument and an effect of power, but also a hindrance, a stumbling-block, a point of resistance and a starting point for an opposing strategy'. To illustrate how power can operate in polyvalent – and consequently paradoxical – ways, Foucault turns to the classification, stigmatization, and surveillance of sexual perversions in the late-nineteenth century:

> There is no question that the appearance in nineteenth-century psychiatry, jurisprudence, and literature of a whole series of discourses on the species and subspecies of homosexuality, inversion, pederasty, and 'psychic hermaphroditism' made possible a strong advance of social controls into this area of 'perversity'; but it also made possible the formation of a 'reverse' discourse: homosexuality began to speak in its own behalf, to demand that its legitimacy or 'naturality' be acknowledged, often in the same vocabulary, using the same categories by which it was medically disqualified.
>
> (Foucault 1978: 101)

Here Foucault claims that no sooner had a dominant pathologizing discourse sought to disqualify homosexuality than a resistant discourse of sexual liberation declared that same-sex desire was a completely natural condition. The very discourse that sought to produce a regulative order managed to empower those it sought to subjugate. In other words, sexological categories could cut either way, depending on who was deploying them. On the one hand, the term 'homosexual' could be used as a clinical definition, thus making men and women who desired their own sex into subjects of disease. On the other, 'homosexuality' could be professed as an entirely healthy congenital condition, thus giving a sexual minority a platform on which to develop concerted campaigns for emancipation.

But historical evidence reveals that there is a significant problem with Foucault's model of 'reverse' discourse. He incorrectly implies that homosexuals were espousing themselves to an identity first devised by doctors, psychiatrists, and social scientists to deleterious ends. For homosexual liberationists were pioneers in theorizing same-sex desire. As Chapter 1 points out, the sex radical Karl Heinrich Ulrichs never used the term homosexuality (see pp. 19–26). Instead, he established the idea that 'man–manly love' was a wholly natural form of inversion, whereby a female soul inhabited a male body. Similarly, the person who conjured the word homosexuality itself, Karoly Benkert (1824–82), was a Hungarian sex radical who maintained a correspondence with Ulrichs. Benkert's earliest use of the word homosexual has been traced to 1869. Such information clearly indicates that it was the sexologists, not the emancipationists, who engaged in a 'reverse' discourse. Krafft-Ebing and his peers seized 'homosexuality' as a term from campaigners seeking to liberate same-sex desire, and thus this category was promptly put into a clinical frame of reference. Yet it must be added that such details do not necessarily invalidate Foucault's general point that power can be refracted through discourse, showing how it is not always burdened by a repressive sovereign law. Instead, power remains in a complex 'polyvalent' condition, as the concept of 'reverse' discourse demonstrates.

If Foucault's 'relational' and thus 'polyvalent' concept of power contests Marxist views of the binary nature of class struggle, then his attack on the belief that power involves submission to a sovereign law is directly angled at psychoanalysis. In his view, a huge theoretical effort was made in the past two hundred years to associate sexuality with an unbending rule of law that sought to put it under severe scrutiny, and psychoanalysis merely confirmed this trend. Yet he argues that, to understand the affiliation between law, psychoanalysis, and sexuality, we require a much broader appreciation of how Western culture was striving to preserve the social order. At one point, Foucault claims that the subjection of sexuality coincided with the late-nineteenth-century scientific discourse of eugenics that spawned racial ideologies, ones that would culminate most terrifyingly in fascism. He argues that sexuality and racism were intertwined. Although this connection between sexuality and racism may at first sound abstruse, there is, he believes, a significant link between the two. The connection is made through the resonant word blood, a word that reveals how the middle classes were compelled to establish their political power on two fronts. First, the bourgeoisie absorbed and transformed the established aristocratic model of patrilineage by 'determining good marriages', 'inducing the desired fertilities', and 'ensuring the health and longevity of children', thus strengthening their ties of blood. Second, the bourgeoisie increasingly respected the 'mythical concern with protecting the purity of the blood and ensuring the triumph of the race' (Foucault 1978: 148–9). The link between these two formations can be best understood if we consider how both incest and racial miscegenation were issues of enduring concern during this period. These two practices were systematically outlawed to uphold sexual purity and respectability, thereby maintaining class and racial power.

If we bear in mind the resonant meanings of 'blood', then it becomes easier to comprehend Foucault's searching critique of psychoanalysis. As Chapter 2 shows, Freud's investigation into the psyche to a large degree broke with the pathologizing tendencies of sexological research. But, in Foucault's view, Freud's inquiries into sexual maturation make perpetual appeals to the cultural laws that regulate the erotic identifications unconsciously achieved by individual subjects. Foucault stresses how the whole apparatus of the Freudian Oedipus and castration complexes (see pp. 62–83), no matter how critical of earlier theories of sexual perversion and degeneration, assimilate prevailing assumptions about the indissociable link between sexuality and cultural prohibition:

> It is to the political credit of psychoanalysis – or at least, of what was most coherent in it – that it regarded with suspicion (and this from its inception, that is, from the moment it broke away from the neuropsychiatry of degenerescence) the irrevocably proliferating aspects which might be contained in these power mechanisms, aimed at controlling and administering the everyday life of sexuality; whence the Freudian endeavour (out of reaction no doubt to the great surge of racism that was contemporary with it) to ground sexuality in the law – the law of alliance, tabooed consanguinity, and the Sovereign-Father, in short, to surround desire with all the trappings of the old order of power. It was owing to this that psychoanalysis was – in the main, with a few exceptions – in theoretical and practical opposition to fascism. But this position of psychoanalysis was tied to a specific historical conjuncture.
>
> (Foucault 1978: 150)

As Foucault says, Freud repudiated the late-nineteenth-century belief that sexuality could be understood in terms of preserving the blood of the race through eugenic efforts to purify and strengthen offspring. Yet here Foucault claims that, in contesting such racialized thought, Freud none the less advanced the view that sexuality was subject to cultural prohibitions that governed an extremely complicated field of erotic identifications between parents and children. In other words, no matter how much psychoanalysis wanted to separate sexuality from a set of laws that upheld the survival of the bourgeoisie's racialized blood, Freud nevertheless elaborated a system of complexes that determined specific erotic identifications which kept sexuality within an abstract framework of prohibition. To Foucault, this particular characteristic of psychoanalytic thought paradoxically binds it to precisely the logic championed by the racist movement to which Freudian thinking was concertedly opposed: namely fascism, which built its horrific politics on the preservation of Aryan purity. Foucault's observation certainly aims to show how deeply Western culture was saturated by the belief that sexuality was defined against a series of injunctions that did their utmost to regulate desire. But the drastic counter-intuitive logic of Foucault's claim may well say more about his own resistance to psychoanalytic laws than its does about Freud's concerted efforts to comprehend group psychology under coercive regimes (see Freud, *Group Psychology and the Analysis of the Ego* [1921] XVIII: 67–143).

Yet it is not just the manner in which psychoanalysis keeps sexuality trapped in a system of subjugating laws that concerns Foucault. He argues that Freud's research into the unconscious simultaneously extends a parallel regulatory model that, since the time of the Middle Ages, has been in place to comprehend human sexuality. The regulatory model in question is the religious confession instituted by the Roman Catholic church. Just as it had sought to interpret the repressed condition of sexuality through the governing mechanisms of cultural law, psychoanalysis exploited the form of the case history already used for some time by sexologists. To Foucault, the case history is simply a modern version of the religious confession that reveals the truth of sinful transgressions. In his view, psychoanalysis builds on the established structure of confession to accentuate how sexual activity is a repressed phenomenon that must be brought into the liberating light of open inquiry. As Foucault declares, in Freud's work 'the great requirement of confession that had taken form so long ago assumed the new meaning of an injunction to lift psychical repression' (Foucault 1978: 130). No one, he suggests, could underestimate the powerful grip that the 'repressive hypothesis' upon which psychoanalysis was based would have on twentieth-century thought. Foucault mentions the notable consequence Freud's research had on the work of the left-wing social theorist Wilhelm Reich (1897–1957). In studies such as *The Invasion of Compulsory Sex-Morality* (1971 [1931]) and *The Sexual Revolution: Towards a Self-Regulating Character Structure* (1945), Reich claimed that society could only be revolutionized if we committed ourselves to a wholehearted anti-repressive struggle that emancipated sexual desire. 'If', writes Reich in 1931, 'there is a lack of social possibilities for genital gratification and sublimation, if the psychic apparatus has been distorted by educational influences to such an extent that it cannot make use of existing possibilities', then the 'results are neuroses, perversions, pathological changes of character, antisocial manifestations of genital life, and, not least, work disturbances' (Reich 1971: 154). From Foucault's perspective, such a theory represented only 'a tactical shift and reversal in the great deployment of sexuality', indicating how Reich's writings were mired in a well-established myth that inextricably linked eroticism with cultural prohibition.

Similar assertions appear in the subsequent two volumes of *The History of Sexuality*, both of which were published in France in 1984. These later volumes, however, lead back to a period well before the emergence of sexology. *The Use of Pleasure* (Volume 2) and *The Care of the Self* (Volume 3) examine the organization of eroticism in antiquity, hundreds of years before the West had granted a name to sexuality. These works bear out a number of illuminating points that form part of Foucault's larger political project to dismantle the hazardous assumptions underpinning modern conceptions of sexuality. Foucault indicates how the modern 'deployment of sexuality' cannot explain the erotic lives of the Greeks and Greco–Romans. Foucault accentuates several ideas about the classical 'use of pleasure' and 'care of the self' that are highly instructive for an analysis of desire in modern Western culture. Both of these classical precepts, he believes, challenge the legalistic prohibitions that throughout the twentieth century have regulated sexuality. If we take a small selection of key passages from these two volumes, together with statements Foucault made in contemporaneous interviews, it becomes possible to see more clearly why his analysis of classical cultures formed part of an ambitious venture to disjoin the modern association of sexuality with systematic interdictions.

In *The Use of Pleasure*, Foucault devotes the larger part of his discussion to the ethical issues raised by sexual relations between male citizens and boys, women, and slaves in ancient Greece. Although the free adult male had the right to penetrate anyone belonging to an inferior group, he had to attend scrupulously to a healthy erotic life in the name of ethically strengthening his self. This concept of ethical strength, however, should not be confused with the narrow modern conception of health as the elimination and prevention of disease. Foucault points out that in classical Greece erotic conduct was organized in terms that demanded the painstaking and thereby healthy exercise of power by the free adult male. A male citizen maintained both his self-respect and his social power by deliberating over his right to penetrate anyone of lesser standing. He was also obliged not to allow himself to be penetrated. Although the free adult males had special sexual prerogatives, there were perceived dangers if they engaged too frequently in sex. Foucault explains why:

> The moral reflection of the Greeks on sexual behaviour did not seek to justify interdictions, but to stylize a freedom – that freedom which the 'free' man exercised in his activity. This produced a state of affairs that might well seem paradoxical at first glance: the Greeks practised, accepted, and valued relations between men and boys; and yet their philosophers dealt with the subject by conceiving and elaborating an ethics of abstention. They were quite willing to grant that a married man might go in search of sexual pleasures outside of marriage, and yet their moralists conceived the principle of a matrimonial life in which the husband would have relations only with his own wife.

> They never imagined that sexual pleasure was in itself an evil or
> that it could be counted among the natural stigmata of a trans-
> gression; and yet their doctors worried over the relationship
> between sexual activity and health, and they developed an entire
> theory concerning the dangers of sexual practice.
>
> (Foucault 1985: 97)

Foucault emphasizes that the ancient Greeks did not make cardinal distinctions between 'normal behaviour' and 'abnormal and
pathological practices', although valuations between what constituted good and bad erotic conduct were undoubtedly at stake.
Instead, this society focused on the 'use of pleasures . . . in terms
of a certain way of caring for one's body', and its free men were
advised to follow a 'regimen aimed at regulating an activity that
was recognized as being important for health' (Foucault 1985:
97–8).

In his analysis, Foucault observes the emphasis placed by the
ancient Greeks on the stylization of erotic conduct. At no point,
he claims, did this classical society stress that repression was the
healthy result of abstention. Rather, the most elevated forms of
self-respect were embodied in male citizens who knew how to
master their desires. This self-mastery constituted an 'ethical
attentiveness towards the self, a point of exceptional significance
to a figure who already wielded mighty power over his children,
his slaves, and his wife. As Foucault observes, this mode of ethical
conduct put no uncertain pressure on the free man to become
'stronger than himself':

> We have seen how sexual behaviour was constituted, in Greek
> thought, as a domain of ethical practice in the form of the
> *aphrodisia*, of pleasurable acts situated in an agonistic field of
> forces difficult to control. In order to take the form of a con-
> duct that was rationally and morally admissible, these acts
> required a strategy aimed at an exact self-mastery – as its
> culmination and consummation – whereby the subject would

be 'stronger than himself' even in the power that he exercised over others. Now, the requirement of austerity that was implied by the constitution of the self-disciplined subject was not presented as a universal law, which each and every individual would have to obey, but rather as a principle of stylization of conduct for those who wished to give their existence the most graceful and accomplished form possible.

(Foucault 1985: 250–1)

In *The Care of the Self*, Foucault reiterates many of these principal points, underscoring how in the Greco–Roman world 'the cultivation of the self produced its effect not in the strengthening of that which can thwart desire, but in certain modifications relating to the formative elements of ethical subjectivity' (Foucault 1986: 67). There is no doubt that he gives his seal of approval to classical models of *askesis*: an ancient Greek word signifying a form of self-questioning that requires the male citizen to reflect on his sexual weaknesses, strengths, and potentialities. Especially attractive to Foucault is how this model of 'ethical subjectivity' presents the possibility to enjoy types of sexual pleasure not dominated by an exterior law. *Askesis*, therefore, should not be confused with its more recent derivation, asceticism. In Christian terms, asceticism implies a self-castigating form of renunciation. By comparison, Foucault contends that in Greco–Roman civilization the self-regulation of desires constitutes a liberating autonomy, for such *askesis* creates a realm of freedom over which the male citizen at last maintains control.

Such practices of freedom were often on Foucault's mind during the last ten years of his life, particularly when he turned his attention towards homosexual minorities who were inventing their own communities of pleasure in the face of considerable hostility. In several of the many interviews Foucault granted in the 1980s, he focuses on how the gay male subcultures of New York City and San Francisco provided models for understanding how it is possible to resist the cultural laws that endeavour to prohibit dissident sexual relationships. 'I think', he remarked in 1982, 'what most bothers those who are not gay about gayness is the gay lifestyle, not sex acts themselves'. Since he believes gay subcultures allow men to interact erotically in ways that do not mimic heterosexual monogamy, Foucault observes that it 'is the prospect that gays will create as yet unforeseen kinds of relations that many people cannot tolerate' (Foucault 1989: 332). Among such 'unforeseen' relationships would be casual sex in the public sphere and engaging in sadomasochism (SM). It is when Foucault elaborates his thoughts on the latter sexual practice that one begins to understand why he thinks genuine forms of sexual freedom might come into being. In an interview first published in the US lesbian and gay journal, *The Advocate*, Foucault's questioner raises the following point about forms of experimental sex dedicated to innovative pleasures. 'Can we be sure that these new pleasures won't be exploited in the way advertising uses the stimulation of pleasure as a means of social control?' The interviewer wants to know if there can be 'unforeseen' sexual relationships that are not bound to the regulative mechanisms enacted by cultural prohibitions. Here is Foucault's reply:

> We can never be sure. In fact, we can always be sure *it will happen*, and that everything that has been created or acquired, any ground that has been gained will, at a certain moment be used in such a way. That's the way we live, that's the way we struggle, that's the way of human history. . . . But you are quite right in underlining that we always have to be quite careful and to be aware of the fact that we have to move on to something else, that we have other needs as well. The SM ghetto in San Francisco is a good example of a community that has experimented with, and formed an identity around, pleasure.
>
> (Foucault 1989: 385)

In the same interview, Foucault remarks that SM is 'a process of invention' that involves an 'acting out of power structures by a strategic game that is able to give sexual pleasure or bodily pleasure' (Foucault 1989: 388). Although many critics of SM would claim that the staging of sexual scenes featuring 'masters' and 'slaves' simply duplicates the most bleakly unequal power structures experienced in the everyday world, Foucault argues to the contrary that SM turns those binary power differences against themselves by allowing participants in this 'strategic game' to take control of the erotic charge factored into domination and subordination. Since this is a 'game' with agreed rules, the 'slave' is not *really* a slave, nor the 'master' *really* a master. In such situations, the masochist or 'bottom' is often thought to command more power than the sadist or 'top' precisely because the 'bottom' controls the moment when the punishments have to stop. Apologists for SM insist that expressly consensual sexual practices of this kind involve complex exchanges of erotic power that may well be unintelligible to outsiders. The not uncommon animosity towards SM points up a distinctly Foucauldian irony. For is not the state taking pleasure in punishing a sexual practice that explores precisely those punishments whose eroticism is ever-present but perpetually denied in everyday life? It is this kind of question that Foucault's transformative research into sexuality certainly provokes. But, like all major theorists, Foucault's work has been the subject of extensive debate because of what it neglects, if not systematically excludes. Even if he praises the 'unforeseen' dimensions to sexual pleasure, there are several highly visible features to the power relayed by eroticism that he ignores. So at this point it is time to examine some of the striking lacunae in his otherwise innovative analyses of sexuality.

FOUCAULT'S EXCLUSIONS

Throughout my overview of *The History of Sexuality*, readers have no doubt already inferred there are many angles from which Foucault's pathbreaking approach to eroticism might come under attack. Among the first critics to seize on weaknesses in his introductory volume were feminists who deplored his marked insensitivity to issues of gender and sexual difference. In an essay published in 1988, Sandra Lee Bartky put a forceful case against Foucault's unstinting sexism, while at the same time recognizing the considerable achievements made by his highly original inquiries into the cultural exercise of power already evident in his earlier study, *Discipline and Punish*:

> Foucault's account in *Discipline and Punish* of the disciplinary practices that produce the 'docile bodies' of modernity is a genuine *tour de force*, incorporating a rich theoretical account of the ways in which instrumental reason takes hold of the body with a mass of historical detail. But Foucault treats the body throughout as if it were one, as if the bodily experiences of men and women did not differ and as if men and women bore the same relationship to the characteristic institutions of modern life. Where is the account of the disciplinary practices that engender the 'docile bodies' of women, bodies more docile than the bodies of men? Women, like men, are subject to many of the same disciplinary practices Foucault describes. But he is blind to those disciplines that produce a modality of embodiment that is particularly feminine. To overlook the forms of subjection that engender the feminine body is to perpetuate the silence and powerlessness of those upon whom the disciplines have been imposed. Hence, even though a liberatory note is sounded in Foucault's critique of power, his analysis as a whole reproduces that sexism which is endemic throughout Western political theory.
>
> (Bartky 1988: 63–4)

It was very probably because of Foucault's obstinate defiance of psychoanalysis that his work refused to attach much significance to the anatomical distinction between the sexes, a distinction fundamental to the sexual laws governing Freud's Oedipus and castration complexes. Instead, Foucault writes of both physicality and sexuality in such a generalized manner that on occasions he makes it almost impossible to see the structural inequalities the West has persistently created between men and women. Given his unobservant attitude to how power differentially affects male and female bodies, it is not surprising that *The History of Sexuality* pays little or no attention to gender, the cultural construction of masculinity and femininity.

This point becomes especially noticeable when one examines Foucault's assessment of male love in classical times. Commenting on the male-centeredness of Volumes 2 and 3 of *The History of Sexuality*, Kate Soper teases out an irony on which Foucault cares not to reflect. Soper argues that the sexual ethics that Foucault strongly admires in both ancient Greek and Greco–Roman civilization depends on forms of domination:

> Foucault has been justly charged with offering an account of power which not only ignores those highly specific forms in which it is exercised in any sexually hierarchical society, but also overlooks the differential impact on the lives of men and women of the general 'disciplining' procedures to which he does attend. In this sense, it can be said that he retains at the very heart of his critique of the liberal-humanist and Marxist accounts of power some of the same universalizing and gender-blind approach to humanity which, for feminism, is a central failing of these theories. Foucault, in other words, might be said to be somewhat implicitly reliant on a masculinist conception of the subject as the support for his polemic with humanism.
>
> There is also something markedly androcentric in the quali-

ty of the attention Foucault brings to his study of the Greek and Greco–Roman sexual ethics in his history of sexuality. It is important, however, to be clear about the nature of this charge. Clearly Foucault does immerse us in the mores of highly patri- archal and patrician societies from which women were *a priori* excluded as significant ethical subjects; his genealogy of ethics is thus very much concerned with the desire and comportment of an elite of male citizens. But in a very real sense, this histori- an (or genealogist) of ideas has no option but to reflect the social pre-eminence of this group since it was largely responsi- ble for the dominant culture.

(Soper 1993: 39)

In her assessment of *The History of Sexuality*, Soper stresses that Foucault's discussion of the 'care of the self' is strangely unaware of how the male citizen's ethical development might involve interaction with women, notably the wives whose voices remain surprisingly muted throughout these volumes. As a consequence, Foucault 'defines the ethical so as to make it appear a very private – and masculine – affair: a matter primarily of self-mastery and authorial self-creation' (Soper 1993: 41). On this view, Foucault's analysis may well appear complicit with the structure of sexual dominance he investigates in classical cultures.

But, as Soper observes, this is not the only place where sexism erupts in *The History of Sexuality*. Foucault's thoughtlessness towards sexual difference makes itself plain when he recounts an event that took place in the French village of Lapcourt in 1867. He relates the story of how a simple-minded farm-hand played a game called 'curdled milk' with a little girl. This episode aims to show how 'discourse aimed at sex' magnified 'people's awareness of it as a constant danger':

At the border of a field, he had obtained a few caresses from a little girl, just as he had done before and seen done by the vil- lage urchins round about him; for, at the edge of the wood, or in the ditch by the road leading to Saint-Nicholas, they would play the familiar game called 'curdled milk'. So he was pointed out by the girl's parents to the mayor of the village, led by the gendarmes to the judges, who indicted him and turned him over first to a doctor, then to two other experts who not only wrote their report but also had it published. What is the significant thing about this story? The pettiness of it all; the fact that this everyday occurrence in the life of village sexuality, these inconsequential bucolic pleasures, could become, for a certain time, the object not only of a collective intolerance but of a judicial action, a medical intervention, a careful clinical examination, and an entire theoretical elaboration.

(Foucault 1978: 31)

Undoubtedly the incident at Lapcourt provides Foucault with a remarkable instance of how various apparatuses of the nineteenth-century state came crashing down to inspect, outlaw, and punish this sexual act. But, on reflection, one is left wondering if the game of 'curdled milk' was both 'bucolic' and 'inconsequential' for the little girl. Rather than see how this incident might involve a terrified child who has been subject to sexual harassment, if not abuse, Foucault shifts our attention, as Soper puts it, 'from the fright of the child victim to the phallic discipline of the academic luminary, whose vision is so dazzling on the issue of "significance" that it all but blinds us to what may really be of most moment' (Soper 1993: 43). Such sobering reflections give one pause when gauging Foucault's receptiveness to the power exercised in and through his primary tool of analysis: discourse.

Just as feminist critiques of *The History of Sexuality* find Foucault inattentive to categories of sex and gender, so too do post-colonial analysts experience disappointment in the way his work repeatedly marginalizes issues of racial difference. Taking her cue from Foucault's passing comments on the bourgeoisie's racialized desire to preserve their blood-line, Ann Laura Stoler asks many searching questions about why he thinks that under a 'new biopolitical regime, modern racism emerges out of the technologies of sex'. To Foucault, observes Stoler, 'racism is a consequence of that "class body" in the making'. But from her own perspective, 'bourgeois bodies were constituted as racially and relationally coded from the outset' (Stoler 1995: 53). Stoler's point is to disclose how ideas about racial difference were factored into a wide range of discursive formations that sought to regulate the social order, making it hard to give priority to one or other category:

> Students of colonial discourses in Africa, Asia, and the Americas have often commented on a common thread: namely, that racialized Others invariably have been compared and equated with children, a representation that conveniently provided a moral justification for imperial policies of tutelage, discipline and specific paternalistic and maternalistic strategies of custodial control. But this equation of children and primitive, of children and colonized savage was not operative in overtly racist, colonial discourse alone. If we look to the childcare manuals of the eighteenth and nineteenth centuries, the same equation is present, but the other way around. Children are invariably othered in ways that compare them to lower-order beings, they are animal-like, lack civility, discipline, and sexual restraint; their instincts are base, they are too close to nature, they are, like racialized others, not fully human beings.
>
> (Stoler 1995: 151)

Stoler's attentive commentary provides a timely reminder of how any discussion of eroticism would be unwise to assume that conceptions of race are subordinate to those of desire. Nor should cultural analysts labour under the misapprehension that race served as a locus for the exercise of power exclusively within colonized territories. Instead, ideas about racial difference had a constitutive role in shaping beliefs about the sexualities of both subaltern peoples and the children of the colonizers themselves. If this observation is not taken into account, then critics run the risk of presuming that sexuality shapes and determines all other relations of power. Bearing this question in mind, Sander Gilman remarks that race and sexuality intertwine when we consider a remark made by Freud in 1926: he claimed not to know the 'dark continent' of psychological research on adult female sexuality. This allusion to a phrase drawn from British imperialism, according to Gilman, ties 'female sexuality to the image of contemporary colonialism and thus to the exoticism and pathology of the Other' (Gilman 1985: 107). This is but one example that indicates how writings and representations of sexuality assume a certain racial definition. Exactly the same could be said about how imperialist concepts of blackness figure a sense of 'undifferentiated, pure sexuality' whose savagery remains unconstrained by cultural laws (Gilman 1985: 126). Both Stoler's and Gilman's critiques accentuate one of the main tendencies in Foucault's exploration of desire. Even if sexuality turns out to be a locus for understanding intense power relations, in Foucault's work the concept becomes the gravitational centre towards which all other social phenomena must fall.

Certainly the very idea that sexuality is an appropriate topic for the exploration of domination, ethics, and power has made several critics suspicious of Foucault's radicalism. Since *The History of Sexuality* applauds how the male citizens of ancient Greece cultivated a carefully stylized *askesis*, Terry Eagleton has argued from a Marxist standpoint that the ethics celebrated in *The Use of Pleasure* comprise little more than a highly individualistic aestheticization of the self. Eagleton sees *askesis* as a characteristic of the ruling classes in both ancient and modern cultures:

> Foucault's Greeks believe that one should temper and refine one's practices not because they are inherently good or bad, but because self-indulgence leads to a depletion of one's vital

powers – a familiar male fantasy if ever there was one. The more one aesthetically restrains oneself, the richer the powers which accrue to one – which is to say that power here would seem in romantic vein an unquestioned good, a wholly undifferentiated category. The positivity of power can thus be maintained, but converted into the basis of a discriminatory ethics by virtue of adding to it the techniques of prudence and temperance. And the ethical theory which is the upshot of this – that 'the physical regimen ought to accord with the principle of a general aesthetics of existence in which the equilibrium of the body was one of the conditions of the proper hierarchy of the soul' [Foucault 1985: 104] – has long been familiar on the playing fields of [the ancient English private school] Eton.

(Eagleton 1990: 394–5)

To Eagleton, Foucault's relentless desire to aestheticize the self in the name of resisting the powers mediated by external subjugatory laws presents far too many intolerable paradoxes for it to be taken seriously. Eagleton observes that, in order to resist the pressures of such laws, the male citizen of ancient Greece simply takes them into his own hands, thus obtaining the privilege to exercise power over himself that he already imposes on all inferiors. Even though Foucault insists that self-regulation of this kind is a practice of freedom, Eagleton cannot help but notice how such *askesis* may well be duplicating the power structures it seeks to overcome. This is how Eagleton puts his case:

The individual must construct a relation with the self that is one of 'domination–submission', 'command–obedience', 'mastery–docility' [see Foucault 1985: 70]. Foucault is thus able to combine the concept of individual autonomy, which stands relatively free of the law, with the pleasures of sado-masochistic power such a law involves. What is gratifying and productive about power, its discipline and dominativeness, is salvaged from political oppressiveness and installed within the

> self. In this way one can enjoy the gains of hegemony without denying the pleasures of power. One might question, however, how far this model really allows Foucault to escape from the lures of traditional hegemony.
>
> (Eagleton 1990: 392)

On this view, Foucault's enduring emphasis on the aestheticization of the self becomes even more baffling when one sees how fiercely *The History of Sexuality* refuses to engage with traditional understandings of human subjectivity. Given his resistance to what he feels are the prohibitive laws governing psychoanalysis, Foucault rarely construes the subject in relation to affective or emotional response. His research has little or no interest in the subject's inner life. Such is Foucault's anti-humanism that he denies the subject any depth or psychological complexity. In this spirit, he firmly repudiates the realm of conflict between conscious and unconscious processes that fascinated Freud.

By refusing the subject the interiority familiar to both humanist, psychoanalytic, as well as certain Marxist orthodoxies, *The History of Sexuality* fashions the subject exclusively in terms of pleasures that rest on a somatic surface. The body, to which Foucault appeals so strongly as the locus of power and transformation, has no deep substance in his work. Placed at the centre of his theory, Foucault's concept of the body remains, so to speak, strategically disembodied – lacking all the features one associates with the humanist subject, such as psychology, intention, motivation, thought, and feeling. Eagleton believes Foucault's idiosyncratic attitude amounts to an 'aestheticizing move towards the subject', and therefore 'leaves love as technique and conduct rather than as tenderness and affection, as praxis rather than interiority'. As a consequence, 'the body stands in for the subject and the aesthetic for the ethical' (Eagleton 1990: 395). Put so starkly, Eagleton's punishing Marxist critique demonstrates how Foucault's subject cannot be understood as an agent of social change, one able to enter into a compassionate and responsive relationship with the needs and desires of a community altogether larger than oneself. Lois McNay elaborates this point: 'Foucault provides no way of going beyond the minimal notion of the subject as a purely determined category to a fuller understanding of the subject as a thinking, willing, responsible agent of choice' (McNay 1994: 103–4). In the case of sexuality, it may well seem that Foucault's model of power requires the very form of psychology he is the first to repudiate. For how do subjects internalize or resist those desires that regulate culture? Is it really the case that discourses lead to institutions that in turn proceed to practices in a seamless continuum? How might subjects operate within discourses in more than a merely instrumental way? Faced with such questions, his critics can therefore argue that Foucault's subject is so minimal that it cannot be seen as an agent of social change.

FOUCAULT'S FOLLOWERS

Taken together, these confrontational feminist, post-colonial, and Marxist appraisals of *The History of Sexuality* may well make it seem that there are so many shortcomings to Foucault's understanding of desire that his work would be of little use to anyone interested in achieving radical political change. But from the first moment it appeared, his introductory volume was quickly welcomed by intellectuals grappling with the limiting critical vocabularies available to discuss sexuality. If Foucault's introductory volume made a distinct advance on earlier theories of desire, it was to show how explanatory categories such as sexuality itself had the devastating effect of naturalizing types of appropriate and inappropriate eroticism. In an essay dating from 1982, Biddy Martin insists on the useful challenge Foucault's work presents to selected strands of feminist thought that claim femininity is an unchanging essence that patriarchal culture brutally distorts. Adopting an anti-essentialist position, Martin outlines the weaknesses in arguments that appeal to the universal spirit of femininity and female sexuality throughout the ages:

> Some American radical feminists thought (the work, for example, of Mary Daly [see Daly 1978]) is, for all its importance and contributions, particularly susceptible to a polemic against patriarchy that ultimately ontologizes woman in terms of an essential superiority and a privileged relationship to nature and truth. The tendency in such polemics is to counter what are considered to be male distortions of reality with what are held to be authentic female representations, and to correct male distortions with the authentic experience that can be read out of women's texts and lives. Unfortunately, this cultural criticism cannot go far beyond the assertion and documentation of a history of sexism, and our own cultural production is based on the premise that we as feminists can speak authentically, can speak the truth of ourselves for all women by virtue of our supposed exclusion from male culture and as a result of our rejection of their meanings.
>
> (Martin 1988: 15)

Foucault's research, contends Martin, reveals why there are considerable dangers in assuming that feminism can recover an authentic and untainted ideal of femininity liberated from patriarchal domination. Indeed, she claims *The History of Sexuality* presents 'a warning against the commitment to any confessional mode as necessarily liberating, and a challenge to the notion that simply speaking or writing frees us in any simple way from patriarchy and phallocentrism' (Martin 1988: 15). According to Martin, once feminist critics accept that femininity has been regulated in historically contingent ways, it becomes possible to appreciate differences between women across eras, across classes, and across cultures. Martin argues that much can be learned from Foucault's emphasis on how social phenomena are understood through power-laden discursive formations, since his theoretical model focuses attention on how femininity and masculinity are redefined over time. The same could be said about the arbitrary distinction that, for more than a century, has been forced between heterosexuality and homosexuality. If we respect this emphasis on the social construction of cultural categories to regulate power relations, the upshot of *The History of Sexuality* is to make us wonder how intellectuals ever came to the conclusion that femininity and masculinity, heterosexuality and homosexuality described phenomena that were unquestionably based in nature. Martin's strongly constructionist position would become increasingly influential among feminist theorists in the 1980s, leading to thorough critiques of essentialist approaches to sex and gender. (The intellectual battle waged between constructionist and essentialist positions has been carefully explored by Diana Fuss [see Fuss 1989].)

It needs to be said, however, that *The History of Sexuality* was not the only work that made the social construction of sexuality a matter of concern among cultural theorists. As early as 1968, Mary McIntosh laid the foundations for such a theory in her classic essay, 'The Homosexual Role' (McIntosh 1981). Likewise, in *Coming Out: Homosexual Politics in Britain, from the Nineteenth Century to the Present*, Jeffrey Weeks revealed 'a changing reality, both in the ways a hostile society labelled homosexuality, and in the way those stigmatized saw themselves' (Weeks 1977: 3). Read alongside Foucault's work, this substantial body of historical and sociological research proved immensely enabling for the area of inquiry that, by the mid-1980s, became known as lesbian and gay studies. Ten years later, this rapidly developing field diversified to such a degree that investigations into the cultural construction of desire were given a much more encompassing label: queer theory. To understand the transformation of lesbian and gay studies into queer theory, I shall examine some of the landmark writings that have transformed the repertoire of available terms to fathom the complexity of human sexuality. In my assessment of these materials, it will become clear that queer theory arose in an intellectual climate when critics were increasingly mindful of the anti-essentialist approach to gender and sexuality we have already encountered in Martin's feminist engagement with Foucault.

Acknowledging how 'The History of Sexuality has been the most influential and most emblematic text of the new scholarship on sex', Gayle Rubin counts among the foremost critics following Foucault's lead to 'identify, describe, explain, and denounce erotic injustice and sexual oppression' (Rubin 1993: 9–10). Trained as an anthropologist, Rubin has for many years been interested in how each society around the world constructs its own 'sex/gender system', 'a set of arrangements by which the biological raw material of human sex and procreation is shaped by human, social intervention and satisfied in a conventional manner, no matter how bizarre some of the conventions may be' (Rubin 1975: 165). First published in 1984, her powerful essay 'Thinking Sex' (Rubin 1993) builds on her earlier work to demonstrate how the contemporary West arranges its beliefs about 'good' sexuality and 'bad' sexuality. To clarify her points, Rubin presents two diagrams that identify degrees of social acceptability and unacceptability among a range of sexual institutions and practices. Under the heading of 'good' or 'normal, natural, healthy, holy' sex, Rubin claims that heterosexual, married, monogamous, reproductive relations that occur 'at home' are regarded as the very 'best'. By contrast, under the heading 'bad' or 'abnormal, unnatural, sick, sinful, "way out"' sex, Rubin catalogues the ensuing group of deviants: transvestites, transsexuals, fetishists, sadomasochists, those engaging in cross-generational sex, as well as those who do it for money. In between these two poles, she designates the 'major area of contest' where one finds sexual behaviours and lifestyles that signal how attitudes are shifting across the moral terrain. In this liminal in-between zone, we find the following: unmarried heterosexual couples; promiscuous heterosexuals; masturbation; and long-term, stable same-sex relationships. Located somewhat closer to 'bad' sex are lesbians in the bar and promiscuous gay men in public places.

In tracing the migration of moral values across the terrain that maps these different styles of sexuality, Rubin observes how relations that are based purely on erotic gratification tend to tumble to the bottom of the hierarchy she has sketched, if with significant qualifications:

> Only sex acts on the good side of the line are accorded moral complexity. For instance, heterosexual encounters may be sublime or disgusting, free or forced, healing or destructive, romantic or mercenary. As long as it does not violate other rules, heterosexuality is acknowledged to represent the full range of human experience. In contrast, all sex acts on the bad side of the line are considered utterly repulsive and devoid of all emotional nuance. The further from the line a sex act is, the more it is depicted as uniformly bad experience.
>
> (Rubin 1993: 14–15)

Rubin's point is to show that a double standard operates when Western culture accords privilege to heterosexual relations. Although opposite-sex encounters may well involve highly unpleasant and even exploitative sex acts, the very fact that these involve a man and a woman grants them much higher status than, for example, various non-consensual activities involving sexual dissidents, such as lesbians or transsexuals. But this is not, Rubin insists, a static model of how the West establishes its moral attitudes towards sexuality. 'Unmarried couples living together, masturbation, and some forms of homosexuality are moving in the direction of respectability'. In the meantime, many other sexual behaviours remain taboo: 'Promiscuous homosexuality, sadomasochism, fetishism, transsexuality, and cross-generational encounters are still viewed as unmodulated horrors incapable of involving affection, love, free choice, kindness, or transcendence' (Rubin 1993: 15). Rubin's belief is that the contested zone in the middle indicates how the moral values attached to sexuality are gradually shifting, as different styles of tolerance permit formally stigmatized erotic behaviours and identities to inch towards those deemed 'good'.

But it should be added that this account of how morality and sexuality are closely intertwined is not altogether as comprehensive as it might first appear. Nowhere does Rubin's mapping of 'good' and 'bad' sex make it clear how differing perceptions of gender can and do affect moral responses to sexuality. Just to give one example, effeminate styles of male homosexuality are frequently more vulnerable to public hostility than those that pass for straight. Similarly, in drawing up these sexual hierarchies, Rubin remains inattentive to how cultural differences might influence moral stances on erotic behaviour – even if later she is careful to note: 'Wealth, white skin, male gender, and ethnic privileges can mitigate the effects of sexual stratification. A rich, white, male pervert will generally be less affected than a poor, black, female pervert' (Rubin 1993: 22). And Rubin would surely not dissent from the view that different ethnic communities within the West adopt variable positions on such issues as monogamy, marriage, and same-sex partnerships. There is no doubt that one major area of contention that she ignores, and which affects many sections of society, is inter-racial desire. These reservations aside, Rubin's 'Thinking Sex' puts the spotlight on how 'a single ideal of sexuality characterizes most systems of thought about sex', whether in terms of religious commitments to 'procreative marriage' or psychological orthodoxies about 'mature heterosexuality' (Rubin 1993: 15).

Since so much value is laid by differing institutions of power upon the 'ideal' sexuality to which we should all aspire, it remains the case in the United States that the 'only adult sexual behaviour that is legal in every state is the placement of the penis in the vagina' (Rubin 1993: 20). Like Foucault, Rubin recognizes how fiercely state legislation seeks to control many types of sexuality that fall short of this 'ideal'. Consequently, she devotes much of her essay to highlighting exactly how 'moral panics' erupt around types of dissident eroticism that simply serve as scapegoats on to which society projects its greatest anxieties:

> Because sexuality in Western societies is so mystified, the wars over it are often fought at oblique angles, aimed at phony targets, conducted with misplaced passions, and are highly, intensely symbolic. Sexual activities often function as signifiers for personal and social apprehensions to which they have no intrinsic connection. During a moral panic, such fears attach to some unfortunate sexual activity or population. The media become ablaze with indignation, the public behaves like a rabid mob, the police are activated, and the state enacts new laws and regulations.
>
> (Rubin 1993: 25)

To clarify this observation, Rubin pinpoints 'two current developments' that absorbed much political energy in the 1980s: 'the attacks on sadomasochists by a segment of the feminist movement, and the right's increasing use of AIDS to incite virulent homophobia'. Noting how, in the early 1980s, anti-porn feminists scapegoated SM imagery to reveal what purportedly caused sexual violence against women (see pp. 151–7), Rubin stresses how this kind of political campaigning was based on a misguided analysis. In declaring that pornography enacted the sexual subordination of women, the feminist anti-porn lobby extended the age-old prejudice that people practising forms of perverse sexuality were largely responsible for committing sex crimes. Rubin observes that feminists crusading against pornography were playing into the censorious hands of the Moral Right. Equally troubling was the emergent 'moral panic' around the AIDS epidemic, which activated 'old fears that sexual activity, homosexuality, and promiscuity led to disease and death' (Rubin 1993: 26).

Both examples, in Rubin's view, show how 'bad' types of desire have served as convenient and defenceless targets when Western culture found itself unable to cope with the fearsome qualities attributed to sexuality. Anti-censorship feminists like Rubin are quick to remark that seemingly violent pornography that draws on SM imagery is the consequence, rather than the cause, of how the West eroticizes structures of domination and submission. She contends that this debate bears parallels with the depressing manner in which many right-wing moralists refused to view gay men as the victims of the AIDS epidemic. Instead, gay men – who still comprise the largest group of sufferers in the West – were blamed for spreading a virus that continues to claim thousands upon thousands of lives. The moralistic imperative to make gay men culpable for the development of an appalling virus had dreadful repercussions: the US and UK governments were at first alarmingly inactive in taking positive steps both to support gay men suffering from the epidemic and to protect those who are uninfected. (Many would argue that, ever since AIDS become known by that acronym in the early 1980s, state funds have never been as forthcoming as they should be in dealing with an urgent health crisis. [On this issue, see Watney 1987].)

Rubin's pathbreaking work has always been notable for the ways in which it has shaped cultural inquiries into sex and gender, especially how and why the West persists in stigmatizing homosexuality. Her earlier essay, 'The Traffic in Women' (1975), provided much inspiration for the book that would be most closely associated with the emergent field of lesbian and gay studies: *Between Men: English Literature and Male Homosocial Desire* by Eve Kosofsky Sedgwick (1985). Although mainly comprising a series of ingenious interpretations of mostly nineteenth-century literary works (by Alfred Tennyson [1809–1892] and Charles Dickens [1812–1870], among others), Sedgwick's book was prefaced with a deft and original introduction that laid out an innovative model for comprehending three related terms:

homosexuality, homosociality, and homophobia. In this distinguished study, Sedgwick explores how relations between men have been consolidated on the basis of 'erotic triangles': a concept adapted from the work of René Girard. Sedgwick claims that male–male desire is legitimated on a *homosocial* basis: that is, through bonds that maintain the privilege accorded to the male sex (Sedgwick 1985: 1–27). Such homosociality, which involves men working in patriarchal league with one another, is regulated by two forms of oppression: *homophobia* and *misogyny*. So, to ensure that relations between men retain their *social* pre-eminence, there have to be two *sexual* structures of oppression in place. On this view, we can see how male-dominated Western society uses marriage as an institution that involves the exchange of women between men. At the same time, heterosexual marriage retains its entitlement because of the stigma attached to male–male eroticism. If somewhat schematic in outline, Sedgwick's arrangement of social and sexual relations has one profound point to make: it remains difficult indeed to keep this particular cultural order intact. For the privilege granted to male–male relations stands in dangerous proximity to the very homosexuality that patriarchal fellowship is obliged to condemn.

Not all of Sedgwick's readers have been entirely convinced by her delineation of the sexual and social order. Lesbian critics have found Sedgwick's mapping of 'hetero-' and 'homo-' relations surprisingly exclusive in its emphasis on male–female and male–male desire (see, for example, Castle 1993: 67–73). But, if this model has a purpose, it is to reveal exactly why the dichotomy between opposite-sex and male same-sex eroticism should be so vigilantly maintained. The reason, of course, is that society has worked hard at dividing sexualities into 'hetero-' and 'homo-' antitheses because there is such a perilous relationship between the two. Since the late Victorian period, we have often assumed that this violent distinction described a natural state of affairs, rather than see how it performed an ideological manoeuvre, one that concealed a deep-seated problem in modern culture. Sedgwick's discussion asks us to ponder how 'in any male-dominated society, there is a special relationship between male homosocial (*including* homosexual) desire and structures for maintaining and transmitting patriarchal power' (Sedgwick 1985: 25). So perhaps *social* and *sexual* relations between men actually lie in much closer proximity, one that the West has found exceptionally discomforting. The troubling closeness between the two, therefore, has been carefully masked by the influential division of male sexuality into antithetical types of 'hetero-' and 'homo-' object-choice.

Sedgwick elaborates this observation in the introduction to her next book, *Epistemology of the Closet* (1990), which makes its critical concerns absolutely clear right on the opening page:

> *Epistemology of the Closet* proposes that many of the major nodes of thought and knowledge in twentieth-century Western culture as a whole are structured – indeed, fractured – by a chronic, now endemic crisis of homo/heterosexual definition, indicatively male, dating from the end of the nineteenth century. The book will argue that an understanding of virtually any aspect of modern Western culture must be, not merely incomplete, but damaged in its central substance to the degree that it does not incorporate a critical analysis of modern homo/heterosexual definition; and it will assume that the appropriate place for that critical analysis to begin is from the relatively decentered perspective of modern gay and antihomophobic theory.
>
> (Sedgwick 1990: 1)

Acknowledging that gay theory is 'decentered' (that is, still not central to academic debate, as well as less theoretically mature as feminist critique), Sedgwick argues that a gay-affirmative appraisal of Western culture needs to recognize how significantly the sharp distinction between 'hetero-' and 'homo-' has shaped many spheres of social life. No sooner has Sedgwick made this declaration than she clarifies her intellectual debt to Foucault. Following *The History of Sexuality*, her book focuses on how sexuality – especially the closeting of male homosexuality – has much to tell us about epistemology, the philosophical consideration of how we come to know what we know. As she says herself:

> [I]n accord with Foucault's demonstration, whose results I take to be axiomatic, that modern Western discourse has placed what it calls sexuality in a more and more distinctively privileged relation to our most prized constructs of individual identity, truth, and knowledge, it becomes truer and truer that the language of sexuality not only intersects with but transforms the other languages and relations by which we know.
>
> (Sedgwick 1990: 3)

Sedgwick, therefore, believes that it is impossible to address sexuality as a phenomenon that can be treated as if it were separate from culture as a whole. Instead, the very system of thought engendered by the term sexuality pervades countless epistemological acts, particularly in the critical methods we use to derive knowledge about our own and other people's public image and personal lives.

On this basis, Sedgwick argues that 'modern homo/heterosexual division' involves ideas about sexuality that are far from stable and complete. She claims that the enduring use of this binary distinction rests on two opposed understandings of how to divide opposite-sex and same-sex desire. Sedgwick's interest lies in how twentieth-century theorists of sexuality tend to fall into two apparently different camps when analysing eroticism. To make her case, Sedgwick identifies two axes that cut between divergent perspectives on sexuality. The first dividing line splits 'minoritizing' from 'universalizing' views of desire, while the second separates 'sexual' from 'gender' definition (Sedgwick 1990: 88). Let me explain what these two distinctions imply.

The first distinction Sedgwick makes between these two standpoints reveals (1) how sexuality is viewed as a matter of inborn essential identity ('minoritizing'), and (2) how desire is seen as part of a continuum that allows for choice ('universalizing'). Put another way, the 'minoritizing' perspective lays an emphasis on fixing sexual desire in terms of *either* 'hetero-' *or* 'homo-' definition. By contrast, the 'universalizing' stance regards sexual desire as spanning the whole gamut of opposite-sex and same-sex eroticism, locating bisexual desire at the centre of a broad range of erotic preferences.

The second distinction Sedgwick makes is between 'sexual' definition and 'gender' definition, and it too identifies a similar antithesis between 'minoritizing' and 'universalizing' perspectives. This time, however, greater stress is put on the sexed body than on desire *per se*. Here we find, on the one hand, a gender 'separatist' standpoint underscoring the specific experiences of what it means to be male or female. One manifestation of this 'minoritizing' position would be lesbian separatism of the kind that developed in the 1970s when groups of women-loving women renounced the heteropatriarchy by living as independently as possible from men. On the other hand, there are 'universalizing' attitudes that celebrate the 'liminality' or 'transitivity' of gender, effacing hard and fast divisions between the male and female sex. Under this heading, Sedgwick includes phenomena like androgyny, as well as styles of political campaigning such as solidarity between lesbians and gay men. One might add that transgendered and transsexual identities present models of gender liminality, since they suggest a transitive movement that eradicates any fixed boundary between male and female, masculinity and femininity.

In effect, these competing outlooks on sexuality contend that it is either an immutable essence ('minoritizing') or a transformable construction ('universalizing'). Put even more crudely, this clash of interests presents the age-old stand-off between those who believe that 'nature' and those who think that 'nurture' determines sexual behaviour. Like Rubin in 'Thinking Sex', Sedgwick is keenly aware that her schematic model can only bear out general tendencies in contemporary understandings of sexuality. By her own admission, this is a 'misleadingly symmetrical map' that fails to show how various theories of desire may hold views emanating from opposing 'minoritizing' and 'universalizing' camps (Sedgwick 1990: 90). But that is the point. In outlining these distinctions, Sedgwick draws attention to the 'highly structured discursive incoherence' inscribed in both 'sexual' and 'gender' positions. Her map provokes many questions about the categories we use to comprehend sexuality. Is erotic identity specific to one's sexed body? Or is it a fluid phenomenon that traverses a complex ensemble of gendered meanings – a whole range of femininities and masculinities that are not necessarily grounded in the anatomical distinction between the sexes? Such inquiries are the result of how painstakingly Sedgwick has followed Foucault's lead, creating the space in which the new academic field of lesbian and gay studies could explore the epistemological structures surrounding sexuality.

Published in the same year as *Epistemology of the Closet*, Judith Butler's *Gender Trouble* (1990) drew on Foucault's writings to produce a fresh analysis of how we construct categories to understand sex, gender, and desire. Throughout her discussion, Butler explores why 'gender' has been a source of 'trouble' in feminist debate. Why should the term gender have been such a vexed issue? In answering this question, Butler draws our attention to how discursive practices frequently create the very problems they are striving to analyse. To explain this point, she focuses on a distinctly Foucauldian paradox of the kind one finds in the introduction to *The History of Sexuality*. Here Butler ponders what it meant for her as a child to get into 'trouble':

> To make trouble was, in the reigning discourse of my childhood,

> something one should never do precisely because that would
> get one *in* trouble. The rebellion and its reprimand seemed to be
> caught up in the same terms, a phenomenon that gave rise to
> my first critical insight into the subtle ruse of power: The prevail-
> ing law threatened one with trouble, even put one in trouble, all
> to keep one out of trouble.
>
> (Butler 1990: ix)

Highly attentive to this type of double bind, Butler proceeds
with her examination of 'gender trouble' by pursuing what
Foucault calls a 'genealogical analysis' (Foucault 1977b: 142). In
his appropriation of the term 'genealogy' from the German
philosopher Friedrich Nietzsche, Foucault was concerned with
tracing how sets of ideas grouped around a phenomenon such as
sexuality. 'A genealogical critique', writes Butler, 'refuses to
search for the origins of gender, the inner truth of female desire, a
genuine or authentic sexual identity that repression has kept from
view'. Instead, 'genealogy investigates the political stakes in des-
ignating as an *origin* and *cause* those identity categories that are in
fact the *effects* of institutions, practices, and discourses with multiple and diffuse points of origin' (Butler 1990: x–xi). Following
Foucault in this way, Butler reaches some impressive conclusions
about exactly why gender has been such a source of intellectual
'trouble'. Not only that, she explores how 'gender trouble' can
open up radical possibilities for social transformation. Such transformation, she argues, comes into view when we consider the *performative* condition of gender. This is an influential concept that
requires careful exposition, not least because it was misconstrued
by many of Butler's earliest readers. In order to understand why
'gender attributes . . . are not expressive but performative', we
need to follow selected aspects of Butler's sedulous genealogical
critique of how distinctions have been made between sex, gender,
and desire (Butler 1990: 141).

One of Butler's principal aims in *Gender Trouble* is to explore how a restrictive binary logic has trapped critical understandings of sex and gender. Since the 1960s at least, modern feminist analysis frequently insisted that sex referred to the sexed body (female or male) while gender signified the sexual meanings attributed to the sexed body (femininity or masculinity). At its most basic, this distinction claimed that sex was determined by nature, while gender was moulded by culture. Although the general assumption was that male bodies were the basis of masculinity, while female bodies were the ground of femininity, seldom did feminist critics examine the potential severance of sex from gender. Butler argues that, if sex is fashioned by nature, while gender is generated by culture, then these two phenomena emerge from divergent sources. Gender, then, does not necessarily proceed from sex:

> If gender is the cultural meanings that the sexed body assumes, then a gender cannot be said to follow from a sex in any one way. Taken to its logical limit, the sex/gender distinction suggests a radical discontinuity between sexed bodies and culturally constructed genders. Assuming for the moment the stability of binary sex, it does not follow that the construction of 'men' will accrue exclusively to the bodies of males or that 'women' will interpret only female bodies. Further, even if the sexes appear to be unproblematically binary in their morphology and constitution (which will become a question), there is no reason to assume that genders ought also to remain as two. The presumption of a binary gender system implicitly retains the belief in a mimetic relation of gender to sex whereby gender mirrors sex or is otherwise restricted by it. When the constructed status of gender is theorized as radically independent of sex, gender itself becomes a free-floating artifice, with the consequence that *man* and *masculine* might just as easily signify a female body as a male one, and *woman* and *feminine* a male body as easily as a female one.
>
> (Butler 1990: 6)

Even if Western culture generally assumes that sex provides the anatomical basis on which the cultural edifice of gender is built, Butler's project is to explain why there can indeed be subversive separations between the two terms. Effeminate mannerisms present one dissident style of manhood that the West often treats with considerable contempt. By comparison, female masculinity often poses a distinct challenge to the social order. One only has to recall how butch lesbians are habitually stigmatized for their unorthodox self-presentation. Both examples suggest that we need to think more subtly about the broad repertoire of gendered styles that men and women may adopt. Butler urges us to contemplate how gender needs to be understood as a pluralizing concept, one that appreciates many different femininities and masculinities in all their variety. At the same time, she casts suspicion on the very idea that 'sex' should be designated as a phenomenon grounded in nature. Culture, after all, has played an undeniable role in naming and understanding 'sex', establishing it as a marker that creates a seemingly natural distinction when in fact it is an arbitrary sign of difference. Sex, therefore, is just as much a cultural construction as gender is presumed to be.

So why has the West maintained such a narrow view of a neatly integrated 'sex/gender system'? Why was it the case that critics rarely questioned the contradictions and tensions at the heart of this approach to sex and gender? Butler claims that it is the assumptions that make heterosexuality an apparently natural institution which keep the binary oppositions of female and male, femininity and masculinity solidly in place. Since heterosexuality appears to have such structural integrity, it remains hard to imagine alternative conceptual frameworks. In the following passage, Butler explains why heterosexuality often had such success in governing how we might think about the relations between sex and gender:

Gender can denote a *unity* of experience, of sex, of gender, and desire, only when sex can be understood in some sense to necessitate gender – where gender is a psychic and/or cultural designation of the self – and desire – where desire is hetero-sexual and therefore differentiates itself through an opposi-tional relation to that other gender it desires. The internal coherence or unity of either gender, man or woman, thereby requires both a stable and oppositional heterosexuality. That institutional heterosexuality both requires and produces the univocity of each of the gendered terms that constitute the limit of gendered possibilities within an oppositional, binary gender system. This conception of gender presupposes not only a causal relation among sex, gender, and desire, but sug-gests as well that desire reflects or expresses gender and that gender reflects or expresses desire.

(Butler 1990: 22)

Here Butler carefully elaborates how dominant ideas about het-erosexuality suppose that sex and gender are terms that can be split into opposite and yet complementary pairs: female and male, feminine and masculine. As a consequence, heterosexual desire proceeds from this system of gendered couplings. That is to say, the binary structure of gender finds its complement in opposite-sex attraction. In heterosexuality, then, desire and gen-der are so mutually reinforcing that it becomes hard to see how its sex/gender system is anything but natural. If gender involves a stable antithesis, and desire requires the reciprocity of each sex, then the apparent coherence of heterosexuality can prove over-whelming – so much so that erotic preferences dissenting from this model can look extremely strange.

Butler's theoretical goal is to *denaturalize* what she calls the 'heterosexual matrix' (Butler 1990: 35). She takes her cue from Foucault to demonstrate, first of all, how influential theoretical work in anthropology (Lévi-Strauss) and psychoanalysis (Freud, Lacan) have appealed to cultural laws that stabilize this sexual system. Testing the limits to these theories, she then examines the exclusionary logics that strive to repel the homosexual and bisexual desires that threaten to overthrow the primacy of opposite-sex eroticism. Unlike Foucault, however, Butler is prepared to explore structures of psychic identification to understand how the subject organizes its desires, particularly in insubordinate ways. In this respect, her model of the subject is not the empty one featured in *The History of Sexuality*. Rather, her interest is in how psychoanalysis can be used against itself to expose the mechanisms through which the subject might experience psychic identifications that repudiate the power of the heterosexual matrix (see Butler 1990: 35–78). In her view, close attention needs to be paid to psychic mechanisms so that we can more fully comprehend why the cultural injunction to become heterosexual does not always work.

The upshot of *Gender Trouble* is to demonstrate exactly how and why sex, gender, and desire do not necessarily fit into the neat binary order of heterosexuality. And it is here that Butler formulates her ideas about the performative condition of gender. Butler uses the word performative to describe how the body provides a surface upon which various acts and gestures accrue gendered meanings. What she calls 'corporeal signification' reveals that gender does not appeal to an ontological essence granted by nature (Butler 1990: 136). Rather, the widespread belief that there is indeed a core gender identity actually depends on performative acts that give the illusion of naturalness. To support her point, Butler discusses gay male drag to illuminate the question of gender performance:

> The notion of an original or primary gender is often parodied within the cultural practices of drag, cross-dressing, and the sexual stylization of butch/femme identities [in lesbian cultures]. Within feminist theory, such parodic identities have been understood to be either degrading to women, in the case

of drag or cross-dressing, or an uncritical appropriation of sex-role stereotyping from within the practice of heterosexuality, especially in the case of butch—femme lesbian identities. But the relation between the 'imitation' and the 'original' is, I think, more complicated than that critique generally allows. Moreover, it gives us a clue to the way in which the relationship between primary identification – that is, the original meanings accorded to gender – and subsequent gender experience might be reframed. The performance of drag plays upon the distinction between the anatomy of the performer and the gender that is being performed. But we are actually in the presence of three contingent dimensions of significant corporeality: anatomical sex, gender identity, and gender performance. If the anatomy of the performer is already distinct from the gender of the performer, and both of those are distinct from the gender of the performance, then the performance suggests a dissonance not only between sex and performance, but sex and gender, and gender and performance.

(Butler 1990: 137)

Butler argues that drag, in principle at least, has the virtue of showing that gender is an emphatically *imitative structure*: that is, a structure that reveals how being female or male, feminine or masculine, entails a performance that requires the production of specific bodily signs. Instead of claiming that drag simply copies an original gender identity, Butler contends that this flamboyant theatricality shows how all gender identities are themselves derivative copies. Through performative acts, each of us learns to *become* a woman or a man, feminine or masculine. Here Butler is adopting a strong constructionist position, thus making her affiliation with Foucault absolutely clear.

Gender Trouble concludes on an inspiring note: to devise ways of confounding the naturalized appearance of gender in its heterosexual guise. Undoubtedly, lesbian and gay cultures have done much to perform what is colloquially known as the 'gender fuck' by engaging with cross-dressing and butch/femme role-playing that baffle the apparently natural link between sex and gender. Yet some critics have been suspicious of Butler's rallying-cry to produce 'a radical proliferation of gender' that will *displace* the very gender norms that enable the repetition' shaping each and every performance (Butler 1990: 148). Ed Cohen, for example, has stated that Butler's model could be viewed as 'voluntarist', since it suggests that genders can be made and remade at will (Cohen 1991: 83). But Butler, in fairness, emphasizes how the 'I' that performs gender does not stand outside the discursive structure that gives femininity and masculinity their multiple meanings. Instead, the subject operates within a field of signification that strives to regulate the production of sex, gender, and desire. That significatory field, however, can none the less be adjusted, contested, if not revolutionized through insubordinate performances of gender.

So that we can see how understandings of sex, gender, and desire might be transformed within performative practices, the time has come to turn to the final topic of this chapter: queer theory. Unquestionably, both *Epistemology of the Closet* and *Gender Trouble* have done much to define this emergent area of inquiry. It is perhaps no accident that both of these books appeared in 1990, the year that brought the activist group Queer Nation to public attention. The imaginative public interventions made by Queer Nation set the terms of a distinctly Foucauldian debate about the labels that have been used to define, limit, and indeed naturalize the distinction between heterosexuality and homosexuality. Employing styles of political protest that developed out of ACT UP (the Aids Coalition to Unleash Power) in New York City, Queer Nation had among its many ambitions the desire to expand the vocabulary used to name and know styles of sexuality. In large part, these activists were frustrated with the complacency of an established lesbian and gay movement that had, from the late 1960s onwards, espoused itself more and more to a constraining and unquestioning 'identity politics'. Sexual liberation, they argued, had been misled by the belief that lesbians and gay men had distinctive and essential identities. Not only that, they felt the lesbian and gay movement had constructed an exclusionary political agenda that made it difficult for anyone who did not conform to these identities to join in their struggles. To take just one example, bisexual men and bisexual women were at times debarred from this political movement, on the grounds that bisexuality involved treacherous intimacy with the heterosexual enemy. Consequently, bisexuals were quick to note the biphobia endemic to lesbian and gay politics. In principle, Queer Nation had no patience with exclusions of this kind. Embracing many communities of sexual dissidents, it promoted a controversial discursive strategy to create an innovative paradigm for thinking about sexuality. Since the 1920s, the word queer had been routinely used as an insult hurled at homosexuals. By wresting the word from the oppressors, this activist group resignified its meaning. In doing so, Queer Nation performed a decisive act of repeating a term only to displace it. In academic contexts, queer theory now encompasses the study of diverse forms of sexual dissidence, each of which questions the heterosexual matrix.

Given her sensitivity to the discursive regimes that have long inhibited our knowledge of sex, gender, and desire, Butler has been quick to respond to the possible fate that might befall queer politics. Since all descriptive terms are in danger of being naturalized through repetition, she contends that the word should remain a subject of productive debate. It would, indeed, be a sad irony if queer ultimately became a token of precisely those kinds of normative thinking it initially sought to contest:

> If the term 'queer' is to be a site of collective contestation, the point of departure for a set of historical considerations and futural imaginings, it will have to remain that which is, in the

present, never fully owned, but always and only redeployed, twisted, queered from a prior usage and in the direction of urgent and expanding political purposes. This also means that it will doubtless have to be yielded in favour of terms that do that political work more effectively. Such a yielding may well become necessary in order to accommodate – without domesticating – democratizing contestations that have and will redraw the contours of the movement in ways that can never be fully anticipated in advance.

(Butler 1993: 228)

Rather than assume that the word queer will resolve the problem of sexual and gender definition once and for all, Butler recognizes that this emergent term may be superseded at some point in the future. There is no doubt that the words we use to interpret sexuality are historically contingent. If we become more reflective in our handling of the terms we use to imagine sex, gender, and desire, then the greater becomes the possibility of resignifying our desires in ways that loosen the naturalizing power of the heterosexual matrix. But this is hardly to claim that opposite-sex relations should not be celebrated. Far from it. Butler's point is that *all* sexualities need to be *denaturalized*, thus maximizing the opportunities to create consensual types of intimacy and to perform our genders in a truly liberated environment. By concentrating on the discursive construction of sexuality, queer theory is a major consequence of Foucault's introduction to *The History of Sexuality*. It is a development in social theory to which he would surely have given his approval.

CONCLUSION
DIVERSE EROTICISMS

In the closing decade of the twentieth century, Western culture has undoubtedly entered an era when erotic behaviours, identities, and styles are diversifying as never before. Since the time of the Civil Rights movement in the late 1960s, there has been an increasing number of vocal sexual minorities struggling for public recognition and political legitimacy. In the process, these heterogeneous groups insist on greatly expanding the available terms which render sexuality intelligible. Especially prominent in recent years have been queer, bisexual, transgender and ethnic minority discourses. This Conclusion takes the opportunity to sketch how each of these movements strives to dismantle the conventional categories that have been used to interpret eroticism. But the decisive impulse to transform the vocabulary for talking about desire is beset with complications. Where, indeed, might the proliferation of sexual identities lead? Will it simply produce a broader repertoire of rigid categories? Will it result in greater social tolerance and acceptance? Or will the outcome be even greater division between communities? These questions are undeniably urgent ones, since they drive at the centre of a social issue that extends beyond sexuality in the contemporary West. If diversity aims at recognizing each distinctive identity, then there may also be the danger of diluting and relativizing the distinguishing characteristics of every one of them. The drive towards diversity could ultimately minimize the differences that activists want the world to recognize.

The concerted movement towards sexual diversity may be viewed as part of an overarching trend that currently affects many spheres of cultural life. This trend has been extensively, if somewhat loosely, understood by the term 'postmodern'. The postmodern extends its net very widely, from defining a period of history ('postmodernity') to explaining a notable shift in how we perceive the world ('postmodernism') (see Harvey 1989). Although it is not possible here to itemize the many features associated with this far-reaching concept, it is possible to risk making a general claim: the postmodern articulates how the present epoch has tried to make a decisive break with Enlightenment models of progress, positivism, and epistemological certainty. It was assuredly in the Enlightenment spirit of progress that the sexologists, the psychoanalysts, and some later theorists of desire felt they could discover the indisputable truth of sexuality. As Foucault observes, no matter how much these researchers laboured to devise sophisticated theoretical models, they tended to produce explanatory categories that drew strict limits around the phenomena they put under scrutiny.

It is in an undoubtedly postmodern spirit that queer theory questions the ideological investments and conceptual biases evident in the categories earlier researchers devised for defining sexuality. Chapter 4 shows that queer interventions have largely followed Foucault in seeking to subvert the longstanding hetero/homo divide. According to Michael Warner, queerness resists 'regimes of the normal' (Warner 1993: xxxvi), especially 'heteronormativity'. But, as Warner adds, rather than assert one specific identity as a point of such definable resistance, queer thinking presents 'an aggressive impulse of generalization'. By this, Warner means that queer politics celebrates many different styles of sexual insubordination that vigorously contest the view that heterosexuality encompasses the most natural, ideal, or suitable model of intimacy.

Yet this patently confrontational attitude can undermine its aims. Discussing human values in a postmodern age of uncertainty, Jeffrey Weeks observes that both queer activism and queer theory are caught in a complicated double bind. It is a commonplace that, in tearing down old orthodoxies, radical politics can easily establish new ones, and queer interventions are no exception in this regard. Weeks implies that, in defining itself broadly against a blanket notion of heteronormativity, queerness paradoxically remains in danger of keeping firmly in place the very structure it seeks to overthrow. Despite these shortcomings, however, Weeks believes that queerness expresses a welcome desire for transforming the criteria through which sexuality has been named and known:

> Queer politics has all the defects of a transgressive style, elevating confrontation over the content of alternatives. . . . Despite this, it is an interesting phenomenon not only because of what it says or does, but because it is a reminder of the perpetual inventiveness of a collective sexual politics which stretches towards different ways of being. Whatever one thinks of it, it illustrates the continuing construction of identities and a sense of community which transcends old certainties and divisions, while challenging the orthodox epistemology of sexuality.
>
> (Weeks 1995: 115)

In producing 'different ways of being', queerness has certainly sought to dissociate itself from what may be called the identitarian assumptions that have underpinned so much thinking about sexuality from the 1860s to the present day. It is this particular impulse to fracture the foundational logic that supports identity-thinking which can be readily construed as postmodern.

But examined from another angle, as Weeks himself declares,

this postmodern queer attitude to sexuality confronts us with some pressing problems. Rather than view the postmodern as the radical subversion of dominant categories, some social theorists have plausibly argued that this trend demonstrates how late capitalism encroaches upon our intimate lives, and from their perspective queer theory is yet one more symptom of the systematic integration of capitalism and desire. Why should this be the case? Part of the answer lies in how the postmodern inclination towards erotic diversity indicates the increasing individualism promoted under a capitalist system that continually diversifies markets by appealing to specialized tastes. Weeks sums up this point concisely when he writes:

> The radical individualism that appears the dominant theme of our age, in sexual and ethical values as much as economic, is an ambiguous phenomenon. On the positive side it undermines the solidity of traditional narratives and relations of domination and subordination. A discourse of choice is a power dissolvant of old verities. . . . But the negative side is a sexual libertarianism that brooks no barrier to individual satisfaction, that makes individual pleasure the sole yardstick of sexual ethics.
>
> (Weeks 1995: 28–9)

Weeks's remarks surely make one cautious when considering sexual diversity as a matter of individual choice, since the very concept of choice presents a moral dilemma. On the one hand, choice celebrates one's right to express a subjugated sexual identity. But on the other, the right to choose a particular erotic lifestyle can well be carried out in an unethical spirit that overemphasizes the satisfaction of personal desires at the expense of other people's needs.

It is precisely the overwhelming stress on individualistic desires that Donald Morton deplores in queer theory. Writing from a strict Marxist standpoint, Morton argues that queerness, if ostensibly resisting heterosexist domination, remains entirely complicit with the postmodern belief that individual freedom exists solely in *laissez-faire* markets where all trade barriers have broken down, enabling commodities to circulate with an almost anarchic energy. 'In this new queer space', writes Morton, 'desire is regarded as autonomous – unregulated and unencumbered' (Morton 1995: 370). In Morton's view, rather than adhere to a Marxist paradigm that evaluates questions of human need, queer theory is mesmerized by sensations stimulated by reckless free market principles. He argues that the consumerist imperative perilously abandons the subject to desire, thus diminishing the capacity for rational calculation. Not surprisingly, then, he protests how queerness thoughtlessly rejects 'Enlightenment views concerning the role of the conceptual, rational, systematic, normative, progressive, liberatory, revolutionary . . . in social change', leaving only '*desire, sensation,* or *jouissance* in their stead' (Morton 1995: 370).

Central to Morton's hard-hitting critique is the belief that queer theory overlooks material conditions of need by erroneously imagining that social change can be achieved at the level of the contestatory sign. One recalls how Queer Nation adapted an insubordinate discursive strategy by wrenching the vilified term 'queer' from homophobes and resignifying it as a term of power and pride. But such manoeuvres do not suggest to Morton that they are tackling fundamental political crises. Instead, playing with the symbolic value of the sign may well prove a distraction at a time when capital is making it hard to see beyond a world saturated with representational media. In the postmodern world, he argues, there is a troubling collapse between reality and representation, most clearly evident in the rapid expansion of computer technologies which manipulate virtual realities in cyberspace. Morton asserts that varieties of thought seduced by the postmodern have misguidedly encouraged queer theorists to think that desire operates, not in relation to material conditions, but purely within a field of significatory activity. As a result, the prevailing ludic – or playful – approach to meaning has led notable writers such as Judith Butler to suggest that sexual subversion can be understood by appealing to notions such as indeterminacy, undecidability, and performativity. There is no doubt that Morton is to some degree correct, since, as the present study shows, much contemporary thinking about sexuality explores intricate connections between desire and representational processes. This issue becomes clear if we momentarily recall the theories of Lacan and Foucault, detailed in Chapters 2 and 4 respectively. Although these influential theorists have completely different understandings of how sexuality is formed, both appeal to powerful systems of meaning-production, whether in terms of the shifting signifier or the 'tactical polyvalence' of discourse. Even if we may feel that Morton somewhat overstates his case (since not every queer theorist has been ideologically duped by the ludic play of signs), his provocative insights prompt important questions. What are sexual dissidents really achieving by shifting the representations through which we comprehend eroticism? Would it not be more productive if they concentrated instead on real inequalities in the social order?

It is unquestionably true that dissident sexual minorities seriously engage with the politics of categorization, and thus with the way desire is construed through discourse. But their theoretical writings show that they regard the political struggle for recognition as much more than a simple matter of toying with indeterminate signifiers. Oppressed erotic communities constantly remark that the nomenclature by which they define themselves has a significant impact on public awareness of who and what they are. On occasions, their chosen categories of self-definition can and will transform how we acknowledge and respect diverse eroticisms.

Take, for example, the politics of naming in relation to bisexuality. Unquestionably, bisexual thinking has become exceptionally powerful in confounding some of the traditional frameworks in which sexual desire has been understood. Long before queerness emerged in the 1990s, bisexuality had presented an often unwelcome challenge to the longstanding hetero/homo divide. Bisexuality presents a third term that upsets this either/or binary, demanding recognition perhaps as both/and. In the past, this defiant bi insurgence against the distinction between hetero- and homo- often proved perplexing. Given the enduring division between straight and gay, bisexuality can still prove hard to fathom because of its unapologetic doubleness ('bi'). Marjorie Garber has explored in detail the pervasive but frequently disavowed biness in Western culture. She argues that by patently refusing to fit into available classifications, bisexuality makes most models for interpreting sexual desire incoherent:

> Bisexuality unsettles certainties: straight, gay, lesbian. It has affinities with all of these, and is delimited by none. It is, then, an identity that is also *not* an identity, a sign of the certainty of ambiguity, the stability of instability, a category that defines and defeats categorizations. . . . No wonder it makes sexual politicians uncomfortable.
>
> (Garber 1995: 70)

Bi thinking, then, definitely shares the postmodern emphasis on the indeterminacy of the sign. Moving across sexes, across genders, across sexualities, bi-ness warmly embraces multiple desires and identifications while repudiating all 'monosexual' imperatives. The paradoxical non-identitarian position of bisexuality – 'an identity that is also *not* an identity' – certainly indicates a desire to defy fixed categorization while maintaining a label that can encompass a very wide diversity of desires.

Just as bi men and bi women have found it hard to convince their listeners that it is perfectly possible not to conform to an unwavering 'monosexuality', so too do cross-dressers and transsexuals routinely encounter puzzlement when presenting their sexualities to the world. Although styles of female impersonation have long been central features of popular culture, it still proves hard for society to tolerate, let alone accept, any type of cross-dressing once it steps off the stage and takes to the streets. Hostility to transgender people has arisen from many different sources, including feminist ones. In 1979, for example, radical feminist Janice Raymond delivered a notorious attack on male-to-female transsexuals, regarding them as patriarchs in drag. 'All transsexuals', writes Raymond, 'rape women's bodies by reducing the real female form to an artifact, appropriating this body for themselves' (Raymond 1979: 104). By any account, this is a severe judgement, presenting gender reassignment as a form of sexual violence as well as sexual conservatism. In her polemical study, Raymond maintains that transsexuality hardly undermines customary definitions of gender but reinforces them instead. In her view, the male-to-female transsexual gives up one gender role and just replaces it with its opposite, keeping the fixed hierarchy between male and female firmly in place.

To combat persistent confusions of this kind, activists have increasingly used the term transgender. This word has sufficient flexibility to include practices of cross-dressing, transsexuality, and intersexual identity. (In previous decades, intersexuality has at times been known as androgyny and hermaphroditism.) The richly expansive meaning of transgender runs so strongly against preconceived notions of masculinity and femininity that it only makes sense once sex and gender are conceptually prised apart. The American writer Leslie Feinberg recounts the following anecdote to explain how s/he has coped with habitual misunderstanding of her/his identity:

> 'You were born female, right?' The reporter asked me for the third time. I nodded patiently. 'So do you identify as female now, or male?'
>
> She rolled her eyes as I repeated my answer. 'I am transgen-

dered. I was born female, but my masculine gender expression is seen as male. It's not my sex that defines me, and it's not my gender expression. It's the fact that my gender expression appears to be at odds with my sex. Do you understand? It's the social contradiction between the two that defines me'.

The reporter's eyes glazed over as I spoke. When I finished she said, 'So you're a *third* sex?' Clearly, I realized we had very little language with which to understand each other.

(Feinberg 1996: 101)

Throughout her/his eloquent cultural history, Feinberg frequently observes that many non-Western cultures have held transgendered people in high esteem, sometimes according them special roles in religious ceremonies. But no matter how postmodern the West has become, it remains the case that almost every time we use a public lavatory a choice has to be made between men and women. Given her/his chosen gender expression, Feinberg has decided to enter her/his sex as male on official documents. Yet in doing so s/he has broken the law, since her/his genital sex remains female. The challenge raised by Feinberg's chosen sexual identity has doubtless become evident in the typographic slashes I have used to designate her/his pronominal position. The slashes, however, are meant to be respectful. Since transgendered identities sometimes powerfully bewilder the line between male and female, even basic pronouns can become obstacles to understanding. Feinberg raises the question whether transgendered people should encourage the use of possessive pronouns such as 'hir', which combine male and female. Yet Feinberg is acutely aware that such a linguistic move might only perpetuate the age-old stereotype of the 'third sex' that the term transgender itself seeks to dislodge.

Even if dissident eroticisms may subvert fundamental categories of sex and gender, they are certainly affected by other markers of difference – such as class, race, and generation – in ways that complicate their expression. This point is drawn into focus by writers belonging to both sexual and ethnic minorities. Addressing patterns of Asian–American same-sex desire, Dana Y. Takagi wryly remarks: 'It is vogue these days to celebrate difference' (Takagi 1996: 23). Suspicious of the trivializing 'vogue' that favours the theoretical celebration of 'difference', she adds that 'underlying much contemporary talk about difference is the assumption that differences are comparable things'. That is why, Takagi argues, one must be cautious of critical viewpoints which assert that sexual identities can be considered like ethnicities, a comparison that has been made by several gay writers (see, for example, Epstein 1987). Differences are not analogous or interchangeable. But an uncritical notion of diversity can give the distinct impression that they are.

Takagi's significant comment recognizes a paradox that continues to haunt many discussions of sexual diversity. In defending difference, there is often a simultaneous incentive to uncover principles of sameness that uniformly link everyone together, especially when campaigners seek platforms on which to campaign for basic human rights. It is this marked tension between sameness and difference that certainly presents the greatest challenge to anyone studying the fast expansion of sexual identities today. Even if we inhabit an age of postmodern uncertainty, one issue remains for sure. There is a desperate need for a common language that respects various expressions of eroticism in a sensitive and non-prescriptive manner. Yet in developing inventive terms through which we can share differences and respect distinctiveness, it would probably be wise to hesitate about one word. Maybe the time has come when diverse desires will no longer be bound together under one constraining label – a label that has for decades proved immensely difficult to analyse. At the close of this book, I think we are well-acquainted with its name. It is known simply as sexuality.

BIBLIOGRAPHY

Ackerley, J.R. (1992), *My Father and Myself* (London: Pimlico).

Adams, Parveen, and Elizabeth Cowie, eds (1990), *The Woman in Question: m/f* (Cambridge, MA: MIT Press).

Barbach, Lonnie (1975), *For Yourself: The Fulfilment of Female Sexuality* (New York: Doubleday).

Barthes, Roland (1975), *The Pleasure of the Text*, trans. Richard Miller (New York: Hill and Wang).

Bartky, Sandra Lee (1988), 'Foucault, Femininity, and the Modernization of Patriarchal Power', in Irene Diamond and Lee Quinby, eds, *Feminism and Foucault: Reflections on Resistance* (Boston: Northeastern University Press).

Bataille, Georges (1962), *Eroticism*, trans. Mary Dalwood (London: Calder and Boyars).

Baudrillard, Jean (1990), *Seduction*, trans. Brian Singer (Basingstoke: Macmillan).

Bennington, Geoffrey (1988), *Lyotard: Writing the Event* (Manchester: Manchester University Press).

Birken, Lawrence (1988), *Consuming Desire: Sexual Science and the Emergence of a Culture of Abundance, 1871–1914* (Ithaca, NY: Cornell University Press).

Bland, Lucy (1995), *Banishing the Beast: Sexuality and the Early Feminists* (Harmondsworth: Penguin Books).

Bloch, Iwan (1908), *The Sexual Life of Our Time In Its Relations to Modern Civilization* (New York: Allied Book Company).

Borch-Jacobsen, Mikkel (1991), *Lacan: The Absolute Master*, trans. Douglas Brick (Stanford, CA: Stanford University Press).

Botting, Fred (1995), *Gothic*, New Critical Idiom (London: Routledge).

Bowie, Malcolm (1991), *Lacan* (Cambridge, MA: Harvard University Press).

Bristow, Joseph (1995), *Effeminate England: Homoerotic Writing after 1885* (Buckingham: Open University Press).

Butler, Judith (1990), *Gender Trouble: Feminism and the Subversion of Identity* (New York: Routledge).

—— (1993), *Bodies That Matter: On the Discursive Limits of 'Sex'* (New York: Routledge).

Carpenter, Edward (1894a), *Marriage in a Free Society* (Manchester: The Labour Press Society).

—— (1894b), *Sex-Love: Its Place in a Free Society* (Manchester: The Labour Press Society)

—— (1894c), *Woman, and Her Place in a Free Society* (Manchester: The Labour Press Society).

Carter, Angela (1979), *The Sadeian Woman: An Exercise in Cultural History* (London: Virago).

Castle, Terry (1993), *The Apparitional Lesbian: Female Homosexuality and Modern Culture* (New York: Columbia University Press).

Cixous, Hélène (1986), 'Sorties', in Hélène Cixous and Catherine Clement, *The Newly-Born Woman*, trans. Betsy Wing (Minneapolis, MN: University of Minnesota Press).

Cohen, Ed (1991), 'Who Are "We": Gay "Identity" as Political (E)motion (A Theoretical Rumination)', in Diana Fuss, ed., *Inside/Out: Lesbian Theories, Gay Theories* (New York: Routledge).

Comfort, Alex (1973), *The Joy of Sex* (New York: Crown).

Cornell, Drucilla (1995), *The Imaginary Domain: Abortion, Pornography, and Sexual Harassment* (New York: Routledge).

Daly, Mary (1978), *Gyn/Ecology: The Metaethics of Radical Feminism* (Boston: Beacon Press).

Darwin, Charles (1871), *The Descent of Man, and Selection in Relation to Sex*, 2 vols (London: John Murray).

Deleuze, Gilles, and Felix Guattari (1984), *Anti-Oedipus: Capitalism and Schizophrenia*, trans. Robert Hurley *et al.* (London: Athlone Press).

—— (1987), *A Thousand Plateaus: Capitalism and Schizophrenia*, trans. Brian Massumi (Minneapolis, MN: University of Minnesota Press).

D'Emilio, John (1992), 'Capitalism and Gay Identity', in John D'Emilio, *Making Trouble: Essays on Gay History, Politics, and the University* (New York: Routledge).

Donne, John (1985), *The Complete English Poems of John Donne*, ed. C.A. Patrides, Everyman's Library (London: Dent).

Dworkin, Andrea (1980), 'Why So-Called Radical Men Love and Need Pornography', in Laura Lederer, ed., *Take Back the Night: Women on Pornography* (New York: William Morrow).

—— (1983), *Right-Wing Women: The Politics of Domesticated Females* (London: Women's Press).

—— (1989), *Pornography: Men Possessing Women* (New York: E.P. Dutton).

Eagleton, Terry (1990), *The Ideology of the Aesthetic* (Oxford: Basil Blackwell).

Ellis, Havelock and John Addington Symonds (1897), *Sexual Inversion* (London: Wilson and Macmillan).

Epstein, Steven (1987), 'Gay Politics, Ethnic Identity: The Limits of Social Constructionism', *Socialist Review* 17: 3–4, 9–56.

Faderman, Lillian (1981), *Surpassing the Love of Men: Romantic Friendship and Love between Women from the Renaissance to the Present* (New York: Morrow).

Feinberg, Leslie (1996), *Transgender Warriors: Making History from Joan of Arc to RuPaul* (Boston: Beacon Press).

Feminists against Censorship (1991), *Pornography and Feminism: The Case against Censorship* (London: Lawrence and Wishart).

Foucault, Michel (1972), *The Archaeology of Knowledge*, trans. A.M. Sheridan Smith (London: Tavistock).

—— (1973), *The Birth of the Clinic: An Archaeology of Medical Perception*, trans. A.M. Sheridan Smith (London: Tavistock).

—— (1977a), *Discipline and Punish: The Birth of the Prison* (New York: Random House).

—— (1977b), *Language, Counter-Memory, Practice: Selected Essays and Interviews*, trans. Donald F. Bouchard and Sherry Simon (Ithaca, NY: Cornell University Press).

—— (1978), *The History of Sexuality, Volume 1: An Introduction*, trans. Robert Hurley (New York: Random House).

—— (1985), *The Use of Pleasure: Volume 2 of The History of Sexuality*, trans. Robert Hurley (New York: Random House).

—— (1986), *The Care of the Self: Volume 3 of The History of Sexuality*, trans. Robert Hurley (New York: Random House).

—— (1989), *Foucault Live (Interviews, 1961–1984)*, ed. Sylvère Lotringer, trans. Lysa Hochroth and John Johnston (New York: Semiotext(e)).

Freud, Sigmund (1953–65), *The Standard Edition of the Complete Psychological Works of Sigmund Freud*, 24 vols, trans. James Strachey *et al.* (London: Hogarth Press and the Institute of Psycho-Analysis).

Fuss, Diana (1989), *Essentially Speaking: Feminism, Nature and Difference* (New York: Routledge).

—— (1995), *Identification Papers* (New York: Routledge).

Gagnon, John and William Simon (1973), *Sexual Conduct: The Social Sources of Human Sexuality* (New York: Aldine de Gruyter).

Gallop, Jane (1982), *Feminism and Psychoanalysis: The Daughter's Seduction* (Basingstoke: Macmillan).

Garber, Marjorie (1995), *Vice Versa: Bisexuality and the Eroticism of Everyday Life* (London: Hamish Hamilton).

Gilman, Sander L. (1985), *Difference and Pathology: Stereotypes of Sexuality, Race, and Madness* (Ithaca, NY: Cornell University Press).

Grosz, Elizabeth (1994), 'A Thousand Tiny Sexes: Feminism and Rhizomatics', in Constantin V. Boundas and Dorothea Olkowski, eds, *Gilles Deleuze and the Theater of Philosophy* (New York: Routledge).

Hall, Radclyffe (1981), *The Well of Loneliness* (New York: Avon Books).

Halperin, David M. (1990), *One Hundred Years of Homosexuality and Other Essays on Greek Love* (New York: Routledge).

Hamilton, Cicely (1909), *Marriage as a Trade* (London: Chapman and Hall).

Harvey, David (1989), *The Condition of Postmodernity* (Oxford: Blackwell).

Hegel, G.W.F. (1975), *The Phenomenology of Spirit*, trans. A.B. Miller (Oxford: Clarendon Press).

Hite, Shere (1976), *The Hite Report: A Nationwide Study of Female Sexuality* (New York: Macmillan).

Hunt, Lynn (1993), 'Introduction: Obscenity and the Origins of Modernity, 1500–1800', in Lynn Hunt, ed., *The Invention of Pornography:*

Obscenity and the Origins of Modernity, 1500–1800 (New York: Zone Books).

Hyams, Barbara (1995), 'Weininger and Nazi Ideology', in Nancy A. Harowitz and Barbara Hyams, eds, *Jews and Gender: Responses to Otto Weininger*, Philadelphia, PA: Temple University Press.

Irigaray, Luce (1985a), *Speculum of the Other Woman*, trans. Gillian C. Gill (Ithaca, NY: Cornell University Press).

—— (1985b), *This Sex Which is Not One*, trans. Catherine Porter with Carolyn Burke (Ithaca, NY: Cornell University Press).

Irvine, Janice (1990), *Disorders of Desire: Sex and Gender in Modern American Sociology* (Philadelphia, PA: Temple University Press).

Itzin, Catherine (1992a), 'A Legal Definition of Pornography', in Catherine Itzin, ed., *Pornography: Women, Violence and Civil Liberties* (Oxford: Oxford University Press).

—— (1992b), 'Pornography and the Social Construction of Sexual Inequality', in Catherine Itzin, ed., *Pornography: Women, Violence and Civil Liberties* (Oxford: Oxford University Press).

Jeffreys, Sheila (1985), *The Spinster and Her Enemies: Feminism and Sexuality, 1880–1930* (London: Pandora).

Johnston, Jill (1973), *Lesbian Nation: The Feminist Solution* (New York: Simon and Schuster).

Kappeler, Susanne (1986), *The Pornography of Representation* (Cambridge: Polity Press).

Kendrick, Walter (1987), *The Secret Museum: Pornography in Modern Culture* (New York: Viking).

Kinsey, Alfred C., Wardell B. Pomeroy, and Clyde E. Morton (1948), *Sexual Behavior in the Human Male* (Philadelphia, PA: W.B. Saunders).

Kinsey, Alfred C., Wardell B. Pomeroy, Clyde E. Morton and Paul H.

Gebhard (1953), *Sexual Behavior in the Human Female* (Philadelphia, PA: W.B. Saunders).

Krafft-Ebing, Richard von (1894), *Psychopathia Sexualis, with Especial Reference to Contrary Sexual Intinct: A Medico-Legal Study*, trans. Charles Gilbert Chaddock (Philadelphia, PA: F.A. Davis).

Kristeva, Julia (1982), *Powers of Horror: An Essay on Abjection*, trans. Leon S. Roudiez (New York: Columbia University Press).

Kristeva, Julia (1984), *Revolution in Poetic Language*, trans. Margaret Waller (New York: Columbia University Press).

Lacan, Jacques (1977), *Écrits: A Selection*, trans. Alan Sheridan (London: Tavistock).

—— (1978), *The Four Fundamental Concepts of Psycho-Analysis*, ed. Jacques-Alain Miller, trans. Alan Sheridan (New York: W.W. Norton).

Lane, Christopher (1995), *The Ruling Passion: British Colonial Allegory and the Paradox of Homosexual Desire* (Durham, NC: Duke University Press).

Laplanche, Jean (1989), *New Foundations for Psychoanalysis*, trans. David Macey (Oxford: Basil Blackwell).

Laplanche, Jean, and Jean-Bertrand Pontalis (1973), *The Language of Psycho-Analysis*, trans. David Nicholson-Smith (London: Hogarth Press).

—— (1986), 'Fantasy and the Origins of Sexuality', in Victor Burgin, James Donald, and Cora Kaplan, eds, *Formations of Fantasy* (London: Methuen).

Laqueur, Thomas (1990), *Making Sex: Body and Gender from the Greeks to Freud* (Cambridge, MA: Harvard University Press).

Laumann, Edward O., *et al.* (1994), *The Social Organization of Sexuality: Sexual Practices in the United States* (Chicago: University of Chicago Press).

Lyotard, Jean-François (1993), *Libidinal Economy*, trans. Iain Hamilton Grant (London: Athlone Press).

McIntosh, Mary (1981), 'The Homosexual Role', in Kenneth Plummer, ed., *The Making of the Modern Homosexual* (London: Hutchinson).

MacKinnon, Catharine A. (1992), 'Pornography, Civil Rights and Speech', in Catherine Itzin, ed., *Pornography: Women, Violence and Civil Liberties* (Oxford: Oxford University Press).

—— (1993), *Only Words* (Cambridge, MA: Harvard University Press).

McNay, Lois (1994), *Foucault: A Critical Introduction* (Cambridge: Polity Press).

Martin, Biddy (1988), 'Feminism, Criticism, and Foucault', in Irene Diamond and Lee Quinby, eds, *Feminism and Foucault: Reflections on Resistance* (Boston: Northeastern University Press).

Masson, Jeffrey Mousaifieff (1984), *Freud, The Assault on Truth: Freud's Suppression of the Seduction Theory* (London: Faber).

Masters, William H. and Virginia E. Johnson (1966), *Human Sexual Response* (Boston: Little, Brown).

Millett, Kate (1970), *Sexual Politics* (New York: Doubleday).

Mitchell, Juliet (1974), *Psychoanalysis and Feminism: Freud, Reich, Laing and Women* (London: Allen Lane).

Mitchell, Juliet and Jacqueline Rose, eds (1982) *Feminine Sexuality: Jacques Lacan and the École freudienne* (Basingstoke: Macmillan).

Morgan, Robin (1980), 'Theory and Practice: Pornography and Rape', in Laura Lederer, ed., *Take Back the Night: Women on Pornography* (New York: William Morrow).

Morton, Donald (1995), 'Birth of the Cyberqueer', *PMLA* 110:3, 369–81.

Newton, Esther (1989), 'The Mythic Mannish Lesbian: Radclyffe Hall and the New Woman', in Martin Bauml Duberman, Martha Vicinus, and George Chauncey, Jr., eds, *Hidden from History: Reclaiming the Lesbian and Gay Past* (New York: New American Library).

Paglia, Camille (1990), *Sexual Personae: Art and Decadence from Nefertiti to Emily Dickinson* (New Haven, CT: Yale University Press).

Pankhurst, Christabel (1913), *The Great Scourge and How to End It* (London: E. Pankhurst).

Porter, Roy, and Lesley Hall (1995), *The Facts of Life: The Creation of Sexual Knowledge in Britain, 1650–1950* (New Haven: Yale University Press).

Raymond, Janice (1979), *The Transsexual Empire: The Making of the She-Male* (Boston: Beacon Press).

Reich, Wilhelm (1945), *The Sexual Revolution: Towards a Self-Regulating Character Structure*, trans. Theodore P. Wolfe (New York: Orgone Institute Press).

—— (1971), *The Invasion of Compulsory Sex-Morality* (New York: Farrar, Straus and Giroux).

Riviere, Joan (1986), 'Womanliness as a Masquerade', in Victor Burgin, James Donald, and Cora Kaplan, eds, *Formations of Fantasy* (London: Methuen).

Rose, Jacqueline (1983), 'Femininity and Its Discontents', *Feminist Review* 14: 5–21.

Rubin, Gayle (1975), 'The Traffic in Women: Notes on the "Political Economy" of Sex', in Rayna R. Reiter, ed., *Toward an Anthropology of Women* (New York: Monthly Review Press).

—— (1993), 'Thinking Sex: Notes for a Radical Theory of the Politics of Sexuality', in Henry Abelove, Michèle Aina Barale, and David M. Halperin, eds, *The Lesbian and Gay Studies Reader* (New York: Routledge).

Russell, Diana E.H. (1992), 'Pornography and Rape: A Causal Model', in

Catherine Itzin, ed., *Pornography: Women, Violence and Civil Liberties* (Oxford: Oxford University Press).

Sayers, Janet (1991), *Mothers of Psychoanalysis: Helene Deutsch, Karen Horney, Anna Freud, Melanie Klein* (New York, W.W. Norton).

Schreiner, Olive [pseud. 'Ralph Iron'] (1883), *The Story of an African Farm*, 2 vols (London: Chapman and Hall).

Schreiner, Olive (1890), *Dreams* (London: T. Fisher Unwin).

—— (1911), *Woman and Labour* (London: T. Fisher Unwin).

Sedgwick, Eve Kosofsky (1985), *Between Men: English Literature and Male Homosocial Desire* (New York: Columbia University Press).

—— (1990), *Epistemology of the Closet* (Berkeley: University of California Press).

Segal, Lynne (1992), 'Sweet Sorrows, Painful Pleasures: Pornography and the Perils of Heterosexual Desire', in Lynne Segal and Mary McIntosh, eds, *Sex Exposed: Sexuality and the Pornography Debate* (London: Virago).

—— (1994), *Straight Sex: The Politics of Pleasure* (London: Virago).

Showalter, Elaine (1990), *Sexual Anarchy: Gender and Culture at the Fin de Siècle* (New York: Viking).

Sontag, Susan (1969), 'The Pornographic Imagination', in Susan Sontag, *Styles of Radical Will* (New York: Farrar, Straus and Giroux).

Soper, Kate (1993), 'Productive Contradictions', in Caroline Ramazanoğlu, ed., *Up against Foucault: Explorations of Some Tensions between Foucault and Feminism* (London: Routledge).

Spencer, Herbert (1862), *First Principles* (London: Williams and Norgate).

Stoler, Laura Ann (1995), *Race and the Education of Desire: Foucault's*

History of Sexuality *and the Colonial Order of Things* (Durham, NC: Duke University Press).

Stopes, Marie (1918), *Married Love: A New Contribution to the Solution of Sex Difficulties* (London: A.C. Fifield).

Sulloway, Frank J. (1983), *Freud, Biologist of the Mind: Beyond the Psychoanalytic Legend* (New York: Basic Books).

Takagi, Dana Y. (1996), 'Maiden Voyage: Excursion into Sexuality and Identity Politics in Asian America', in Russell Leong, ed., *Asian American Sexualities: Dimensions of Gay and Lesbian Experience* (New York: Routledge).

Theweleit, Karl (1987), *Male Fantasies: Volume One. Women, Floods, Bodies*, trans. Stephen Conway *et al.* (Minneapolis, MN: University of Minnesota Press).

Tiefer, Leonore (1995), *Sex Is Not a Natural Act and Other Essays* (Boulder, CO: Westview Press).

Ulrichs, Karl Heinrich (1994), *The Riddle of "Man–Manly" Love: The Pioneering Work on Male Homosexuality*, 2 vols, trans. Michael A. Lombardi-Nash (Buffalo, NY: Prometheus Books).

Warner, Michael (1993), 'Introduction', in Michael Warner, ed., *Fear of a Queer Planet: Queer Politics and Social Theory* (Minneapolis, MN: University of Minnesota Press).

Watney, Simon (1987) *Policing Desire: Pornography, AIDS, and the Media* (London: Methuen/Comedia).

Weber, Samuel (1991), *Return to Freud: Jacques Lacan's Dislocation of Psychoanalysis*, trans. Michael Levine (Cambridge: Cambridge University Press).

Weeks, Jeffrey (1977), *Coming Out: Homosexual Politics in Britain from the Nineteenth Century to the Present* (London: Quartet).

—— (1986), *Sexuality* (London: Tavistock).

—— (1995), *Invented Moralities: Sexual Values in an Age of Uncertainity* (Cambridge: Polity Press).

Weininger, Otto (1975), *Sex and Character* (New York: AMS Press).

Williams, Linda (1989), *Hard Core: Power, Pleasure, and the 'Frenzy of the Visible'* (Berkeley: University of California Press).

—— (1992), 'Pornographies On/Scene, or Diff'rent Strokes for Diff'rent Folks', in Lynne Segal and Mary McIntosh, eds, *Sex Exposed: Sexuality and the Pornography Debate* (London: Virago Press).

Wilson, Elizabeth (1981), 'Psychoanalysis: Psychic Law and Order?', *Feminist Review* 8: 63–78.

Wright, Elizabeth, ed. (1992), *Feminism and Psychoanalysis: A Critical Dictionary* (Oxford: Basil Blackwell).

INDEX